Uexküll's Surroundings

Future Ecologies Series

Edited by Petra Löffler, Claudia Mareis and Florian Sprenger

Gottfried Schnödl works at the Institute for Culture and Aesthetics of Digital Media (ICAM) at Leuphana University Lüneburg.

Florian Sprenger is professor of virtual humanities at Ruhr-Universität Bochum.

Uexküll's Surroundings: Umwelt Theory and Right-Wing Thought

Gottfried Schnödl and Florian Sprenger

Translated by

Michael Thomas Taylor and Wayne Yung

meson press

Bibliographical Information of the German National Library
The German National Library lists this publication in the Deutsche Nationalbibliografie (German National Bibliography); detailed bibliographic information is available online at http://dnb.d-nb.de.

Published in 2021 by meson press, Lüneburg, Germany
www.meson.press

Design concept: Torsten Köchlin, Silke Krieg
Cover image: Mashup of photos by @betogaletto on Unsplash and takoyaki_king on Flickr

The print edition of this book is printed by Lightning Source, Milton Keynes, United Kingdom.

ISBN (Print): 978-3-95796-201-0
ISBN (PDF): 978-3-95796-202-7
ISBN (EPUB): 978-3-95796-203-4
DOI: 10.14619/2010

The digital editions of this publication can be downloaded freely at: www.meson.press.

Contents

Series Foreword: Future Ecologies 9

[1] **Introduction 11**
Gottfried Schnödl and Florian Sprenger

[2] **Uexküll and Nazism: 'Planmäßigkeit' and 'Placelessness' 23**
Florian Sprenger

[3] **Uexküll as a Whole: On the Totality of Planmäßigkeit 107**
Gottfried Schnödl

[4] **Umwelten and their Surrounding(s) 175**
Florian Sprenger

[5] **Conclusion: Politics and the Future of Umwelt Theory 229**
Gottfried Schnödl and Florian Sprenger

Jakob Johann von Uexküll: Biographical Overview 233

Bibliography 235

Series Foreword: Future Ecologies

Edited by Petra Löffler, Claudia Mareis, and Florian Sprenger

The future of life on Earth has generated ongoing debates in academia, through which the concept of ecology has gained status by being able to connect disciplines across the natural sciences, humanities, arts, design and architecture. Criticism of the effects of climate change, which exacerbate existing inequalities in our global population, has spread from academia to the political and public spheres. At a time when the future of life on this planet is more uncertain than ever, the urgency of exploring other ways of thinking, acting and dwelling together is evident. This book series investigates emerging ecologies in uncertain worlds—ecologies that are open to the interests of other-than-humans and that care for plural modes of existence. By providing a platform for these topics and debates, we hope to contribute to a nature contract with the Earth as the shared common ground of water and minerals, air and birds, earth and woods, living and non-living, active and passive matter.

Future Ecologies is about a "time-space-mattering" that calls into question common knowledges about the relationship between space, place, territory, and the linearity of time in light of the circulation of matter, energies, and affect. It also questions the meaning of past ecologies and unsustainable futures for emergent ecologies, while problematizing the ambivalent histories of environmental knowledge, especially in the interplay of modernity and coloniality. Reading research in the *Future Ecologies* series allows you to take the many facets of past ecological thinking into account, to reveal its differentiated and often contradictory political implications and effects—and to criticize its, sometimes, naïve promises. Studying *Future Ecologies* means not taking for granted what ecology means.

The series promotes a relational thinking that is aware of the environmental, economic, social, and individual complexities of such a pluriverse driven by equally complex technologies and infrastructures. As Donna J. Haraway said, in a shared world "nothing is connected to everything, but everything is connected to something". This connection generates and discloses different scales of responsibility. We dedicate this book series to all earthly critters who want to invent and try out new forms of life and styles of cohabitation, who ask which risks we want to and are able to take, and which futures we dream of. We invite contributions that address the geopolitical inequalities of climate change and capitalist extractivism, that deal with politics of (un)sustainability and (de)futuring, technologies of recycling and environing, non-anthropocentric epistemologies and practices of world-making.

The *Future Ecologies* series advocates for interdisciplinary approaches towards the numerous aspects of ecology. We invite junior and senior scholars from various disciplines in media, cultural and literary studies, anthropology, design, architecture, and the arts to build collaborations between different voices, practices and knowledges—that is: heterogeneous communities of practice. By endorsing open access publishing, the series also aims to partake in the current transformation of the ecologies and economies of knowledge production.

[1]

Introduction

Gottfried Schnödl and Florian Sprenger

Today, the Baltic-German biologist Jakob von Uexküll (1864–1944) is regarded as a pioneer of the ecological movement, with his way of looking at the world often seen as a credible response to the problems of the Anthropocene, although he never saw himself as an ecologist. He is taken as an authority who spoke up for the diversity of human and animal Umwelten (the plural of Umwelt, literally "around-world," referring not only to the environment, but in this context particularly to what he called an organism's receptor world and effector world, its "Merkwelt" and "Wirkwelt"). He is regarded as a biologist who champions a holistic view of nature that provides a place for every living entity. To some, then, his holism might seem to take the uniqueness of every living entity seriously. His work is seen as an overcoming of subject-object dualisms, a turning away from a mechanistic understanding of the organism as essentially a machine governed by reflexes, a turning toward the subject's active creation of the world, a different way of thinking about nonhuman life, and, it would seem, an antianthropocentrism capable of addressing the challenges of the Anthropocene.

His ideas have moreover been adopted and built upon in diverse ways by a wide variety of sometimes very different schools of thought, ranging from philosophical anthropology and speculative realism to semiotics and cybernetics to robotics and posthumanism. Uexküll's provocative act of assigning to ticks, snails, and sea urchins the same subjectivity formerly reserved for human beings still influences debates today. But this all comes at the price of a structural conservatism and an identitarian logic in which everything should stay in its place and nothing should mix—be it biologically or politically. To put it bluntly, Uexküll's Umwelt theory is antidemocratic, totalitarian, and holistic in the worst sense. And beyond that, Uexküll was much more deeply involved in Nazism than previously thought.

The present volume does not ask what Uexküll might teach us today. It does not explore the question of why we need to read Uexküll right now. Instead, it looks at his popularity as a symptom, embedded within a historical constellation that the book aims to reconstruct in detail. It examines his theoretical framework not as an answer, but as something whose plausibility is to be questioned. Such an approach necessarily distances itself from simply applying his theories, and from using particular components of his thought to answer today's most pressing problems. Instead, the aim here is to explore the historical place of Umwelt theory in the current moment: What makes an exploration of Uexküll's surroundings worthwhile, even politically necessary, for us right now? In light of recent efforts by New Right, identitarian, and racist movements to reestablish lines of connection from Uexküll to what is labeled a "conservative ecology," this question becomes even more urgent. It goes beyond research on Uexküll himself and extends into how scholars working on the history of ecology are positioning themselves in today's political debates.

The present investigation will contextualize Umwelt theory (and its sometimes highly selective readings) within the tensions and disputes of the holistically oriented German-language biology of the first third of the twentieth century, a time and milieu in which biological and political ideas were inextricably intertwined. The starting point is to be found in the holistic and organicist currents within biology and natural philosophy (i.e., ones explaining phenomena from the holistic interactions of their elements) that Uexküll referenced in his work. Given the profound conflicts of the time, these are currents that can only be understood if one also examines what they were directed against. The holism of the period, which proposed that the individual case can only be explained within the context of the whole, took on very different forms, and Uexküll's Umwelt theory was certainly not at the core of efforts to formulate holistic theories.[1] Nonetheless, he positioned his theory firmly in this field, both scientifically and politically. Despite the idiosyncrasies of Umwelt theory, it therefore makes sense to see Uexküll himself as a holist, thereby allowing us to understand his anti-Darwinism and antidemocracy, along with his pandering to the Nazis, within the context of certain discursive frameworks—ones that have lately enjoyed a renewed influence. This book will demonstrate that these aspects are deeply embedded in the foundations of Uexküll's Umwelt theory and play an important role in his current popularity—all across the political spectrum of his readership today.

The analysis will show that Uexküll's Umwelt theory is structurally conservative, leads to a holistically justified rejection of democracy, and results in an identitarian logic where everything has its place according to a plan and whatever is wrongly placed

1 Holism is not itself a coherent philosophy and is characterized above all by a diversity of intellectual positions. Heavily debated among scholars, it is the site of intensive clashes between worldviews that are themselves in conflict with mechanistic ones. On this, see D. C. Phillips, "Organicism in the Late Nineteenth and Early Twentieth Centuries," *Journal of the History of Ideas* 31, no. 3 (1970): 413–32; Hilde Hein, "The Endurance of the Mechanism-Vitalism Controversy," *Journal of the History of Biology* 5, no. 1 (1972): 159–88; and Donna J. Haraway, *Crystals, Fabrics, and Fields: Metaphors of Organicism in Twentieth-Century Developmental Biology* (New Haven: Yale University Press, 1976).

is to be excluded. For Uexküll, difference can only be seen as a deviation from oneness and thus as a threat to holism—despite the fact that the perspectivism of Umwelt theory would seem to affirm a diversity of worlds. Umwelt theory is a theory of correct placement—and thus also wrong placement. Whoever is different belongs to a different holistic unity, whose place is elsewhere. Uexküll's biology is always political, his Umwelt theory always a worldview.

It is precisely these aspects that are regaining their fraught power today with the emergence (or reemergence) of a "conservative ecology," as promoted by the identitarian movement and the New Right.[2] Where this conservative ecology points back to Uexküll (as do its proponents Michael Beleites and Alain de Benoist), it presents itself as both holistic and ethnonationalist, and thus politically and biologically conservative. Taking up the ideology of "blood and soil" more or less explicitly and seeing itself as a continuation of the interwar period's "Conservative Revolution," conservative ecology wants to frame the "Umwelt" or "environment" as the authentic "Lebensraum" (living space) of a "Volk" (people or nation, but in this context also ethnonation) and to integrate the Umwelt into "Heimatschutz" (which means here both homeland protection and habitat protection), thereby taking a racist population policy and making it a topic of ecology. In accordance with Umwelt theory, the mixing of Umwelten is seen as the greatest threat to the holistic order and the integrity of the Volk's supposed cultural and biological oneness: to each his own Umwelt, but please not in our Lebensraum.

Conservative ecology shares many antidemocratic, antiliberal, and antiegalitarian lines of thought with Umwelt theory. It sees itself as a continuation of the interwar period's Conservative

2 Conservative ecology does not represent a well-defined theory with unambiguous statements but instead a loosely connected political movement sharing the ideas noted here and disseminating its message through corresponding books, magazines, websites, videos, and chat forums. A detailed analysis is presented at the end of the first chapter.

Revolution, with Uexküll counted as one of its protagonists by Armin Mohler, who helped shape the New Right movement in Germany.[3] It is therefore no accident that Umwelt theory has once again proven so compatible with right-wing viewpoints.

It is the availability of new source materials that have made this book's analyses particularly groundbreaking, with recent years witnessing the publication of historical documents casting a new light on Uexküll's role in Nazism.[4] The fact that he was, at least until 1934, much more deeply involved in it than was previously known, and that he tried at the time to expand his "biology of the state" into a doctrine of the "total state" for the Nazis, inevitably changes the traditionally dominant perspective on his biography.[5]

Uexküll has long been described (especially with reference to the 1964 hagiographical biography written by his wife Gudrun) as an upstanding and unsuspecting conservative aristocrat, one

3 See Armin Mohler, *Die konservative Revolution in Deutschland 1918–1932: Ein Handbuch* (Darmstadt: Wissenschaftliche Buchgesellschaft, 1989), 79 and 313.

4 Uexküll's problematic statements about Judaism, his praise of Hitler in the revised second edition of *Staatsbiologie*, and his friendship with the racial hygienist Houston Stewart Chamberlain have all been noted in important previous works, which have also discussed the connection between biological and ideological debates. The historical research detailed in the present book not only substantiates these observations, which are often neglected by scholars who favor a rehabilitation of Uexküllian theory, but also demonstrate a previously unknown dimension of his entanglement with Nazism; see E. Scheerer, "Organische Weltanschauung und Ganzheitspsychologie," in *Psychologie im Nationalsozialismus*, ed. C. F. Graumann (Berlin: Springer, 1985); Anne Harrington, *Reenchanted Science: Holism in German Culture from Wilhelm II to Hitler* (Princeton: Princeton University Press, 1999); Marco Stella and Karl Kleisner, "Uexküllian Umwelt as Science and as Ideology: The Light and the Dark Side of a Concept," *Theory in Biosciences* 129, no. 1 (2010): 39–50; Geoffrey Winthrop-Young, "Afterword: Bubbles and Webs; A Backdoor Stroll through the Readings of Uexküll," in *A Foray into the Worlds of Animals and Humans: With a Theory of Meaning*, ed. Geoffrey Winthrop-Young (Minneapolis: University of Minnesota Press, 2010).

5 A tabular overview of Uexküll's biography is presented at the end of this book.

who made a few mistakes at most but still opposed the regime on certain points, and so was ultimately blameless. According to commentators such as Giorgio Agamben, Uexküll's occasional flashes of antisemitism were simply a "curious episode" in the biography of "this very sober scientist."[6] But this image of Uexküll is shattered by newly published archival materials on his role in the Committee for Legal Philosophy at the Academy for German Law (which was deeply anchored in Nazism), materials that this book is now been systematically bringing together for the first time. Uexküll was not just an "advantage-seeking bit player,"[7] and the assertion that he turned away from Nazi politics and ideology after Hitler's takeover in 1933 is mistaken.[8] In light of the new sources, reports of Uexküll's alleged acts of resistance in 1933, as claimed by his wife and her subsequent readers, have turned out to be historical revisionism downplaying his involvement. Uexküll took an active part in the development of a Nazi legal philosophy, using Umwelt theory to help underpin it. Starting in the 1930s, he began justifying his antisemitism with the idea that Germany was the incorrect place for the Umwelt of the Jews.

But it is not just new biographical details that we are presenting with this book. In fact, our argument is that Umwelt theory itself cannot be extricated from this historical constellation. Uexküll's thought cannot be broken down into a forward-thinking side and a problematic side, and his pandering to the Nazis was not some temporary aberration of an otherwise blameless aristocrat. His political stance is built upon his theoretical foundations, and his book Staatsbiologie, whose revised 1933 edition calls upon Hitler to combat the "parasites" in the "body of the state," manifests this intellectual concordance—one whose roots, however, go

6 Giorgio Agamben, *The Open: Man and Animal*, ed. Werner Hamacher, trans. Kevin Attell (Stanford: Stanford University Press, 2004), 43.

7 Florian Mildenberger, "Überlegungen zu Jakob von Uexküll (1864–1944): Vorläufiger Forschungsbericht," *Österreichische Zeitschrift für Geschichtswissenschaften* 13, no. 3 (2002): 147.

8 See for example Carlo Brentari, *Jakob von Uexküll: The Discovery of the Umwelt Between Biosemiotics and Theoretical Biology* (Berlin: Springer, 2015), 39.

back much further. As early as World War I, Uexküll was using both biological and ideological arguments to justify his anti-Darwinism, which was congruent with his political conservatism. The latter abhorred any changes to the whole and implied a conception of the individual that could not be reconciled with liberal or egalitarian notions, making it even easier to do so with totalitarian ones. For Uexküll, rejecting the theory of evolution was the same as rejecting democracy, which he considered the rule of the mob. The identitarian logic of Umwelt theory converged with Uexküll's antisemitism from the very start.

This structural conservatism is the fulcrum between Umwelt theory's biological side and its political side—one that cannot be excised. It abhors any change and withdraws into the naturally given immutability of what Uexküll calls Planmäßigkeit ("conformity with a plan," indicating a purposiveness, systematicity, or planned quality). The world in which the baker does "baker things" and Mr. Schulz perceives "Schulz things" is to stay the way it is, precisely because it cannot be otherwise. If Mr. Schulz never gets to know Mr. Meyer's Umwelt and perceives "his world through his own sensory glasses,"[9] he will have to accept that the world is the way it is and cannot be changed. He has to find his place within the holism of the state so that it can give him, in turn, the security of everything being kept in its place. In this world, there is no room for a confrontation with that which is different. By 1933, Uexküll is calling whoever fails to fit into this holistic order a "parasite."

Anchored in the structural conservatism of Umwelt theory from the very start is a vision of the world that would become more than just a vision in 1933. And right from the start, this vision makes space for an antisemitism that does not come across as explicit racism but instead uses the sober facade of Umwelt theory to feign acceptance of all Umwelten, before then denying

9 Jakob von Uexküll, "Zum Verständnis der Umweltlehre," *Deutsche Rundschau* 256, no. 7 (1938): 64.

the right to remain for all those who allegedly have no place on this soil. This results in Uexküll's calling upon Hitler to remedy the problematic intermingling of Umwelten, and to fight off the parasites that have beset Germany—namely Jews, the press, and democracy itself.[10] Even though Nazism would turn out to be other than what Uexküll had hoped for—with his disdain for mass movements, modernity, and Darwinism—he still participated in the restructuring of the Nazi state until at least the summer of 1934 (there are no surviving records after this date), trying to make Umwelt theory the foundational bedrock of the new total state.

It is true that Uexküll's attempts remained just that, with the Nazis never giving his work the recognition he might have hoped for (a fate shared by many of the German holists and most of the thinkers associated with the Conservative Revolution, some of whom sat in the same Committee for Legal Philosophy alongside Uexküll); his ideas seemed too incompatible with Nazi biology's scientism and social Darwinism.[11] But it is still important to reconstruct Uexküll's conceptual connections, because this is the only way to make clear his closeness to the Conservative Revolution and to conservative ecology, and to highlight all the other problems that arise if one makes use of Umwelt theory without also considering its political entanglements and implications. Commentaries on Uexküll have generally assumed a fissure running through his work, allowing the productive parts to be separated from the problematic ones (insofar as this problematic aspect is recognized at all) and further developed on their own. We want to show that there is no such fissure. This does not mean that reading Uexküll is no longer worthwhile—but it does mean that this can no longer be done without also reflecting on the political consequences of Umwelt theory.

10 Jakob von Uexküll, *Staatsbiologie: Anatomie, Physiologie, Pathologie des Staates* (Hamburg: Hanseatische Verlagsanstalt, 1933), 2nd ed., 71.

11 On Nazi biology, see Änne Bäumer, *NS-Biologie* (Stuttgart: S. Hirzel, 1990).

The points of contact between holistic ecological thought and fascist ideology have been known for some time. The history of nature conservation under Nazism is just as well researched as the role of right-wing forces (particularly those grouped under the label of "ecofascism") in the environmental movements of the 1970s, especially in the founding of Germany's Green Party.[12] Considering the dangers involved in uncritically making Uexküll into a champion of diverse and equally deserving Umwelten, a new look at these lines of connection is necessary for an understanding of what "conservative ecology" meant in 1933 and what it means today.

This should certainly not be seen as an attempt to "cancel" Uexküll. Not only are we highly skeptical of the supposed existence of such a "cancel culture," we actually want to encourage people to read Uexküll's works—but to do so differently than before. In order to understand the broader constellation in which lines of connection can be drawn from holistic theories to today's New Right ideas, it is critically important to contextualize the historical texts—thereby allowing for a fresh new reading.

The three chapters of this book offer critical rereadings of Umwelt theory, with new historical findings as their starting point. The first step is to take Uexküll's most important ideas (especially Planmäßigkeit and its promise of order) and detail their entanglements with Nazism before relating them to the present day. The second step is to demonstrate the central position of this Planmäßigkeit in Uexküll's biology and to trace its historical discursive roots. This section closes with a look at the significance of this line of thought within the Conservative Revolution, which is understood as a collective term covering a

12 For example, see Janet Biehl and Peter Staudenmaier, *Ecofascism Revisited: Lessons from the German Experience* (Porsgrunn: New Compass Press, 2011); Oliver Geden, *Rechte Ökologie: Umweltschutz zwischen Emanzipation und Faschismus* (Berlin: Elefanten, 1999); Joachim Radkau and Frank Uekötter, eds., *Naturschutz und Nationalsozialismus* (Frankfurt am Main: Campus, 2003).

multitude of different conservatisms during the interwar period, not all of which were ultimately subsumed into Nazism, but which nonetheless helped pave the way for it. Finally, in the third step, the focus is on the relationship between Umwelt and Umgebung (meaning both "surroundings" and "the act of surrounding"), in order to work out the epistemologies of surrounding(s) upon which Umwelt theory is built. Here is where irresolvable internal contradictions emerge, culminating in an assumed plurality and multiplicity of Umwelten despite the alleged existence of a unifying Planmäßigkeit behind it all. And finally, the question is posed once again of a how a new reading of Uexküll should be conducted in this context, so that tomorrow's scholars of ecology can better arm themselves against the ghosts of their own history.

The question of Uexküll's Surroundings therefore presents itself in several ways. First, in any discussion of Uexküll's "Umgebungen" or "surroundings," there must be an examination of what exists outside the Umwelten and surrounds them. This raises the issue of the accessibility of other Umwelten, the question of intersubjectivity, change, and mixing, and consequently of the epistemologies of surrounding(s) that provide the foundation for Umwelt theory and establish these very relationships. Second, the question of Uexküll's surroundings also concerns the historical context in which he formulated his ideas, including his philosophical, biological, and political contexts, his sources of inspiration and his scorned opponents, his entanglements and his contradictions. Third, the book's title also raises the question of what happens when Uexküll's theory is transplanted from one "surroundings" to another, i.e., when it is transferred to the present day. In other words: How should Uexküll be handled today—and in the future—if we now know more about the history of his theory and how compatible it was and is with both the old and the New Right?

In addition to all the other challenges of our current situation, the Anthropocene, as a period marked by an advancing and possibly unstoppable climate change, there is also the question of how we conceptually describe today's state of affairs. While our own readings of Uexküll do not offer any solution in this regard, they do show that his Umwelt theory cannot actually provide answers for problems marked by constant change—at least if such change is not itself understood as inherent in holistic concepts such as Uexküll's Planmäßigkeit. On the contrary: Uexküll's conceptual framework can only be used with extreme caution as a kind of quarry from which theoretical fragments can be chiseled out; otherwise there is a risk that its epistemological and political problems will tag along and reproduce themselves all too quickly in a new context. Our premise is that the theoretical currents permeating Uexküll's work, along with the political positions it takes, are in some ways diametrically opposed to that which is sought by many of those who would reappropriate his ideas. Certainly, it is entirely possible to use Uexküll's ideas to develop arguments for a plurality of possible worlds, a coexistence of equally deserving life forms, and an undermining of anthropocentric thinking. But this should nonetheless be grounded in a precise reconstruction of the historical background surrounding Umwelt theory's development and spread. The aim of this book is to investigate its attendant problems—also in contrast to the more affirmative readings of Uexküll—and to show that Uexküll's political entanglements back then are now acquiring a new relevance in the modern day.

Today's ecology movement suffers from a lack of awareness of its own roots: it has never been entirely innocent, pure, or natural. If ecological theory is to be applied to the urgent tasks of tomorrow and this is to be informed by an understanding of the challenges anchored within it, then its history needs to be much more closely examined than has so far been the case. Furthermore, an investigation of ecological thinking's current popularity among scholars working in cultural studies and the philosophy of science could then be more firmly grounded in the history of ecology. If today's New Right can inscribe holistic thinking—here equated with ecological thinking—on their fluttering banners, then this should elicit a more critical view within academic discussions of ecology. That is why we declare that ecology has never been entirely innocent, pure, or natural. It was and is embedded in social contexts. Uexküll's surroundings must therefore be understood as a part of today's political confrontations.

[2]

Uexküll and Nazism: 'Planmäßigkeit' and 'Placelessness'

Florian Sprenger

Uexküll's entanglements with Nazism are fundamental—much more so than has been acknowledged. They consist above all in his attempt to make Umwelt theory compatible with an ideology of "blood and soil" and to expand this theory into an organicist notion of the "total state." The task of the following two chapters will be to elaborate the theoretical foundations that made Uexküll's theories susceptible to these connections with Nazi thought, in addition to the fascist tendencies of holistic thinking. This chapter will begin, however, by reconstructing the historical contexts for these discourses by turning to previously unexamined sources, while also making clear what Uexküll's Umwelt theory was able to offer to Nazism.

Uexküll was ambivalent about Nazi racial policy: he initially rejected the concept of "race" as too Darwinian, replacing it with the concept of "Volk" (generally meaning "people" or "nation," but here additionally with the sense of "ethnonation").[1] As early as

1 Concerning Uexküll's conception of race, see the detailed description of sources that shaped his ideas presented by Florian Mildenberger and Bernd

1915 he nevertheless conjured up the image of "racial chaos" as the specific danger posed by the interbreeding of "human races."[2] And by the early 1930s, he was conflating the antisemitism that had been more or less overt in his writings since the early 1920s with an immunitarian logic. This logic ultimately implied removing the "homeless" and thus "placeless" Jews and other groups he deemed unfitting, democratic, or liberal from the state in order to maintain its internal protection against foreign bodies. As a member of the Committee for Legal Philosophy within the Academy for German Law (the Akademie für Deutsches Recht, which was staunchly Nazi), he refashioned his work on "state biology" into a theory of the total state. This state, as he conceives it, is organized organically. It not only subordinates everything in it to politics but also assigns each component a fixed place in the whole.

From the outset, Umwelt theory is also a theory of correct placement, of being in the right place. Its first thesis is that every subject has a genuine *Umwelt* (pl. *Umwelten*, literally "around-world," referring not only to the environment, but in this context particularly to an organism's receptor world and effector world, its "Merkwelt" and "Wirkwelt"); its second is that these Umwelten are adapted to their *Umgebungen* (surroundings, sing. *Umgebung*) in accordance with a *Planmäßigkeit*—"conformity with a plan," indicating a purposiveness, systematicity, or planned quality given by nature. From these principles, it follows that changes of place endanger the whole. Behind the tendency in this theory's structure to conserve existing relations lies a structural conservatism that not only nurtures antimodern, antidemocratic, and antiliberal resentments but also explains the world as a structure in which everything has its naturally determined place. Hence the mixing of Umwelten—which is for epistemological

Herrmann, "Nachwort," in Jakob von Uexküll, *Umwelt und Innenwelt der Tiere*, ed. Florian Mildenberger and Bernd Herrmann (1909; repr., Berlin: Springer, 2014).

2 Jakob von Uexküll, "Volk und Staat," *Neue Rundschau* 26, no. 1 (1915): 54.

reasons impossible in Uexküll's theoretical biology—is to be avoided at all costs in politics, too.

This is why questions about the "right place" within an Umwelt are equally important for Uexküll in biology and politics: the Umwelt of every living entity assigns it a proper place according to the Planmäßigkeit of nature, just as the organic state—and later the "total state"—assigns every human being a proper place according to its own Planmäßigkeit. When a being is in the wrong place, this order is jeopardized. The metaphor of the soap bubble that Uexküll repeatedly uses to describe the subjectivity of Umwelten is telling here: a being who looks out at the world from within its soap bubble sees everything as refracted through this optical sphere.[3] Bubbles cannot overlap and they burst when they collide. Each bubble surrounds its place and gives its subject its own unique identity, which cannot be exchanged or changed without destroying the bubble itself. And though these bubbles can form a kind of flexible foam, this comprises a structurally immutable framework in which each cell is fixed in place.

The question of the right or wrong place of each living entity within the whole will serve as a key in this chapter to draw out the connections between Uexküll's Umwelt theory and his commitment to Nazism. In 1933 Uexküll incorporated into his theory the idea that the Jews in Germany were not in the right place—even though they have their Umwelt—and therefore that "Adolf Hitler and his movement"[4] should end this "racial chaos"[5] by removing the "parasitic network"[6] of the Jews from the body of the Volk.

3 See Jakob von Uexküll, *Theoretical Biology*, trans. Doris L. Mackinnon (New York: Harcourt, Brace & Company, 1926), 81–83. This translation is based on the 1920 first edition of Uexküll's *Theoretische Biologie*, which was later reworked for the 1928 second edition.

4 Jakob von Uexküll, *Staatsbiologie: Anatomie, Physiologie, Pathologie des Staates* (Hamburg: Hanseatische Verlagsanstalt, 1933), 2nd edition, 71.

5 Jakob von Uexküll, "Volk und Staat," *Neue Rundschau* 26, no. 1 (1915): 54.

6 Letter from Uexküll to Richard Chamberlain, April 10, 1921, quoted in Anne Harrington, *Reenchanted Science: Holism in German Culture from Wilhelm II to Hitler* (Princeton: Princeton University Press, 1999), 231.

1. Umwelt and Umgebungen

Uexküll's initial thesis posits that every living entity has "its own, unique Umwelt . . . that is mutually conditioned by the animal's Bauplan [building plan]."[7] In his 1920 book *Theoretical Biology*, he formulates this basic premise as follows: "The external world offers to the organism a certain number of properties separated in space and in time, from which to select, and therewith the possibility of making a poorer or a richer surrounding-world [Umwelt]."[8] Every living entity thus operates in its own authentic Umwelt because it inhabits a particular inner world that depends on its biological apparatus, and because it perceives particular objects (what Uexküll calls receptor cue carriers or "Merkmalsträger") existing in its surrounding or outer world, which allows it to react in its own specific way in its particular effector world.

Uexküll builds on the thesis developed by Johannes Müller in 1826 that sensory perception is based on nerve impulses specific to the respective sensory organ. Perception is accordingly a mental representation of the respectively stimulated nerves.[9] Uexküll finds in this premise the physiological proof for Kant's thesis that perception does not provide access to the world. But Uexküll goes one step further: for him, every living entity has its own apparatus for processing stimuli, which also means that it has its own Umwelt. The idea within Müller's vitalistic concept of life energy, that every stimulus has specific characteristics depending

7 Uexküll, *Umwelt und Innenwelt der Tiere*, 4. The conceptual history of "Umwelt" has been elucidated in detail by Georg Toepfer, who nevertheless uses the term synonymously with "milieu" and "environment." Georg Toepfer, ed., *Historisches Wörterbuch der Biologie* (Stuttgart: Metzler, 2011), 560–607. On the history of the concept of Umwelt, see also Geoffrey Winthrop-Young, "Afterword: Bubbles and Webs: A Backdoor Stroll through the Readings of Uexküll," in *A Foray into the Worlds of Animals and Humans: With a Theory of Meaning*, ed. Geoffrey Winthrop-Young, trans. Joseph D. O'Neil (Minneapolis: University of Minnesota Press, 2010).

8 Uexküll, *Theoretical Biology*, 317.

9 See ibid., 117–20.

on which sensory organ is perceiving it, becomes for Uexküll the Umwelt generated by all of a being's sensory organs: "But then, one has discovered the gateway to the [Umwelten], for everything a subject perceives belongs to its perception world [Merkwelt], and everything it produces, to its effect world [Wirkwelt]. These two worlds, of perception and production of effects, form one closed unit, the [Umwelt]."[10] Instead of providing access to reality, the sensory organs transform stimuli into carriers of meaning whose form and content depend on an organism's building plan. Herein lies the constructivist part of Uexküll's Umwelt theory: there is no privileged physiological access to the external world. A living entity has only what Uexküll calls a functional cycle ("Funktionskreis"), that is, the coupling of receptor and effector organs, which Uexküll elaborates as a model of all relations between subjects and their Umwelten. The functional cycle replaces the reflex model that Uexküll had developed in order to more sharply differentiate his position, in which the living entity reacts to a stimulus from outside and exhibits a predetermined behavior, with a circular structure in which perception and behavior flow into each other in the functional cycle.[11]

This foundation, increasingly refined by Uexküll since the 1910s and worked out mainly in popular science publications, produced a research agenda that was no longer able to treat organisms as isolated entities but viewed them instead as components of the mutual entanglement of the organism and its surrounding, or to cite Christina Wessely's terminology, as designed for "the

10 Uexküll, *Foray*, 42. See also Gregor Schmieg, "Die Systematik der Umwelt: Leben, Reiz und Reaktion bei Uexküll und Plessner," in *Das Leben im Menschen oder der Mensch im Leben? Deutsch-französische Genealogien zwischen Anthropologie und Anti-Humanismus*, ed. Thomas Ebke and Caterina Zanfi (Potsdam: Universitätsverlag Potsdam, 2017), 358.

11 As Carlo Brentari has noted, the second edition of *Umwelt und Innenwelt der Tiere* replaces the chapter on reflexes with a chapter on the functional cycle, which has also been interpreted as a precursor of cybernetic feedback; see Carlo Brentari, *Jakob von Uexküll: The Discovery of the Umwelt between Biosemiotics and Theoretical Biology* (Berlin: Springer, 2015), 97–98.

study of surroundings (*Umgebungswissen*)."[12] Mostly undertaken before 1920, Uexküll's experimental studies demonstrated that this knowledge is initially to be gained only from living animals, which also focused his attention on their observable behavior.[13] Beginning in the interwar period, the Umwelt theory he developed on the basis of this research then became the basis for his theoretical biology.

This theory immediately raises fundamental questions concerning worldview, with Uexküll's approach is premised on the idea that every living entity lives in a unique world accessible only to itself. The world in which we live—in which I live—is thus always only an excerpt from a multitude of possible individual Umwelten that remain inaccessible to each other. Each tick lives in its own tick Umwelt, each sea urchin in its own urchin Umwelt, and each snail in its own snail Umwelt. Although the Umwelten of individual species are similar in the sense that the species' perception organs are analogous, these worlds are never congruent. Every living entity has its own possibilities for cognition—and herein lies the Kantianism of Uexküll's position, which also fundamentally transforms Kant—that are rooted in the form of its own receptor organs. Analogous in terms of their position within Uexküll's theory, but structurally distinct from Kant's forms of intuition, these organs determine what the living entity cognizes, that is, what becomes part of its Umwelt and what does not, in addition to the forms of space and time. From this follows a concept of life that focuses not on the individual nor on a hierarchy of life forms but instead sees the principle of life equally at work in all of life's manifestations. Uexküll's vitalism draws its force

12 See Christina Wessely, "Watery Milieus: Marine Biology, Aquariums, and the Limits of Ecological Knowledge circa 1900," *Grey Room* 75, no. 6 (2019): 37. On this point, see also Kijan M. Espahangizi, *Wissenschaft im Glas: Eine historische Ökologie moderner Laborforschung* (dissertation, ETH Zürich, 2010).

13 It is for this reason that Uexküll is often considered to be one of the founders of behavioral science, influencing Konrad Lorenz among others; see Carlo Brentari, "Konrad Lorenz's Epistemological Criticism toward Jakob von Uexküll," *Sign Systems Studies* 37, no. 3/4 (2009): 637–59.

and coherence from this equality of Umwelten in their respective places within a whole of Planmäßigkeit. For Uexküll, life is based on the principle of Planmäßigkeit as defined by its various Umwelten. It is these Umwelten that give all individual elements their place in the whole.

Corresponding to Kant's unknowable thing in itself, this premise is based on the distinction between Umwelt and Umgebung that Uexküll initially employed to delineate his concept of Umwelt in 1909:[14] seen from an "objective" point of view, an Umgebung is the geographical, physical space comprising an Umwelt. They include those conditions for the organism's existence that the organism need not directly access, such as climate, soil conditions, light, or humidity. Umgebungen are not, however, comprised of what is known or recognized in these Umwelten, which themselves only ever contain certain excerpts of or perspectives on their Umgebungen.

Compared to terms like "environment" or "milieu," which are related but not congruent, Uexküll's use of "Umwelt" (an as yet uncommon word that he himself did not invent, but advanced in a new way) is more emphatic in incorporating the role of a subject, one around which a world is constituted. These terms should thus not be used interchangeably. They each convey different causalities of interaction between a surrounding and what it surrounds; each conveys different spatial and temporal relations and different horizons of what can be said about Umgebungen per se. In short, each has its own epistemology of surrounding(s), as both an activity of surrounding and state of being surrounded. Among these related terms, Uexküll's notion of Umwelt most strongly emphasizes the subjective constitution of an Umwelt by the subject who is surrounded, and this is a concept that simultaneously endows each living entity with a specific place. This raises questions that will prove key to Uexküll's epistemology of surrounding(s). How does one achieve the "objective"

14 See Uexküll, *Umwelt und Innenwelt der Tiere*.

point of view from which a certain Umgebung, and thereby indirectly other Umwelten, are accessible? How can Umwelten be observable at all, that is to say, capable of being studied scientifically at all, if they are purely subjective? Uexküll develops a methodology that works through this problem, reformulating it over and over again as time goes by, sometimes in ways that contradict his earlier positions, only to repeatedly fail to find a solution.[15]

The fact that the multiplicity of Umwelten does not form a cacophony but a harmony—precisely in the narrower musical sense that Uexküll often plays with[16]—is also a consequence of what Uexküll calls Planmäßigkeit. His holism ensures that the whole of nature corresponds to an order that is more than the sum of its parts while also unfolding its effect in each of those parts.[17] The primacy of the whole runs through all levels touched by Uexküll's theory—from an individual Umwelt bubble to all of nature as a subject ("Subjekt-Natur").

For Uexküll, the mechanistic biology of his day was characterized by the positing of an objective Umgebung for all living entities, the negation of their respective subjectivity, and the elision of

15 For a general discussion of epistemologies of surrounding(s), see Florian Sprenger, *Epistemologien des Umgebens: Zur Geschichte, Ökologie und Biopolitik künstlicher Environments* (Bielefeld: Transcript, 2019).

16 See Veit Erlmann, "Klang, Raum und Umwelt: Jakob von Uexkülls Musiktheorie des Lebens," *Zeitschrift für Semiotik* 34, no. 1/2 (2012): 145–58, as well as Sara A. Schroer, "Jakob von Uexküll: The Concept of Umwelt and its Potentials for an Anthropology Beyond the Human," *Ethnos* 6, no. 3 (2019): 1–21.

17 As Mildenberger's biography makes clear, Uexküll's intellectual trajectory is by no means clearly directed toward the development of a holistic theory. His publications at the beginning of the twentieth century are more multifaceted and also hint at other intellectual movements, which are nevertheless increasingly omitted in his later texts. It is precisely in the role of a holistic biologist, which is what Uexküll increasingly becomes, that he came to be embroiled in the political and philosophical debates of the 1930s; see Florian Georg Mildenberger, *Umwelt als Vision: Leben und Werk Jakob von Uexkülls (1864–1944)* (Wiesbaden: Steiner, 2007).

behavior as a category of observation. In his view, these had resulted in a purely deterministic conception of living entities as stimulus-response machines.[18] Such an approach would not be able to grasp Planmäßigkeit in his sense. Seen against this foil, Umwelt theory becomes legible as an attempt to place biology on new foundations, to ground it holistically. Because of the radicality with which Uexküll transforms this antianthropocentric subjectivity of the Umwelt (which accords no priority to human beings) into the epistemological basis of biology and beyond that into a worldview, his contemporaries saw him as a pioneer for a new way of conceptualizing human beings in nature, as do many of his readers today, though not necessarily in the discipline of biology.[19]

2. The Promise of Order in Planmäßigkeit

For Uexküll, nature is subject to a universal principle that he calls Planmäßigkeit, a "conformity with plan." This principle is expressed in a harmony between the structure of an organism, which Uexküll also calls its "Bauplan" or building plan, and the

18 The fact that hardly any biologists have ever advocated such a simplistic form of mechanism and determinism is typical of the extremely polemical debate between holism and mechanism.

19 Umwelt theory can accordingly be connected to philosophical anthropology, as can be seen, for example, in Helmuth Plessner's in-depth engagement with Uexküll, which had already begun in 1927. However, it is precisely the boundaries of Uexküll's bubbles that Plessner pierces with his "positionality of the excentric form," which sees in Umwelt theory a chance to dissolve the dichotomy of subject and object through the interweaving of each human being in its Umwelt; see Helmuth Plessner, *Levels of Organic Life and the Human: An Introduction to Philosophical Anthropology*, trans. Millay Hyatt (New York: Fordham University Press, 2019 [1928]), 58–64; see also, more recently, Katharina Block, *Von der Umwelt zur Welt: Der Weltbegriff in der Umweltsoziologie* (Bielefeld: transcript, 2015); Benjamin Bühler, *Ökologische Gouvernementalität: Zur Geschichte einer Regierungsform* (Bielefeld: transcript, 2018); and Kristian Köchy, "Helmuth Plessners Biophilosophie als Erweiterung des Uexküll-Programms," in *Zwischen den Kulturen: Plessners "Stufen des Organischen" im zeithistorischen Kontext*, ed. Kristian Köchy and Francesca Michelini (Freiburg: Karl Alber, 2016).

structure of its Umwelt. These two structures always correspond to each other. Planmäßigkeit is the principle that gives each individual—whether human or animal—its place in nature and in society. It keeps all Umwelten in place and ensures that they remain hidden from each other because they are "fitted into" the Umgebung according to the principle of Planmäßigkeit, thus also negating any need for adaptation (*Anpassung*, which is contrasted here against *Einpassung* or being "fitted into" something). One consequence is that evolution is superfluous. The chance, haphazard order of nature that follows from evolution is not compatible with Uexküll's Umwelt theory. Whereas evolutionarily adapted living entities are shaped by their surroundings, to which they are passively subjected, living entities who are "fitted into" their Umgebung in Uexküll's sense actively produce their Umwelt. In an analogous way, for Uexküll the concept of "milieu" conveys liberal and democratic ideas because it implies a deterministic relationship of an Umgebung to a passively shaped individual, that is to say, it does not grant the latter any autonomy. Hence Uexküll distinguishes "milieu" from the German term "Umwelt," which he sees as being resistant to democracy and as the only term for an Umgebung that could capture Planmäßigkeit.[20] In its Umwelt, the subject is autonomous and not subject to external forces. At the same time, as the following chapter will show, the conception of subjectivity this presupposes is devoid of any spontaneity and itself comes to be indistinguishable from the naturally given principle of Planmäßigkeit.[21] In Uexküll's Umwelt, subjectivist-relativist and determinist lines of thought thus coincide—but not in a way that blunts their difference; rather,

20 See Wolf Feuerhahn, "A Specter Is Haunting Germany—The French Specter of Milieu: On the Nomadicity and Nationality of Cultural Vocabularies," *Contributions to the History of Concepts* 9, no. 2 (2014): 33–50.

21 Maurizio Esposito also emphasizes the merging of Uexküll's notions of "subject" and "Planmäßigkeit": "Kantian Ticks, Uexküllian Melodies, and the Transformation of Transcendental Philosophy," in *Jakob von Uexküll and Philosophy: Life, Environments, Anthropology,* ed. Francesca Michelini and Kristian Köchy (London: Routledge, 2020), 39.

both of these seemingly opposing tendencies are thereby sharpened to extremes. Uexküll's Planmäßigkeit makes life appear as at once radically subjectivistic and completely predetermined.

Uexküll thus founds his theory on a fundamentally different footing compared to other models of the time, ones that try to explain how natural laws govern contingency, or how random chance governs the evolution of species. For Uexküll, Planmäßigkeit is present in all manifestations of nature, and recognizing this quality is the true aim of biology. Planmäßigkeit stands in contrast to the planlessness of Darwinism, which Uexküll argues would never be able explain the order of nature. It thus functions as what Julian Jochmaring calls a "vitalistic wild card" in assigning everything its place within the order of nature,[22] though this can only be inferred by observing how living entities are "fitted into" nature.

Planmäßigkeit thus not only governs forms of natural manifestations; it also determines the social forms of organization used by human beings. Uexküll's *Staatsbiologie: Anatomie, Physiologie, Pathologie des Staates* (State biology: anatomy, physiology, and pathology of the state) was first published in 1920, initially as a separate appendix to Uexküll's book *Theoretische Biologie*, which itself contained a chapter on the state as an organism. His *Staatsbiologie* is a project of naturalization that not only declares all institutions to be organs within a body constituted by the state but also posits relations between classes, ethnicities, and genders as natural and thus grounded in the principle of Planmäßigkeit. The book is premised upon a pathology of decay as manifested in a society that is now breaking loose from this principle. It tellingly displays all the dangers that come with a biologistic transferring of biological facts to social reality, especially of Planmäßigkeit as something that promises order,

22 Julian Jochmaring, "Im gläsernen Gehäuse: Zur Medialität der Umwelt bei Uexküll und Merleau-Ponty," in *Gehäuse: Mediale Einkapselungen*, ed. Christina Bartz et al. (Munich: Fink, 2017), 261.

 and that Uexküll also characterizes as a "Weltmacht," or "world-defining power."[23]

Uexküll's *Staatsbiologie* sketches a reactionary organicism in which the state is presented as a living entity with a monarchical head as its brain governing various estates of executive organs. This hierarchy of the state as propagated by Uexküll is based in biology. Accordingly, his *Staatsbiologie*, which he politically sharpens in 1933, attempts to return both the state and nature into a structure completely organized as a "multiform honeycomb of Umwelt cells."[24] In this static order determined by Planmäßigkeit, all changes in the placement of an Umwelt are threats to stability. For Uexküll, the anatomy of the state consists in a strictly ordered hierarchy of occupations, which ideally not only accords each one a fixed status within a desired order of estates, but is also to be understood as a chain of Umwelten: every citizen—and here Uexküll only refers to males—has one, and only one, specific task within the organism of the state.[25] Each citizen has a defined place where he must stay lest the continuity of the state be endangered. Each occupation accordingly has its own receptor world and effector world, rendering it incompatible with other positions:

> If one compares each Umwelt enclosing a single, human individual with the cell of a honeycomb, then the whole organ forms a gigantic honeycomb in which no building block may be destroyed . . . The question is only whether one can interchange the individuals encased within the different

23 Jakob von Uexküll, "Biologische Briefe an eine Dame, Brief 4–12," *Deutsche Rundschau* 179 (1919): 281.

24 Jakob von Uexküll, *Staatsbiologie: Anatomie, Physiologie, Pathologie des Staates*, 1st ed. (Paetel: Berlin, 1920), 24.

25 The corporatist estate-based society, just like the holistic conception of the state organism, was also propagated at the same time by other Conservative Revolution thinkers such as Othmar Spann; see Othmar Spann, *Der wahre Staat: Vorlesungen über Abbruch und Neubau des Staates* (Leipzig: Quelle und Meyer, 1921).

> Umwelten, like the honey in the cells, without damaging the whole.[26]

Uexküll's answer to this question is no. In this sense, the organization of the state, which he sees as necessarily centered on a monarchical Umwelt,[27] forms the Umgebung of individual Umwelten, giving them their innate and unchanging place. A change of occupation would thus be a violation of the duties that each individual has within the organism of the state. Attempts to leave one's innate place are biologically impossible and endanger the state. The baker bakes, the tailor sews, and the minister rules. "Each of them lives in a different occupational world into which he slowly grows and which eventually belongs to him as closely as does his own body."[28] This also makes the family the biological prerequisite for the continued existence of the state.

Faced with the newly established freedom of the press in Weimar Germany, and with what he saw as a generally declining sense of duty, Uexküll accordingly conjured up a scenario of decay among the organs of the state. By elevating the closure of Umwelten and its associated subjectivity to a general a model of order, one that manifests nature's Planmäßigkeit (as an ordering of all Umwelten) on a social level as well, Uexküll's *Staatsbiologie* thus implies a social complexity without any negotiation or mediation. This order cannot be mediated: any mediation, any negotiation, any election—in a word, democracy—would disrupt it. As Uexküll writes: "Attempting to impose laws on the state, which is solidly rooted in what is given by nature, is childish. Its rules can certainly be explored, but not changed."[29] Since Uexküll does not believe that exchange between these closed Umwelten is directly

26 Uexküll, *Staatsbiologie*, 1st ed., 21.

27 Ibid., 23.

28 Jakob von Uexküll, "Die Universitäten als Sinnesorgane des Staates," *Ärzteblatt für Sachsen, Provinz Sachsen, Anhalt und Thüringen* 13, no. 1 (1934): 145.

29 Jakob von Uexküll, "Die Biologie des Staates," *Nationale Erziehung* 6, no. 7/8 (1925): 180.

possible, his notion of a state manages to operate without communities formed on the basis of individual interests: Uexküll's attacks on the free press as society's "greatest enemy"[30] reveals the potential threat he believed it posed to this order. The economic workings of labor and property, including social contract theories and models of trade union organization, play no role for Uexküll. Instead, his focus lies on an organic "metabolism with its functional regulation."[31]

From this perspective, solidarity movements appear more like an attempt to collectively break loose from the position prescribed by Planmäßigkeit. The masses are dangerous precisely because they are forcing their way out of their Umwelten. Instead, what is required, and also presumed as naturally given, is being "fitted into" the order of estates. Uexküll invokes, for instance, an image of a human chain through whose hands grain passes from the countryside to arrive in the city as bread. This chain is necessary to give the Umwelten of these various occupations their own space—in contrast to the masses, in which each individual constantly changes their place and it remains impossible to realize any order at all. Uexküll has nothing but contempt for a republic of citizens.

In this convergence of what is given by nature and what is demanded by society, Uexküll shows himself to be a biologist of what is often called the "Conservative Revolution," the collection of antiliberal, antidemocratic, and antiegalitarian movements that arose in Germany during the Weimar Republic. Because Uexküll believes that subjects *cannot* and *should not* leave their place, that they cannot change their being and their thinking, and that they cannot come to agreement even discursively, the state is needed as an authoritative higher level, one possessing its own laws that accord with Planmäßigkeit (and hence express Uexküllian

30 Uexküll, *Staatsbiologie*, 2nd ed., 67.

31 Ibid.

"subjectivity") and having access to the Umgebung of these Umwelten. For Uexküll, only monarchs and a group of aristocratic state officials close to the sovereign can guarantee Planmäßigkeit. "From this it necessarily follows that the only organizational form to be manifested by every state is that of monarchy."[32] The monarch thus represents for Uexküll the counterpart of a subject who is the absolute ruler of his own, individual Umwelt. For Uexküll, it is biological reasons that make democracy an impossible form of government, and political reasons an unsuitable one.

Even by 1920, then, Uexküll assigned primacy to the state—and thus to the whole—over the people. Whereas he saw the Volk as composed of familial Umwelten, he saw the state as composed of occupational Umwelten. In the works he published from 1933 on, following the new edition of *Staatsbiologie,* Uexküll tends to undo the distinction between the Volk and the state in favor of what he considers the "totality of the state." In this totality, the Volk and the state work together as an organic unit. Since the "occupants of the state honeycomb spend only a fraction of their lives in their occupational Umwelten," he argues, the Volk and the state are not identical.[33] It is nevertheless the task of an organic and "total" state to enable both to work together.

At first glance, it seems tempting to explain these ideas biographically. As an aristocrat and former feudal landowner who had been displaced from his estate in the Baltics, Uexküll was "a member of a ruling class that inwardly sought to maintain a medieval state organized according to estates, and outwardly took the absolutist ruling principle of tsarist autocracy as its sole ideal."[34] Uexküll's self-image that repeatedly emerges in

32 Uexküll, *Staatsbiologie*, 1st ed., 18.

33 Ibid., 24.

34 Florian Mildenberger and Bernd Herrmann, "Nachwort," in *Umwelt und Innenwelt der Tiere*, 269. In the wake of the Russian Revolution and World War I, Uexküll lost his family's lands in the Baltic states, along with his savings. Mildenberger and Herrmann offer a plausible but insufficient explanation when they propose that Uexküll's loss of financial security

his writings is shaped by this social position—and the ignominy of its loss. That said, a purely biographical explanation cannot adequately explain the close epistemological entanglement of his holistic Umwelt theory with a certain manifestation of Nazism; nor can it explain the "increasingly right-wing conservative attitude" in the 1920s that Mildenberger finds in Uexküll. For this, we need the historical perspective proposed in the present book.[35]

Only then does it become clear that Uexküll's contempt for democratic and egalitarian forms of organization, his "disgust . . . at the sight of the political battle of opinions in the press and parliament," is founded not only in politics but in biology.[36] Seen thus, democracy is biologically dysfunctional because it contradicts the organic wholeness of the state. The democratic equality of all individuals is not compatible with the organic order—meaning the hierarchy of estates—that Uexküll propagated; this is an order in which each part has a specific task that can only be performed in its respective place: "One cannot play a symphony on an organ that is made up entirely of identical organ pipes, because they will all make the same sound. Likewise, one cannot create a state out of a Volk made up entirely of like individuals."[37] Similar views are apparent as early as 1923: because it rests upon "facts" rather than opinions, Uexküll affirms the "aristocratic worldview of modern science . . . we have become true aristocrats by entrusting ourselves only to the leadership of the best, and no longer of the majority."[38] By describing the pursuit of knowledge in political terms, Uexküll shows that his "aristocratism" is not

during the interwar period led to a temporary radicalization of his antisemitism (Mildenberger, *Umwelt als Vision*, 241). Harrington, too, derives Uexküll's antisemitism and his rejection of democracy from his biography; see Harrington, *Reenchanted Science*, 38–39.

35 Mildenberger, *Umwelt als Vision*, 110.

36 Uexküll, "Die Biologie des Staates," 181.

37 Uexküll, "Volk und Staat," 62.

38 Jakob von Uexküll, "Die Aristokratie in Wissenschaft und Politik," *Das Gewissen* 9, no. 1 (March 5, 1923): 9.

something that can be separated from his scientific self-conception. For Uexküll, a democratic takeover of science can only be seen as mob rule. This is why he demands constant submission to authority: "Where in the world does there exist a joint effort by free or equal factors? Coercion and subordination are the basic conditions for any thriving coordinated work."[39] For him, this hierarchy can in turn only be secured by an organic order, as envisioned in his *Staatsbiologie*, thus enabling the final abandonment of "democracy to the well-deserved damnation of laughableness."[40]

Uexküll used the same argument in 1918 to protest against universal suffrage in the January 1919 election for the constituent Weimar National Assembly. He justified his opposition by saying that the "men elected are neither representatives of the Volk nor representatives of the state. They are nothing more than representatives of the masses."[41] Democracy, he believed, leads only to the chaos of the masses, who are "united into a whole by no common ideal, no common sense for what is holy,"[42] and who therefore cannot represent a stable state and a strong Volk. The electoral law, he writes, is "completely blind to the fabric of the body of the state and can thus only bring about disaster."[43] For him, the voting mass resembled "an animal without a brain that embodies stupidity in its purest form."[44] It was only in his *Staatsbiologie*, composed two years later, that Uexküll was able to holistically construct an organic order based on estates and Umwelten, an order embedded in the state and the Volk, and thus offer a model of politics promising political stability. Uexküll

39 Ibid.

40 Ibid.

41 Jakob von Uexküll, "Biologie und Wahlrecht," *Deutsche Rundschau* 174, no. 1 (1918): 202.

42 Jakob von Uexküll, "Trebitsch und Blüher über die Judenfrage," *Deutsche Rundschau* 193 (1922): 97.

43 Uexküll, "Biologie und Wahlrecht," 202.

44 Ibid., 203.

consequently refuses to accept the "mass ritual" of the election—but for reasons of biology:

> That is why biologists are demanding an exemption clause in the electoral law, which they can only consider an indecent assault on the life of the state. Their conscience forbids them from making themselves complicit by exercising their right to vote.[45]

The dangers of biologism become especially apparent in these examples taken from Uexküll's political-biological writings. He does not ground his demands in normative claims but always with reference to what he takes to be the biological facts of his investigations: his own personal demands become demands of nature. Uexküll's *Staatsbiologie* is not just a normative political model (or rather, the model's resulting diagnosis of the existing state's pathology). It claims to describe the state as a biological structure that is subject to the same Planmäßigkeit as nature. While the incomparable Umwelten of all living entities can coexist alongside each other in nature, a viable state (meaning an organic one) can only exist if it takes this Planmäßigkeit as its model, giving it reality as a biological order.[46] If not, the natural law of life entails that the state must perish. All deviations from this order are threats to the life of the whole.

According to Umwelt theory, the world of the baker and that of the minister are fundamentally incompatible; similarly, the viability of a state depends on heeding the incompatibility of different Umwelten. This incompatibility, in turn, results in the

45 Ibid.

46 As Jonathan Beever and Morten Tønnessen have shown, Uexküll's egalitarian description of all Umwelten being equal circumvents the methodological problem of making normative deductions from biological observations; but he replaces it with the no less problematic concept of Planmäßigkeit; see Jonathan Beever and Morten Tønnessen, "'Darwin und die englische Moral': The Moral Consequences of Uexküll's Umwelt Theory" *Biosemiotics* 6, no. 3 (2013): 443.

orderly placement of all Umwelten according to Planmäßigkeit. Uexküll's writings are permeated by a promise of order in which everything has its place. If everything has its place, it also follows from this promise that whatever is not in the right place must disappear lest it endanger the whole. One consequence of this promise of order, as we will see, is an identitarian logic. This premise resulted in concrete political demands that became explicit in the 1933 revised edition of *Staatsbiologie,* and that form the foundation for Uexküll's participation in Nazi Germany's Committee for Legal Philosophy.

This promise of order can itself be understood as a particular conception of Umgebung (which semantically echoes the ancient Greek term *periechon*, "that which surrounds, encompasses"): it is not just the space surrounding a thing, it is also what gives that surrounded thing its place, precisely by surrounding it.[47] The dyad of surrounding and surrounded—which for Uexküll is the dyad of Umwelt and subject—is a relational principle in which one side is related to the other in such a way that their natural relationship determines the place of what is surrounded. Uexküll's Umwelt theory formulates this structuring principle of the Umwelt (which surrounds a thing in a particular way and thus gives it its place) for both biology and politics within the framework of an epistemology of surrounding(s) in which the surrounded subject produces its Umwelt and thus, based on its biological features, occupies its own place in accordance with the principle of Planmäßigkeit. One may argue that there is no living entity without an Umwelt—a thought that becomes explicit in Uexküll's writings around 1933. But for him, there are certainly human beings who are not in the right place, and who therefore (with

47 See Leo Spitzer, "Milieu and Ambiance," *Philosophy and Phenomenological Research* 3, no. 1 (1942): 2; and Werner Hamacher, "Amphora (Extracts)," *Assemblage* 20 (April 1993): 40–41. For Spitzer, this spatial dimension of surrounding(s) has been relegated to the background in modern scholarly inquiries into the causal interactions between surrounding and being surrounded, with the result that the '"warmth" and "depth" of *periechon* have been lost.

their Umwelt) are not "fitted into" the place where they currently are: the Jews.

3. Uexküll and Nazism

The promise of order, conceived in terms of the subject, that lies within Umwelt theory offers the prospect of a social and biological world in which the whole stands above its parts, but in which the place of the parts in the whole can only be determined because these parts are ordered in accordance with Planmäßigkeit. This approach is deeply rooted in a historical moment when order was becoming the preeminent social issue. The holistic and vitalistic theories that emerged in the German-speaking world during the interwar period with constant reference to older, natural-philosophical and biological concepts of holism belong to this historical situation, and their worldview opens up interpretations of the present and solutions for the future. With its structural conservatism and its aversion to liberalism and individualism, this holistic tradition has not been able to sufficiently arm itself against totalizing or even totalitarian blandishments; it was and is defenseless against the intentional erasure of difference and thus also against the ethnonationalist concepts of Nazi biology.[48] Uexküll, too, was susceptible especially in the early 1920s to the "power of enchantment that emanated from ethnonationalist ideals, influencing the holistic

48 See Änne Bäumer, *NS-Biologie* (Stuttgart: S. Hirzel, 1990); Jozef Keulartz, *Struggle for Nature: A Critique of Radical Ecology* (London: Routledge, 1998); Harrington, *Reenchanted Science*; Mitchell G. Ash, *Gestalt Psychology in German Culture, 1890–1967: Holism and the Quest for Objectivity* (Cambridge: Cambridge University Press, 2007). On holism in general, see D. C. Phillips, "Organicism in the Late Nineteenth and Early Twentieth Centuries," *Journal of the History of Ideas* 31, no. 3 (1970): 413–32; and Garland E. Allen, "Mechanism, Vitalism and Organicism in Late Nineteenth and Twentieth-Century Biology: The Importance of Historical Context," *Studies in History and Philosophy of Science Part C: Studies in History and Philosophy of Biological and Biomedical Sciences* 36, no. 2 (2005): 261–81.

and romantic tendencies of science in Germany at the beginning of the twentieth century."[49] Mildenberger has shown that this enthusiasm weakened between 1925 and 1933, a time when Uexküll no longer pursued his biology of the state.[50] But since he had incorporated these thoughts into the foundation of his Umwelt theory, they were positioned to return with renewed vehemence in 1933. Uexküll's example shows that there were often convergent affinities between holism and Nazism in the 1930s.[51] Holistic thinking did not necessarily have to become fascist, and fascist thinking was by no means necessarily holistic, but both showed a tendency toward one another. This observation suggests particular caution with regard to the present day.

3.1 Ideologies of Holism

In 1933—the year of the revised new edition of *Staatsbiologie*—several prominent German holists were among those who signed the *Vow of Allegiance of the Professors of the German Universities and High-Schools* [sic., Institutions of Higher Education] *to Adolf Hitler and the National Socialistic State*. Signatories included Adolf Meyer-Abich, the editor of Jan Smuts who held an extraordinary professorship in philosophy and history of natural science at Hamburg both before and after the war, and who was

49 Andreas Weber, *Die Natur als Bedeutung* (Würzburg: Königshausen & Neumann, 2003), 78.

50 See Mildenberger, *Umwelt als Vision*, 111.

51 Marco Stella and Karel Kleisner already clearly pointed out this affinity in 2010. More recent research allows us to take their warnings even more pointedly; see Marco Stella and Karel Kleisner, "Uexküllian Umwelt as Science and as Ideology: The Light and the Dark Side of a Concept," *Theory in Biosciences* 129, no. 1 (2010): 39–51; and E. Scheerer, "Organische Weltanschauung und Ganzheitspsychologie," in *Psychologie im Nationalsozialismus*, ed. C. F. Graumann (Berlin: Springer, 1985).

a friend of Uexküll;[52] Richard Woltereck;[53] Hermann Weber, a member of the Nazi Party since 1933 and of the governing body of the Reichsbund für Biologie (Reich Federation for Biology); and Jakob von Uexküll.[54] A brief glance at the writings of these professors shows that this was not just opportunism. In his 1937 book Ökologie als Wissenschaft von der Natur oder biologische Raumforschung (Ecology as the science of nature or biological spatial research), Karl Friederichs writes of the bond between a Volk and its space and refers to ecology as the "doctrine of

52 See Brentari, *Jakob von Uexküll*, 35. On the lines of connection as well as ruptures between Nazism and Meyer-Abich's holism, see Kevin S. Amidon, "Adolf Meyer-Abich, Holism, and the Negotiation of Theoretical Biology," *Biological Theory* 3, no. 4 (2008): 357–70; and Ryan Dahn, "Big Science, Nazified? Pascual Jordan, Adolf Meyer-Abich, and the Abortive Scientific Journal Physis," *Isis* 109, no. 4 (2018): 68–90.

53 See Richard Woltereck, *Grundzüge einer allgemeinen Biologie: Die Organismen als Gefüge/Getriebe, als Normen und als erlebende Subjekte* (Stuttgart: Enke, 1932). For a more detailed discussion of Woltereck, see Jonathan Harwood, "Weimar Culture and Biological Theory: A Study of Richard Woltereck (1877–1944)," *History of Science* 34, no. 3 (1996): 347–77; and Sabine Brauckmann, "From the Haptic-Optic Space to Our Environment: Jakob von Uexküll and Richard Woltereck," *Semiotica* 134, no. 1/4 (2001): 293–309.

54 The question of whether these biologists were Nazis and whether they consistently backed the regime is beside the point, because it diverts attention away from the ease with which their theories could be aligned with the ideology of the time. To cite Thomas Potthast: "This 'synthetic' vision of ecology fit into Nazism via references to biology as a worldview and, above all, by equating [the Nazi terms of] 'Lebensgemeinschaft und Lebensraum' [a living commonality and living space] with 'blood and soil,' and by insisting on 'Gemeinschaft als Lebensform der Natur' [commonality as nature's life form], without fully subscribing on the theoretical level to biologistic-deterministic racism." See Tomas Potthast, "Wissenschaftliche Ökologie und Naturschutz: Szenen einer Annäherung," in *Naturschutz und Nationalsozialismus*, ed. Joachim Radkau and Frank Uekötter (Frankfurt am Main: Campus, 2003), 238. Ute Deichmann emphasizes that in contrast to other sciences, biology saw no mass exodus of established researchers, because large parts of the discipline fell in line behind this new direction; see Ute Deichmann, *Biologists under Hitler* (Cambridge: Harvard University Press, 1996).

blood and soil."[55] Similar thoughts were expressed by August Thienemann, who is not listed as a signatory of this pledge but nonetheless brought his holism in line with Nazism. Directly referring to Uexküll, Thienemann likewise transforms the ecological premise that organisms can only be explained in their interaction with each other and with their surrounding into a doctrine of "blood and soil," which he sees as a step toward realizing a Nazi biology: "When one hears today: 'Biology' is a crucial part of the Nazi worldview,' this entails for biologists not only joy at the recognition of a long-desired position but above all a serious, weighty duty."[56] Weber writes analogously in 1942, with reference to Uexküll:

> In the language of biologists, the pair of terms 'organism and Umwelt' . . . means the same thing as what is meant, in the language of politics, by the expression 'blood and soil.' They are not, in other words, an antithesis but on the contrary the expression of a close connection, an interlocking that is naturally necessary and governed by laws of two highly complex structures.[57]

55 Karl Friederichs, *Ökologie als Wissenschaft von der Natur oder biologische Raumforschung* (Leipzig: Barth, 1937), 91. For a historical contextualization of Friederich, see Deichmann, *Biologen unter Hitler*, 124.

56 August Thienemann, *Leben und Umwelt* (Leipzig: Barth, 1941), 74. The last observation in Thienemann's book, however, is a remark that there is not yet any chair of ecology in Germany (see ibid., 118). As Thomas Potthast has shown, Thienemann's book *Grundzüge einer allgemeinen Ökologie* (Outlines of a general ecology), first published in 1939, appeared in the 1956 series Rowohlts Deutsche Enzyklopädie with many sections couched in Nazi rhetoric deleted. See Thomas Potthast, "Wissenschaftliche Ökologie und Naturschutz," in *Naturschutz und Nationalsozialismus*, 252, as well as Kurt Jax, "'Organismic' Positions in Early German-Speaking Ecology and Its (Almost) Forgotten Dissidents," *History and Philosophy of the Life Sciences* 42, no. 4 (2020): 9.

57 Hermann Weber, "Organismus und Umwelt," *Der Biologe*, no. 11 (1942): 57. For a more detailed discussion of Weber, see Stella and Kleisner, "Uexküllian Umwelt as Science and as Ideology."

Hans Böker, who had been working on a holistic theory of anatomy, became a nonactive sustaining member of the SS in 1934.[58] Meyer-Abich proclaimed in 1939 that holism is the view "most clearly capable of outlining the epistemological program of our generation," which he saw as standing at "decisive turning points in Western intellectual history."[59]

The German-language holism of the years before the war demanded that all individual interests should be subordinated to the whole—whether in biology or politics. The holistic biologists and ecologists of the interwar period were more or less actively engaged in trying to provide policymakers with such a language of the whole. With the new edition of his *Staatsbiologie*, Uexküll, too, offered his conservatism as a holistic worldview for the new movement with the hope that biological science could become the foundation for policy decisions in the new political constellation.

For the holists mentioned here, who dominated the field of scientific debate in Germany, Nazism (at least in the mid-1930s) promised a future purified of democracy, individualism, and liberalism, and in which the whole would stand above the individual. For Nazism, holism was attractive because it offered a countermodel to the mechanistic concept of nature, which it

58 See Alejandro Fábregas-Tejeda, Abigail Nieves Delgado, and Jan Baedke, "Reconstructing 'Umkonstruktion': Hans Böker's Organism-Centered Approach to Evolution," *Classics in Biological Theory* 16 (2021).

59 Adolf Meyer-Abich, "Hauptgedanken des Holismus," *Acta Biotheoretica* 5, no. 2 (1940): 89–90. At the time Meyer-Abich was working at the German-Dominican Institute in Ciudad Trujillo, the Dominican Republic, researching the "living spaces" of former colonies that he hoped to soon resettle with a new generation of scientists, as he wrote in a report to Nazi Party's office for colonial policy: "Of course, it was certainly with good reason, namely to prevent the squandering of valuable German blood, that the position was once taken years ago by those in charge that only married civil servants should be sent from Germany to the colonies." Adolf Meyer-Abich, "Gedanken über die Organisation der wissenschaftlichen Forschung in den Kolonien, 12. November 1940," quoted in Deichmann, *Biologen unter Hitler*, 106.

saw as Jewish.[60] Historians have already shown how the Nazis tried to conceive of Volk and nature together, through policies toward nature that were quite innovative (without, however, ever mentioning "Umwelt"), such as their Reich Hunting Law of 1934 and the Reich Nature Protection Law of 1935.[61] As Ludwig Trepl and Anette Voigt point out, the Nazis did not invent nature conservation but rather incorporated it as an existing conservative movement.

The Nazi version of *Naturschutz*—the conservation or protection of nature—was also capable of creating "Heimat" (meaning both "homeland" and "habitat") through the conversion of annexed territories. This meant breaking with the idea of an unchanging and already given Heimat: "Hence what was specifically Nazi was not the idea of *Heimatschutz* [both 'homeland protection' and 'habitat protection'] but the idea of producing landscapes of German Heimat in conquered territories."[62] Based on an ideology of "blood and soil," the laws passed by the Nazis not only served to protect endangered *Lebensräume*, or living spaces, but always conceived of these areas as living spaces for the German Volk. This "blood and soil" ideology emerged as early as the late nineteenth century to justify the exclusivity of German

60 For a more detailed account, see Harrington, *Reenchanted Science*.

61 On the environmental policies of Nazism, see Anna Bramwell, *Blood and Soil: Richard Walther Darré and Hitler's Green Party* (Abbotsbrook: Kensal Press, 1985); Joachim Radkau and Frank Uekötter, eds., *Naturschutz und Nationalsozialismus* (Frankfurt am Main: Campus, 2003); and Franz-Josef Brüggemeier, Mark Cioc, and Thomas Zeller, eds., *How Green were the Nazis? Nature, Environment, and Nation in the Third Reich* (Athens, OH: Ohio University Press, 2005).

62 See Ludwig Trepl and Annette Voigt, "Von einer Kulturaufgabe zur angewandten Ökologie: Welche Verwissenschaftlichung hat der Naturschutz nötig?," *Jahrbuch des Vereins zum Schutz der Bergwelt* 73 (2008): 168 (emphasis in the original). Since annexation only becomes possible at the end of the 1930s, these fault lines do not yet play a role in Uexküll's work. Whether the Nazi masterminds really argued exclusively in such biologistic terms, as Trepl and Voigt suggest, and not also in terms of culture, is an issue that would have to be discussed at more length elsewhere.

 soil for German blood—as we find, for example, in the demands made since 1930 by Richard Walther Darré, later Reich Minister for Food and Agriculture, to bring the two back together.[63] This implied that both had to be cleansed of everything foreign. As Margit Bensch points out, this is not a theory of adapting to nature but a demand for natural space to be appropriated by an actively shaping subject who is part of a Volk collectivity—and it is precisely this train of thought that we find in Uexküll's Umwelt theory.[64]

From this holistic view of nature follows the necessity of excluding everything that does not belong to this whole—leading ultimately to extreme forms of eugenic selection aimed in particular against liberal, "overcivilized," urban forms of life that were considered to have lost contact with the very ground from which they had sprung. Above all, however, this line of thought is profoundly antisemitic, because it denies the Jewish people, which it characterizes as "groundless" ("bodenlos"), the right to live on German soil and describes them as parasites. Such ideas can already be found with authors such as the philosopher Ludwig Klages, the architect and later Nazi Reichstag deputy Paul Schultze-Naumburg, and the founder of Heimatschutz Ernst Rudorff, who are today cited as masterminds of the New Right.[65]

63 Anne Bramwell has described Darré's policies as a precursor to green environmental policies: Bramwell, *Blood and Soil*.

64 See Margit Bensch, "Blut und Boden: Welche Natur bestimmt den Rassismus," in *Landschaftsentwicklung und Umweltforschung*, ed. Stefan Körner et al. (Berlin: Schriftenreihe im Fachbereich Umwelt und Gesellschaft, TU Berlin, 1999).

65 Schultze-Naumburg and Rudorff founded the German Heimatschutz Federation in 1904, which maintained close ties with the ethnonationalist movement and served as a model for the Nazis' policies of Naturschutz and Heimatschutz; see Thomas Bogner, "Zur Bedeutung von Ernst Rudorff für den Diskurs über Eigenart im Naturschutzdiskurs," in *Projektionsfläche Natur: Zum Zusammenhang von Naturbildern und gesellschaftlichen Verhältnissen*, ed. Ludwig Fischer (Hamburg: Hamburg University Press, 2004).

But they also run—often less radically, but buttressed by philosophical arguments—through the writings of these holists.

Uexküll, too, as part of this antimodern, antidemocratic tradition, repeatedly spelled out this line of thought in his Umwelt theory. In 1933, he also called for the subordination of the individual to the state, which he began calling the "total state" in 1934 and which purportedly needed to be cleansed of all parasites. This rhetoric is particularly evident in his correspondence with the racial hygienist Houston Stewart Chamberlain in the 1920s, which Anne Harrington has analyzed in detail. Harrington shows that Uexküll also tended to take more radical political positions in these letters, sometimes including antisemitism and anti-Zionism, which he then repackaged in his published writings under the guise of Umwelt theory.[66]

For example, Uexküll imagines in a letter to Chamberlain in 1921 the existence of a "parasitic network formed by the Jews, which is everywhere causing the structure of the state to disintegrate and turning nations [Völker] into festering heaps of tripe."[67] The rhetoric of the parasite that must be eradicated is first employed in Uexküll's writings around 1920, then falling into relative disuse before he takes it up once again in the 1933 revised edition of *Staatsbiologie*. Even if Uexküll protested in an unanswered letter to Chamberlain's widow, Richard Wagner's daughter Eva (who died in 1927), against the dismissal of Jewish colleagues such as

66 See Harrington, *Reenchanted Science*, 33ff. and Jutta Schmidt, "Jakob von Uexküll und Houston Stewart Chamberlain: Ein Briefwechsel in Auszügen," *Medizinhistorisches Journal* 10, no. 2 (1975): 121–29, as well as the documents cited in Florian Mildenberger and Bernd Herrmann, "Nachwort," in *Umwelt und Innenwelt der Tiere*, 295 and 308–9. Chamberlain's writings, published by Uexküll in 1928 under the title *Natur und Leben* (*Nature and life*), consist mainly of texts that mythologize nature while implying a biologistic conception of society. Antidemocratism, antisemitism, and holism go hand in hand here. See Houston Stewart Chamberlain, *Natur und Leben*, ed. Jakob von Uexküll (Munich: Bruckmann, 1928).

67 Letter from Uexküll to Richard Chamberlain, April 10, 1921, quoted in Harrington, *Reenchanted Science*, 231.

Ernst Cassirer, Otto Cohnheim, and Otto Kestner from the University of Hamburg,[68] his letters to her husband remain an expression of a stance that was anything but oppositional. Quite to the contrary, they show the ease with which Umwelt theory could be aligned with the Nazism's theory of state—which then became a concrete reality in 1933.

The holists' attempts to ingratiate themselves nevertheless ultimately remained unsuccessful, and their approach, including Umwelt theory, never achieved the influence within Nazi science that its proponents had hoped for.[69] Ecology was at this time by no means an established science but rather subject to attacks from various quarters, especially from experimental science.[70] Like so many other leading figures in the Conservative Revolution, Uexküll also seems to have hoped for something else from Nazism: as an aristocrat, he was skeptical of populist mass movements from the very start, and he rejected both eugenics and the Nazi concept of race because of what he considered to be their Darwinism. However, this did not prevent him from being actively and institutionally involved in elaborating a Nazi legal philosophy for a "total state" that was conceived in organic terms and derived from his Umwelt theory.

68 Letter from von Uexküll to Eva Chamberlain, May 5, 1933, quoted in Schmidt, "Jakob von Uexküll und Houston Stewart Chamberlain," 127. Uexküll dedicated his 1934 *Streifzüge durch die Umwelten von Tieren und Menschen* (*A Foray into the Worlds of Animals and Humans*) to Kestner.

69 Mildenberger writes of this: "Overall, it can be surmised that because of the expansionist wars of the 'Third Reich' and the role of biology as the leading scientific discipline underpinning the purpose of the state, a statically formulated Umwelt theory seemed wholly unacceptable"; see Mildenberger, *Umwelt als Vision*, 202.

70 Ecological, holistic, and organicist positions nevertheless established a firm place in the journal of the Deutscher Biologenverband (German Biologists' Association), a staunchly Nazi publication. See, for example, Friedrich Alverdes, "Organizismus und Holismus," *Der Biologe* 5, no. 4 (1936): 121–28.

In 1933, Uexküll revised *Staatsbiologie*, first published in 1920, with the goal of attracting a new readership and examining the "entirely new diseases of the state" that had since erupted.[71] Ideally, these were to be cured with the help of the new movement that had come to power. The prescription for this cure was part of Uexküll's *Staatsbiologie*: a state reorganization effort that understands the state as an organism, one in which everything has its place in the whole, and where parasites and disease producers need to be fought off.

The two editions of *Staatsbiologie* are identical except for a few passages, but it is precisely these passages that illustrate some of Uexküll's hopes—and fears—under the new regime. Reconstructing the differences between the two editions thus helps to better contextualize Uexküll's involvement in the Committee for Legal Philosophy and, in particular, to understand the role played by the image of the parasite in his antisemitism.

In the chapter devoted to the pathology of the state, Uexküll shortens the section on the "Growing together of the Tissue of the State" by cutting several paragraphs on the "ribbon-like freeloaders"[72] represented by the factory worker class (here using the German word "Band," meaning both ribbon and conveyor belt) as a "dangerous enemy of the state"[73] that, according to the 1920 edition, has made itself the "master of the country."[74] This contempt for the worker no longer seemed appropriate in 1933 given the successes of the Nazi Party, and Uexküll substituted the following sentences:

> For more than a decade, we have been compelled to witness how state-subverting collusions of every kind have

71 Uexküll, "Vorwort," in *Staatsbiologie*, 2nd ed.

72 Uexküll, *Staatsbiologie*, 1st. ed., 42.

73 Ibid.

74 Ibid.

> undermined every regulation defending the state's interests. Let us hope the day has now come that will bring the individual organs of state back to life.[75]

In the subsequent section on the dissolution of the organs of state, Uexküll adds that "no dictatorship . . . however draconian, can repair this dissolution."[76] And finally, before the section on parasites, i.e., "those of a foreign race [fremdrassigen] who are living in the state,"[77] one finds the sentence that in 1920 still carried a pessimistic cast: "Hence the downfall of the European states is only a question of time."[78] In 1933 Uexküll added: "For Germany, the danger has been averted only by Adolf Hitler and his movement."[79]

In the section on parasites of the state (discussed in more detail below), Uexküll expands the 1933 version with racial theory ideas on defending against the "inundation of individual organs by members of a foreign race."[80] Uexküll goes on by justifying the "state leader's"[81] actions against "racial diseases afflicting

75 Uexküll, *Staatsbiologie*, 2nd ed., 62.

76 Ibid.

77 Uexküll, *Staatsbiologie*, 1st ed., 49, as well as 2nd ed., 72.

78 Uexküll, *Staatsbiologie*, 1st ed., 49, as well as 2nd ed., 71.

79 Ibid. It was in this sense that Ernst Lehmann, the chairman of the Nazi-aligned Biologists' Association, reviewed the new edition of *Staatsbiologie* in 1934, while reversing the roles of trailblazer and follower (although he would later reject Umwelt theory in 1938); see Florian Mildenberger and Bernd Herrmann, "Nachwort," in *Umwelt und Innenwelt der Tiere*, 308. According to Lehmann, Hitler was carrying out what biologists like Uexküll had long been demanding: "What is, after all, the ultimate cause of the radical change brought by Adolf Hitler: he has drawn the logical conclusions from the realization that it was necessary to put the state back on the foundation of organic living. . . . It is a twofold joy to see how those who now control the state are working to take biological realities as the guide for their actions." Ernst Lehmann, "Rezension J. v. Uexküll, Staatsbiologie," *Der Biologe* 3, no. 1 (1934): 25.

80 Uexküll, *Staatsbiologie*, 2nd ed., 73.

81 Ibid.

the state,"[82] but also notes that in the case of "racial diseases afflicting the Volk . . . the absolute purity of the Volk"[83] is no elixir ensuring a thriving state. Uexküll's remarks at this point can be read as indicating the importance of ethnic polyphony: "A conductor who wanted to eliminate all horns from his orchestra would do it serious harm."[84] But here, too, behind his criticism of the determinism that he finds in race theory, we find an argument grounded in his Umwelt theory that posits Planmäßigkeit as an ineluctable order. With reference to Mendel's principles of inheritance, Uexküll states that even in the case of "racial cross-breeding"[85] no characteristics would mix and no inferior individuals would arise, as was assumed by Nazi ideology, but that "just as the bad characteristics of inferior individuals will also appear in their offspring, so too will the good characteristics of superior individuals."[86]

Thus, while Uexküll saw nothing wrong with intermarriage from the point of view of genetics, from the point of view of Umwelt theory it could very well be problematic—or salutary—under certain circumstances. The premise of this argument is that although different individuals have different Umwelten, they are all equivalent because, according to Uexküll's biological theory, a hierarchization of Umwelten is not reconcilable with the Planmäßigkeit of Umwelten.[87] This supposed tolerance is

82 Ibid.

83 Ibid.

84 Ibid.

85 Ibid.

86 Ibid., 75.

87 For example, Uexküll already writes in his 1922 essay "Leben und Tod": "In their relationship to Planmäßigkeit, all men are alike"; see Jakob von Uexküll, "Leben und Tod," *Deutsche Rundschau* 190 (1922): 180. Their Umwelten, though, are completely different, as Uexküll explains directly afterwards using the example of the encounter with a Maasai in East Africa. Uexküll establishes no hierarchy here between the Umwelten of different peoples. But he does do so between the "desolate world" of people who strive only for possessions and, on the other hand, the "wealth and diversity of nature" (ibid.) that are accessible to children and to people living in nature.

particularly evident in remarks he makes on religion in order to explain why a mixed marriage poses a problem: "The pious Christian who devotes himself to prayer in a baroque church will feel equally repelled by a Jewish synagogue as will the pious Jew by a baroque church."[88] The mutual repulsion described here looks nothing like a coexistence of equally valid Umwelten; Uexküll's model is based less on tolerance and more on exclusion and agonality, as will be shown in the following chapter. Uexküll does say that "only respect for a foreign personality and its Umwelt"[89] can be the basis for successful coexistence. This is only possible, however, if one recognizes the Planmäßigkeit that surreptitiously introduces a hierarchy of Umwelten. "It is not the sum of notes that makes the melody, nor the racially defined given sum of qualities that makes a personality, but the plan that unites them, and that is created anew for each human being."[90]

Uexküll's Umwelt theory thus does not ultimately imply a recognition of the other but the idea that one cannot in any way transcend what is one's own. It is in principle granted that others, too, have an Umwelt of their own. But in any concrete case, the Umwelt of another being remains inaccessible. It is an utterly unchangeable postulate of this theory that one cannot get outside of one's own skin, i.e., Umwelt. Every religion, to take the example from Uexküll's *Staatsbiologie*, has its own Umwelt and its own place, which cannot coincide with that of other Umwelten and places. It is easy to conclude from these ideas, as Uexküll does in the quote given above, that Germany is no place for synagogues. Beginning in 1933, an antisemitic strand appeared once again in Uexküll's writings—but this time, in the guise of dispassionate Umwelt theory rather than open aggression.

As early as 1915, Uexküll evokes the genetic danger of intermixing human races that he would later return to as a problem:

88 Uexküll, *Staatsbiologie*, 2nd ed., 75.

89 Ibid., 76.

90 Ibid.

> When individuals of different races are mixed, either a new combination of genes conforming to plan may occur, producing specific high-quality individuals; or a new race may emerge. In most cases, however, the result will be individuals who, by themselves and among each other, are ill matched. And this, following Chamberlain, can be characterized as racial chaos.[91]

In 1933, it seems, this chaos had ensued—as a chaos of Umwelten. Uexküll, though, traced it not to a mixing of genes but of Umwelten. However, salvation appeared closer in 1933 than it had in 1920: "For Germany the danger has been averted only by Adolf Hitler and his movement."[92] These words set the new agenda of *Staatsbiologie*. Uexküll names the removal of "parasites" from the body of the state as an essential feature of the policies that will soon be implemented—an immunitarian rhetoric that clearly has antisemitic connotations in the context of this period and especially of the letters cited above, even if Uexküll does not directly refer to Judaism as parasitic in his book: "Thus no one will blame a state's leader if he curbs this over-foreignization of the state's organs by a foreign race."[93]

Even though Uexküll speaks only of curbing and not of exterminating, his "parasite" rhetoric suggests that Jews should be treated just like parasites. In the context of an organic theory of the state, this word choice is not simply a metaphorical comparison (nor is any other description of state features in his text, which rejects any interpretation of the state organism idea as simply an analogy),[94] but instead a characterizing of specific biological features. In order to understand how Uexküll's 1933 edition of *Staatsbiologie* implements a Nazi program in its own particular way—not down to every detail, but by producing a

91 Uexküll, "Volk und Staat," 54.

92 Uexküll, *Staatsbiologie*, 1933, 71.

93 Ibid., 73.

94 Ibid., 5.

"total state" in the Nazi sense—it is important to highlight this rhetorical figure. It betrays the deep connection of Umwelt theory to an aristocratic conservatism that, while expecting more from Nazism and differing at times in its details, was more than sympathetic to Nazi principles—and that seized the opportunity it found to make its own contribution to the cause.

At first glance, the rhetoric of "parasites" does not accord with the equality of Umwelten in Umwelt theory. Yet this dissonance is something that should draw our attention. Uexküll does present all Umwelten as equal, but it is precisely because they have their place in the organic whole according to the principle of Planmäßigkeit that they must not mix. Whatever does not belong in the place of German Umwelten—that is to say, in the Umgebung encompassing this Umwelt—must disappear lest it endanger the order of the state.

As a biologist, Uexküll does not speak of parasites without reflection; he is well aware of their particular living conditions. A parasitic creature, like a symbiotic one, is always next to, in, or on something else that gives it its place. Parasitism as a form of life is always associated with a spatially contiguous relationship of surrounding and being surrounded.[95] Etymologically, the term comes from *para* for *beside* and *sitos* for *food* or *grain. Parasitos* originally referred to a priest who attends the meal of the gods at a sacrifice, as the representative of a community. The *parasitos* participates in the feeding of the gods, completing the ritual without contributing anything. In Greek comedy, the parasite is a beggar who entertains a table party in exchange for a meal.[96] As a biological term, the word first appeared in the sixteenth century

95 On the epistemology of surrounding(s) in the context of symbiosis, see Florian Sprenger, "Neben-, Mit-, In- und Durcheinander: Zur Wissensgeschichte der Symbiose," *Zeitschrift für theoretische Soziologie* 9, no. 2 (2020): 274–91.

96 On the conceptual history of "parasites," see Heiko Stullich, "Parasiten, eine Begriffsgeschichte," *Forum interdisziplinäre Begriffsgeschichte* 2, no. 1 (2013): 21–29.

but it was only in the early nineteenth century that it became more systematically developed. In the context of the study of insects in particular, as Georg Toepfer has elaborated, it initially denoted a one-sided relationship in which the parasite lives at the expense of the host.[97] The term became increasingly complex, ultimately leaving it unclear whether there is a general form of parasitism at all, despite the fact that this is one of the most common forms of life.

Outside biology, the term has served to convey antisemitic stereotypes at least since the eighteenth century, and thus not coincidentally since the modern nation-state began to develop.[98] It is used to insinuate that the Jews, like the Sinti and Roma, are unable to form a state of their own in diaspora, which compels them to become parasitic wherever they appear. Here, the writings of Johann Gottfried Herder provide a crucial point of reference; Herder's rhetorical figures would be reworked again and again until the Nazi era:

> The people [Volk] of God, to whom Heaven itself once gave a fatherland of their own, have been for thousands of years, nay, almost since their origin, a parasitic plant on the tribes [Stämme: the word means both tribes and stems or trunks] of other nations; a lineage [Geschlecht] of cunning middlemen almost all over the earth, who, in spite of all oppression, yearn nowhere for their own honor or a dwelling of their own, nowhere for a fatherland.[99]

97 See Georg Toepfer, "Parasitismus," in Toepfer, *Historisches Wörterbuch der Biologie*, 3.

98 On the history of this metaphor, see Alexander Bein, "'Der jüdische Parasit': Bemerkungen zur Semantik der Judenfrage," *Vierteljahreshefte zur Zeitgeschichte* 13, no. 2 (1965): 121–47.

99 Johann Gottfried Herder, *Ideen zur Philosophie der Geschichte der Menschheit: Dritter Teil* (Riga: Johann Friedrich Hartknoch, 1787), 98. In contrast to the antisemitism of the twentieth century, Herder hoped that the Jews might be integrated into the European states.

As Andreas Musolff has shown, the metaphor of the parasite changes at the end of the nineteenth century with the emergence of the idea of the "Volkskörper," the "Volk's body," capable of being infested in its entirety by parasites, an idea closely associated with holistic and organicist thinking.[100] This discourse is the basis for the mobilization of zoological and, above all, infectological science in order to fight the "parasites of the Volk [Volksparasiten]." A rhetoric of purity demands that parasites must be eradicated to protect the wholeness and immunity of the body of the Volk or the state. The foundation for these eradication measures is already laid with this appropriation of a biological understanding of parasite control.

Although Uexküll devotes what are perhaps the most forceful passages to the tick in his *Foray into the Worlds of Animals and Humans*, it is as a negative foil that parasites are used in his *Staatsbiologie*. Hence it is worth looking at the relations that Uexküll's parasites have to their Umgebungen to understand how a tick can simultaneously have an Umwelt and be "placeless"—and what this means when this discourse is transferred to Judaism. Uexküll argues that a tick is particularly well "fitted into" its Umwelt, precisely because it cannot exist as a parasite without its host, but this also means that its Umwelt is very poor. For Uexküll, just three "receptor/effector cues" [Merkmale and Wirkmale] suffice to characterize a tick's Umwelt: heat, butyric acid, and the mechanical stimulus of the host animal's skin surface.

The whole rich world surrounding the tick is constricted and transformed into an impoverished structure that, most importantly of all, consists only of three features and effect marks [Merkmale and Wirkmale]—the tick's environment [Umwelt]. However, the poverty of this environment is needful

100 See Andreas Musolff, *Metaphor, Nation and the Holocaust: The Concept of the Body Politic* (London: Routledge, 2010), 121–22.

for the certainty of action, and certainty is more important than riches.[101]

This poverty, though, is only possible because the tick has a host on which it depends for long-term survival and reproduction. Without this host, the tick loses its place in the order of nature—and the host can deprive the tick of its place. The life form of parasites is accordingly always characterized by dependency: its Umwelt can be simple because it is oriented toward another living entity as an Umwelt.

Any fascination with the poor but certain Umwelt of parasites has disappeared with the publication of *Staatsbiologie* in 1920—immediately after World War I, and against the background of the omnipresent legend that Germany had been "stabbed in the back," a rhetorical claim that was itself also an attempt to identify Germany's inner enemy. Here, the analogy between parasitic organisms and Völker (the plural of Volk) goes beyond any question of mere survival. For Uexküll, the parasites in question are not only the Jews but all those who refuse their place in the state, that is to say: foreign Völker, as well as democrats and liberals. In the first edition of *Staatsbiologie*, Uexküll refers to German factory workers as "ribbon-like freeloaders,"[102] but he uses the term "parasite" only in contexts where he is talking about foreign Völker, including the Jews. Unlike an organism, a Volk does not become a parasite to keep itself alive but as a consequence of its character. Uexküll explains this by turning to the example of England as a "Volksparasit" (a parasite upon other Völker).[103]

If a state is a parasite by its very nature, this is because of its Volk's character. Of course, not every inhabitant of a parasitic

101 Uexküll, *Foray*, 51. It is precisely this idea that Giorgio Agamben will later take up; see Giorgio Agamben, *The Open: Man and Animal* (Stanford: Stanford University Press, 2004), 39. The "poverty" of which Uexküll speaks contradicts the ostensibly equal ranking of all Umwelten.

102 Uexküll, *Staatsbiologie*, 1st ed., 42.

103 Ibid., 51.

state is himself a parasite. In the same way, it is not at all the case that each cell of a leech is itself a small leech. But just as the gametes of a leech always grow into a leech, so too is it that even if the individual Englishman is not a parasite, wherever Englishmen found a state, it will necessarily become a parasite.[104]

In a text published in 1917 at the height of World War I, "Darwin und die englische Moral" (the German word "Moral" encompasses both morals in the sense of ethics, and the morale of a population at war), Uexküll explains that Darwin's theory of evolution was received differently in England and Germany because of the countries' differing Umwelten. Above all, it is parliamentarism and the idea of "common sense" that Uexküll finds problematic. He cites the numerous crimes committed by the British against millions of Indians and Irish, which he argues Germany would never have committed because the country would never try to enslave the rest of the world. This could only be possible, he continues, in a country with parliamentarism and a free, internationally oriented press.[105]

For Uexküll, then, parasitism is not just a biological fact but also something that shapes politics: the dominant basic idea of later Nazi geopolitics, as inspired by the anthropogeographer Friedrich Ratzel (1844–1904), was that every Volk has a genuine "Lebensraum," or "living space," with which it is so connected that it can survive in other living spaces only if it is strong enough to dominate and subjugate them.[106] In this geopolitics of "blood

104 Ibid., 53.

105 See Jakob von Uexküll, "Darwin und die englische Moral," *Deutsche Rundschau* 173 (1917): 438–47, as well as Uexküll, *Staatsbiologie*, 1st ed., 51.

106 Nazism continued to develop this idea in Darwinist terms: in the struggle for survival in a harsh environment, it is only races with a good genetic makeup that persist, while inferior races either avoid the struggle to adapt and become "placeless" nomads or become extinct through natural selection; see Peter Weingart, Jürgen Kroll, and Kurt Bayertz, *Rasse, Blut und Gene*: *Geschichte der Eugenik und Rassenhygiene in Deutschland* (Frankfurt am Main: Suhrkamp, 1992). Of course, such approaches are not found in Uexküll's work, which is defined by its anti-Darwinism.

and soil," a victorious race can even make foreign lands into its own homeland, and any Volk that does not live in its place is a parasite unless it succeeds in transforming that place into a new Lebensraum of its own. Although Uexküll does not directly refer to Ratzel, the association of geographic location with an innate Umwelt is central in his application of Umwelt theory to the state.

As Roberto Esposito has pointed out in his work on immunitarian biopolitics, it is not only an abstract theory of state organs that Uexküll elaborates in 1933.[107] In his new edition of *Staatsbiologie*, he speaks not of just any state as he did in 1920, but instead outlines his concrete perceptions of Germany's situation in 1933. Even in 1920, Uexküll is already sketching out the panorama of a new German state, one that needed to be cleansed of not only "parasites of the Volk," but also the diseases of liberalism and democracy: "Thus a condition has occurred that would also occur in our body if, instead of the cells of the cerebrum, the majority of the body's cells had to decide which impulses to transmit to the nerves. Such a state of affairs is called 'nonsense.'"[108] In 1933 he demands, as an antidote to Germany's concrete endangerment, that "state physicians" be trained to fight these diseases and parasites; he demands, in other words, an immunitarian biopolitics aiming to eradicate everything that is "foreign" to the state body, and he furthermore names the instruments for doing so.[109] Parasite prophylaxis appears here as a form of collective self-defense.

For Uexküll, otherness means not being "fitted into" a particular Umgebung. This applies to all those who do not belong to this particular place, meaning they are not fused with "its blood and its soil." And "placelessness," as one might call this situation, either results from abandoning one's designated Umwelt cell

107 Roberto Esposito, *Bíos: Biopolitics and Philosophy* (Minneapolis: University of Minnesota Press, 2008), 17.

108 Uexküll, *Staatsbiologie*, 1st ed., 46.

109 On the metaphor of the "sick state"—without reference to Uexküll—see also Musolff, *Metaphor, Nation and the Holocaust*.

in the state honeycomb (something that happens because of the evils of democracy) or it is ostensibly inherent in a Volk's character.[110] Moreover, when it is not only individual living entities but a whole Volk that becomes as "placeless" as the Jews in the diaspora, it endangers the organic order of the state in which such a "placeless" Volk resides. Someone who has no place in the state, or who is deprived of a place, necessarily upsets its order, because this order consists of the organic arrangement of individually surrounding places. According to this immunitarian logic, every Umwelt is located somewhere, but not every Umwelt is allowed to have its place where it is.

Uexküll's characterization of Judaism in his letters and in other parts of his work, for example in his 1936 memoir *Niegeschaute Welten: Die Umwelten meiner Freunde* (Worlds never seen: the Umwelten of my friends) can also be read in this light.[111] In impressions from his first encounters with Jews in his youth, one finds all the elements of parasitism, even if Uexküll does not use the term:

> A completely foreign Volk lived here, corralled together in a country otherwise densely inhabited by Germans and Latvians. A crowded urban Volk, linked to the countryside only by loose economic ties. One could have excised this Volk in its entirety and transplanted it elsewhere without changing the face of the country.[112]

110 Uexküll, *Staatsbiologie*, 1st ed., 52.

111 We could not find any evidence for Gudrun von Uexküll's claim that, although this book had not been banned, its sales had been restricted and it could not be displayed in shop windows; see Gudrun *von Uexküll, Jakob von Uexküll, seine Welt und seine Umwelt* (Hamburg: Wegner, 1964), 176. The book is not listed in the 1938 censorship list, the *Liste des schädlichen und unerwünschten Schrifttums*. Brentari restates this unsubstantiated claim by writing that the book was "officially banned"; see Brentari, *Jakob von Uexküll*, 42; see also Juan M. Heredia, "Jakob von Uexküll, An Intellectual History," in Michelini and Köchy, *Jakob von Uexküll and Philosophy*, 30.

112 Jakob von Uexküll, *Niegeschaute Welten*: *Die Umwelten meiner Freunde; Ein Erinnerungsbuch* (Berlin: Fischer, 1936), 160.

With this image, Uexküll directly takes up the "parasitic plant" that Herder writes about.[113] Here, he articulates the antisemitism of the 1930s in sophisticated form, spinning further tales about the "small Umwelten" of the "simple Jews," who in his telling always correspond to common stereotypes.[114] The Jews are guests of a friendly host Volk, but soon turn out to be parasites.[115] They are described as profiteers of an exchange in which they themselves contribute nothing. This rhetoric already holds the germ of the idea that the host must rid itself of this parasite, despite all sympathies he may harbor for individual members of the alien race, and thus end the supposed abuse of his hospitality. It is precisely because the Jewish population is understood as a parasite that it can, in Uexküll's representation, be so easily expelled: transplanted elsewhere, it will be able to live just as well; but there, too, it may also spread parasitically.[116]

The account of the Jews in the Russian Empire ends with a conversation with a Jewish student who was also studying in Dorpat (now Tartu) at the same time as Uexküll. This student hopes for a "ruthless antisemitism" to remind the Jews, "who have assimilated themselves to their host Völker," that they "are one Volk under one God, and that they have a common task to fulfill for the good of mankind."[117] By appropriating this opinion and having it spoken by a Jew in his narrative, Uexküll endorses this distorted

113 Herder, *Ideen zur Philosophie der Geschichte der Menschheit*, 98.

114 Uexküll, *Niegeschaute Welten*, 161.

115 On the figure of the Jew-as-guest, see Manfred Schneider, "Der Jude als Gast," in *Gastlichkeit: Erkundungen einer Schwellensituation*, ed. Peter Friedrich and Rolf Parr (Heidelberg: synchron, 2009).

116 In his 2002 pamphlet on Jewish Bolshevism, the right-wing historian Johannes Rogalla von Bieberstein refers to a sentence that follows this statement, in order to give evidence for the positive relationship that Uexküll supposedly had with the Jews: "The pious, law-abiding Jew can be relied upon even today, but one should beware of an apostate, faithless Jew"; see Uexküll, *Niegeschaute Welten*, 166, quoted in Johannes Rogalla von Bieberstein, *"Jüdischer Bolschewismus": Mythos und Realität*, 4th ed. (Schnellroda: Edition Antaios, 2004), 30.

117 Uexküll, *Niegeschaute Welten*, 167.

self-incrimination. Despite the story's talk of the "good of mankind," it displays nothing but naked antisemitism, for which the Jews, as a "placeless Volk," are themselves to blame, and from which they will ultimately only benefit.[118]

Geoffrey Winthrop-Young has suggested reading the characterization of the Jews in Uexküll's letters as "'Umweltvergessenheit' or the 'forgetfulness of Umwelt'—an inability to grasp and experience one's own preordained environment that is both brought about and glossed over by vague appeals." One could argue about whether the analogy to Heidegger's notion of "Seinsvergessenheit," or a "forgetfulness of being," is apt.[119] But in the context of the passage quoted above, this proposed term makes it clear that for Uexküll the Jewish Volk may have an Umwelt like all other living entities, but it has ostensibly forgotten that while it may live in an Umwelt, it nonetheless has no place. If, however, in the organic "total state" (which Germany was to become from 1933 onwards), the Umwelt is bound to the place that an individual occupies in terms of spatial geography and sociopolitical order, then the absence of this place—or its deprival—has concrete political consequences. In this framework, a mixing of Umwelten must be avoided at all costs.[120]

118 Brentari, by contrast, refers to these statements as "words of appreciation for the Russian Jews"; see Brentari, *Jakob von Uexküll*, 42.

119 Geoffrey Winthrop-Young, "Afterword," in *A Foray into the Worlds of Animals and Humans*, 229. I am grateful to Erhard Schüttpelz for a discussion of the following ideas.

120 Taking up this thought of Uexküll's and drawing an equivalence between animal and human races, the staunch Nazi holist Hermann Weber wrote in 1939: "If miscegenation occurs, however, the danger to the resulting mixed population will be all the greater depending on how different the specific organization of the two races is, and hence how different their racial Umwelten are, since Umwelt always means Umgebung appropriation within a particular Umgebung. . . . If, by contrast, the races are quite different and have developed under very unequal conditions and spatial separation, the better equipped race can only lose through this mixing, even if one only applies the criteria of suitability for an Umgebung." Hermann Weber, "Der Umweltbegriff der Biologie und seine Anwendung," *Der Biologe* 8, no. 7/8

The "placelessness" of Jews as an "uprooted Volk" thus consists not only in the loss of a given place, their "homeland": it threatens the biological-political order wherever they resettle. Uexküll explains the radicalization of individual Jews—that is, their enthusiasm for Marxism and socialism—with the original loss of their natural Umwelt (just as it was only in leaving their Umwelt, he argued, that Germans could become Marxists or socialists). Since they have no place of their own, they need a host to give them a place, which means they will unavoidably become parasites. According to this logic, a "placeless" Volk is necessarily a parasitic Volk. The English may very well have a place of their own, while also being parasites occupying other places as colonies; but the Jews lack any proper place of their own at all. Their "groundlessness" (which Heidegger mentions in his *Black Notebooks*[121]) means that Jews are not only stateless and "placeless," but also that (in Uexküllian terms) even if their Umwelten are located somewhere, they have no place of their own. The problem is thus not only that they hinder a "total state"—they simply have no place in its spatial hierarchy. And because they have no place, they must disappear. Uexküll's biology sees the Jews as impossible; his politics sees them as intolerable. The Jews put into question the order in which everything is in its place. The historical consequences of this line of thought are obvious even if Uexküll, as should be emphasized once again, does not speak of murdering the Jews.

The particular type of Nazi rhetoric found in Uexküll's *Staatsbiologie* is grounded in his Umwelt theory, and with its thesis that different but equal Umwelten are incompatible it provides a

(1939): 257. Weber calls for "selection and eradication through lawmaking measures" in order to secure a "bonding" of Umwelt and human that is "grounded in the law of life" for the good of the "ethnonational [völkisch] reality" (ibid., 259). Weber further argues that "the Umwelt of a Nordic person includes a superior" (ibid., 261).

121 Martin Heidegger, *Ponderings VII–XI: Black Notebooks 1938–1939*, trans. Richard Rojcewicz (Bloomington: Indiana University Press, 2014), 75.

foundation for racist policies.[122] Uexküll's antisemitism and racism do not refer to the supposed "inferiority" of foreign races. Rather, he ascribes to these races an equal value that is nevertheless canceled out by the "placelessness" that comes with Judaism, democracy, internationalism, and liberalism. As Mildenberger has pointed out, Uexküll refuses to accept the racism of his day, which ascribes different innate characteristics to the various human races it postulated.[123] It can nevertheless be shown, in contrast to this conclusion, how Uexküll provides arguments for a form of racism that assigns to each race its own Umwelt, that demands the demarcation of each Umwelt from others, and that ties Umwelten to geographic locations while depriving some Umwelten of a place of their own, and thus eliminates any basis for their biological possibility and political legitimacy.

One might of course object that Uexküll did in fact have Jewish friends and sought to defend his fellow Jewish professors.[124] In a 1922 review of Chamberlain's book *Mensch und Gott*, Uexküll makes it clear that he sees no hierarchy between "Semitic" and "Aryan" worldviews and calls for the "moral qualities of the opponent to no longer be doubted."[125] He likewise recognizes, as Mildenberger has pointed out, that there are Jews who "are Germans in a far deeper sense than all the many thousands of pure-blood Aryans who aspire to the delusion of internationalism."[126] The fact that Uexküll writes the latter in an

122 Mildenberger has also found evidence of similar reasoning in the work of Uexküll's former collaborator Lothar Gottlieb Tirala, who became a professor of racial hygiene in Munich in 1933; see Florian Mildenberger, "Race and Breathing Therapy: The Career of Lothar Gottlieb Tirala (1886–1974)," *Sign Systems Studies* 32, no. 1–2 (2004): 253–75.

123 See Florian Mildenberger, "Überlegungen zu Jakob von Uexküll (1864–1944): "Vorläufiger Forschungsbericht," *Österreichische Zeitschrift für Geschichtswissenschaften* 13, no. 3 (2002): 145–49.

124 See Mildenberger, *Umwelt als Vision*, 158.

125 Jakob von Uexküll, "Mensch und Gott," *Deutsche Rundschau* 190 (1922): 86.

126 Uexküll, "Trebitsch und Blüher über die Judenfrage," 97. Also quoted in Florian Mildenberger and Bernd Herrmann, "Nachwort," in *Umwelt und*

essentially approving review of deeply antisemitic books by Arthur Trebitsch and Hans Blüher, however, renders this statement ambivalent at the very least. In 1933, too, Uexküll did not refer to the "inferiority" of the Jews or other antisemitic or racist stereotypes, but rather to their "placelessness." His antisemitism does not rely on sweeping attacks against a supposedly inferior race; it is rooted in his Umwelt theory. Hence his support of Jewish colleagues in no way contradicts his antisemitism. He can fully recognize the Umwelt of the Jews, but their "placelessness" leads him to demand that they be checked by the Führer. By formulating the characteristics of the parasite according to Umwelt theory and then transferring these to the Jews, Uexküll can pay respect to their Umwelt while also describing them as a Volk whose "placelessness" means it must be expelled.[127] With this rhetorical trick, Uexküll is able support the regime's fascist measures without getting his hands dirty. This is why Uexküll can write, only a few pages after calling for Hitler to expel the parasites: "Respect for the foreign personality and its Umwelt is the only basis for developing humane forms of interaction."[128]

Innenwelt der Tiere, 296.

127 In his book on the parasite, Michel Serres posited that the host exists only because the parasite exists, with the consequence that their coexistence is in no way one-sided. Serres's attempt to reinterpret the parasite becomes charged precisely in the context of the history pursued here, in that it reveals the host's inner dependence on that of which it seeks to rid itself; see Michel Serres, *The Parasite*, trans. Lawrence R. Schehr (Minneapolis: University of Minnesota Press, 1987). This idea has been further elaborated by Jonathan Inda in an examination of descriptions of migrants as parasites: "What this means is that the host and the parasite are each already inhabited, so to speak, by the other as a difference within"; see Jonathan Inda, "Foreign Bodies: Migrants, Parasites, and the Pathological Nation," *Discourse* 22, no. 3 (2000): 54.

128 Uexküll, *Staatsbiologie*, 2nd ed., 76.

In 1933 Uexküll attempts to employ the antisemitism described above not only to support his Umwelt theory but also to gain the attention of the Nazi party. He fuses the structural conservatism of his Umwelt theory with a form of fascist racist rhetoric, generating an identitarian logic that is again gaining currency today: to each Volk its own Umwelt. Uexküll dismisses ethnonationalist thinking, propagating instead a return to a Prussian state governed by a civil service and a monarchy—or now in the Nazi context, a Führer-focused state lacking a parliament and staffed by civil servants from the aristocracy (a group among which he counted himself as a former feudal landowner). But his attempt to pander to the Nazis with a holistic reading of his *Staatsbiologie*, with all its concrete political consequences for "parasites," the press, labor unions, democrats, and liberals, is obvious.

Uexküll's first direct encounter with Nazism was initially unpleasant, if Gudrun von Uexküll is to be believed. She recounts that Joseph Goebbels wrote an article in the *Völkischer Beobachter* about a conference in Hamburg—presumably the Twelfth Congress of the German Psychological Society, held from April 12 to 16, 1931, where Uexküll presented his work on the olfactory field of dogs.[129] Goebbels supposedly called Uexküll's research the "diddling of a German professor" and denounced the irrelevance of studies like his that made no contribution to the further development of the German Reich.[130] However, despite a diligent search, it has not been possible to find such an article in the *Völkischer Beobachter.* In an entry from the Goebbels diaries dated May 19, 1930, there is a hint that Goebbels may have personally met Uexküll:

129 See Jakob von Uexküll, "Das Duftfeld des Hundes," in *Bericht über den XII. Kongreß der Deutschen Gesellschaft für Psychologie in Hamburg vom 12.–16. April 1931*, ed. Gustav Kafka (Jena: Gustav Fischer, 1932).

130 See Gudrun von Uexküll, *Jakob von Uexküll, seine Welt und seine Umwelt*, 169.

> Dinner at Mrs. v. Dircksen's. I have now completely won over Court Preacher Döring. As well as a certain Prince Reuss, who immediately understood what we are after. I gave up with a certain 'Baron' Uexküll, however, who is a true white Jew.[131] It is pointless here to educate him.[132]

Although Gudrun von Uexküll suggests that her husband thus became *persona non grata*, the files of the Reich Research Council (Reichsforschungsrat) as well as the Emergency Association of German Science (Notgemeinschaft der Deutschen Wissenschaft) prove that his research on guide dogs also continued to receive funding. In 1935, 700 reichsmarks were granted out of a request for 1200 to support research on "the language of dogs." A film camera from equipment owned by the German Research Foundation (Deutsche Forschungsgemeinschaft) was also transferred to Uexküll. Until 1942, none of the eight applications for material support submitted under Uexküll's name by his Institute for Umwelt Research (Institut für Umweltforschung) were rejected.[133] It can thus be said that Uexküll—and following his retirement, the staff of the institute he built up—faced no difficulties in obtaining funding, even in difficult times.

131 From the 1930s onwards, "white Jew" was a derogatory term used primarily to describe scientists who were not seen as Jewish by virtue of their ancestry or religion, but who were considered to harbor "Jewish sentiments" and, in particular, to work in research fields that were identified as Jewish. The most prominent example is Werner Heisenberg, who had deemed Einstein's theory of relativity to be of interest. See Hermann, Armin, "Physik und Physiker im Dritten Reich," in *Wissenschaft, Gesellschaft und politische Macht*, ed. Erwin Neuenschwander (Basel: Birkhäuser, 1993), 105–25.

132 Joseph Goebbels, *Tagebücher: Teil 1, Aufzeichnungen 1923–1941, vol. 2/I Dezember 1929–Mai 1931*, ed. Elke Fröhlich (Munich: Saur, 2008), 159, entry dated May 19, 1930.

133 See the file on Jakob von Uexküll, German Federal Archives at Berlin-Lichterfelde, R 26-III (Siegel BDC) and BArch R 73/15316, https://invenio.bundesarchiv.de/invenio/direktlink/0b0b4054-f28b-46f6-8d67-e0dfe8650a3b/.

Despite these conflicts, Uexküll's strategy succeeded in at least one respect. Only one year after the revised edition of *Staatsbiologie*, he was appointed to the Committee for Legal Philosophy (Ausschuss für Rechtsphilosophie) at the Academy for German Law by Hans Frank—a man who, before the war, was Reich Leader of the National Socialist Legal Professionals Association (Nationalsozialistischer Rechtswahrerbund); during the war, was Governor General of Poland; and after the war, was sentenced to death as one of the main defendants at the Nuremberg trials. With his appointment, Uexküll became one of seventeen members on the committee, alongside Martin Heidegger, Alfred Rosenberg (who was also sentenced to death at the Nuremberg trials), Erich Rothacker, and Carl Schmitt, in addition to professors who expressed no particular affinity to Nazism, such as the neo-Kantian Rudolf Stammler and the international law expert Viktor Bruns.[134] This committee—the only one among the academy's

134 There were close links between certain committee members, especially apparent in the years 1933 and 1934: as is well known, Heidegger's lecture course from 1929/1930 *The Fundamental Concepts of Metaphysics* extensively refers to Uexküll, and in many other passages to Rothacker, with whom Heidegger had a decades-long correspondence. See Christina Vagt, "'Umzu Wohnen': Umwelt und Maschine bei Heidegger und Uexküll," in *Ambiente: Das Leben und seine Räume*, ed. Thomas Brandstetter and Karin Harrasser (Vienna: Turia + Kant, 2010). In his 1934 cultural anthropology text *Geschichtsphilosophie* (Philosophy of history), Rothacker in turn extended Uexküll's Umwelt theory to human beings, developing the thesis that there is a close correlation between lifestyle, culture, and living space. See Erich Rothacker, *Geschichtsphilosophie* (Munich: Oldenbourg, 1934), 91. For Rothacker, cultural history is a struggle between lifestyles; and since he considers these to be characteristics of races, this is a racial struggle, too. The political zeal of Rothacker, a member of the Nazi Party since 1933, has long been known. See Volker Böhnigk, "Die nationalsozialistische Kulturphilosophie Erich Rothackers," in *Philosophie im Nationalsozialismus*, ed. Hans J. Sandkühler (Hamburg: Meiner, 2009). For instance, Rothacker signed the declaration *Die deutsche Geisteswelt für Liste 1* (The German intellectual world for List 1), which was published in the Nazi newspaper, the *Völkischer Beobachter*, on March 3, 1933, two days before the Reichstag elections, followed up in November 1933 by the *Vow of Allegiance of the Professors of the German Universities*, which included the signatures of every important German

nearly sixty committees that Frank personally chaired—strove to provide legal-philosophical support to a new legal code designed to implement the Nazi agenda, a code that would be appropriate to "Deutschtum," or "Germandom." There was no coherent view of the Nazi state shared by all members of the committee, and by no means did all of its members later act in ways supportive of such a vision. But all those invited were trusted by Frank and Emge to make future contributions to such a legal philosophy.

Since the files of the committee were mostly destroyed in 1938, its work can only be reconstructed from fragments in the files of the Academy for German Law together with corresponding archival material from the Nietzsche Archive in Weimar, the Bavarian State Archives in Munich, and the German Federal Archives in Berlin. Since 2019, these files have been available in a critical edition edited by Werner Schubert. These documents make it possible for the first time to reconstruct Uexküll's role in detail. On top of this is the source-material research of Miriam Wildenauer and Kaveh Nassirin, focusing on the surviving files and later statements of the deputy head of the committee, the legal philosopher Carl Emge, who was teaching in Jena at the time in addition to

holist. Meanwhile, Carl Schmitt (himself closely read by Heidegger and Rothacker) wrote in his 1942 book *Land und Meer*: "Nonetheless, man is not a creature wholly conditioned by his medium [Umwelt]. Through history, he has the ability to get the better of his existence and his consciousness"; see Carl Schmitt, *Land and Sea*, trans. with foreword by Simona Draghici (Washington DC: Plutarch Press, 1997), 5. I thank Friedrich Balke for this reference. Schmitt, who later sought to legitimize the Nazi racial laws from the perspective of legal philosophy, had agreed to attend the committee's inaugural event, but he is not named in the attendance list, which also makes it unlikely that he met Heidegger. See Werner Schubert, "Einleitung," in *Akademie für Deutsches Recht, 1933–1945, Protokolle der Ausschüsse, Weitere Nachträge (1934–1939)*, ed. Werner Schubert XXIII (Berlin: De Gruyter, 2019), 11. Mildenberger points out that at this time Uexküll may have already personally known Rosenberg, a Baltic exile, especially since Rosenberg also translated the *Protocols of the Elders of Zion* that Uexküll cited in his letters to Chamberlain. See Mildenberger, *Umwelt als Vision*, 109.

directing the "historical-critical edition" of Nietzsche's writings.[135] The reconstruction of this material shows that the commonly accepted image of Uexküll's role in this period is untenable.

Known among historians but otherwise largely ignored until now, the committee has become (despite the scarcity of sources) the subject of intense debate in recent years, particularly due to growing controversies about Martin Heidegger's Nazi involvement, ignited by the question of whether it—and thus Heidegger—was directly involved in the creation and subsequent implementation of the Nuremberg Race Laws.[136] There is, however, no evidence that the committee influenced these laws, which were passed in September 1935;[137] and the lack of surviving archival material means there is no proof for activities

135 See Miriam Wildenauer, "Grundlegendes über den Ausschuss für Rechtsphilosophie der Akademie für Deutsches Recht," last updated May 11, 2019, https://entnazifiziert.com/; and Kaveh Nassirin, "Martin Heidegger und die 'Rechtsphilosophie' der NS-Zeit," *FORVM*, last accessed August 15, 2020, http://forvm.contextxxi.org/martin-heidegger-und-die.html. On Emge, see Stephan Günzel, "Philosophie des Führens: Carl August Emge in Jena and Weimar," in *Angst vor der Moderne: Philosophische Antworten auf Krisenerfahrungen, Der Mikrokosmos Jena 1900–1940*, ed. Klaus-Michael Kodalle (Würzburg: Königshausen & Neumann, 2000) and Christian Tilitzki, "Der Rechtsphilosoph Carl August Emge: Vom Schüler Hermann Cohens zum Stellvertreter Hans Franks," *Archiv für Rechts- und Sozialphilosophie* 89, no. 4 (2003): 459–96.

136 See François Rastier, "Heidegger, théoricien et acteur de l'extermination des juifs?," *The Conversation*, last updated November 1, 2017, last accessed August 15, 2020, https://theconversation.com/heidegger-theoricien-et-acteur-de-lextermination-des-juifs-86334; Kaveh Nassirin, "Den Völkermördern entgegengearbeitet?," *Frankfurter Allgemeine Zeitung*, July 11, 2018; Nassirin, "Martin Heidegger und die 'Rechtsphilosophie' der NS-Zeit"; and Sidonie Kellerer and François Rastier, "Den Völkermördern entgegen gearbeitet," *FORVM*, last accessed August 15, 2020, http://forvm.contextxxi.org/den-volkermordern-entgegen.html.

137 Hans-Rainer Pichinot, *Die Akademie für deutsches Recht: Aufbau und Entwicklung einer öffentlich-rechtlichen Körperschaft des Dritten Reichs* (dissertation, University of Kiel, 1981), 62ff.

after 1934.[138] Evidence regarding the end of the committee is contradictory. Officially, it was dissolved on Frank's orders in 1938, and Frank himself was stripped of all offices by Hitler on August 20, 1942.[139] A list of members is nevertheless extant that must date to sometime after July 17, 1941, given Rosenberg's designation as Reich Minister; its publication by Wildenauer in 2017 sparked intense discussions. The list indicates that the committee continued to exist until at least 1941, and at most until January 1943, but does not prove that the committee actually met.[140] The document thus does not serve to help reconstruct whether and in what form the body was still active at the time. That said, since many of the activities of the Academy for German Law were shrouded in secrecy, we cannot entirely rule out the possibility that the committee continued to operate. Equally controversial is the role played by this list of names—reduced from the original slate to only twelve remaining members that do not include Uexküll. At the very least, it proves that the unknown individual who compiled it was still involved with the committee in the early 1940s and that the availability of members was indicated by check marks. This still leaves it unclear what form and, above all, what influence on policy the committee might still have had after 1934.

While Sidonie Kellerer and François Rastier have concluded from this list of names that the committee, and thus Heidegger in

138 See Dennis LeRoy Anderson, *The Academy for German Law: 1933–1944* (New York: Taylor & Francis, 1987), 138, 347, and 578, as well as Werner Johe, *Die gleichgeschaltete Justiz: Organisation des Rechtswesens und Politisierung der Rechtsprechung 1933–1945, dargestellt am Beispiel des Oberlandesgerichtsbezirks Hamburg* (Hamburg: Christians, 1983), 29. But as Kellerer and Rastier point out, Johe's claims are only based on Frank's self-disclosures of 1946; see Kellerer and Rastier, "Den Völkermördern entgegen gearbeitet."

139 See Werner Schubert, "Einleitung," in *Akademie für Deutsches Recht*, 14. On Frank's removal, see Nassirin, "Martin Heidegger und die 'Rechtsphilosophie' der NS-Zeit."

140 For arguments that the committee had ceased activity, see ibid. In January 1943, the committee was included in an official list of academy committees that were terminated; see Wildenauer, "Grundlegendes über den Ausschuss für Rechtsphilosophie der Akademie für Deutsches Recht," section 9.1.2.

particular, was involved in the formulation and implementation of the Nazi race laws, Kaveh Nassirin rejects this view and interprets this list as simply naming potential reviewers.[141] It is not possible that the document is an actual attendance list, because the psychiatrist Max Mikorey was stationed at the front at the time; moreover, there was such deep animosity between Rosenberg and Schmitt that it was unlikely they would have worked together during this period.

In any case: Uexküll—who retired in 1936 and emigrated to Capri in 1940, where he died in 1944—is unlikely to have played a role in the process and is no longer included on the list in question. Its significance in terms of the early days of the committee in 1934 has, however, been hitherto ignored in Uexküll research.[142] Reconstructing Uexküll's role also means refuting the picture of naïveté that was painted by his wife Gudrun in her 1964 biography of her husband—and thus rejecting the most important "source" for Uexküll's life that some scholars still rely on today.

Replying to the invitation sent to him by Frank and his deputy Emge, Uexküll wrote a letter signed "Heil Hitler" and inquired about the tasks with which the committee would be charged. Implicitly, the letter refers to his *Staatsbiologie*: "Since I am convinced that the state is a living entity, I would particularly welcome the establishment of an academy dedicated to the care of its health."[143] Here, there is not much of a leap left between healthcare concerns and antiparasite rhetoric. In a letter confirming his participation, dated April 28, 1934, Uexküll expresses

141 See Rastier, "Heidegger, théoricien et acteur de l'extermination des juifs?" and Nassirin, "Martin Heidegger und die 'Rechtsphilosophie' der NS-Zeit."

142 It has been known since at least the 1980s among historians, as well as in the discussions about Heidegger, that Uexküll was involved in this committee; see Victor Farías, *Heidegger and Nazism* (Philadelphia: Temple University Press, 1990), 205–6.

143 From the Emge file in the archives of the Academy for German Law, German Federal Archives (GSA 72/1588), quoted in Wildenauer, "Grundlegendes über den Ausschuss für Rechtsphilosophie der Akademie für Deutsches Recht," part 3.5.6.

his wish to give a twenty-minute lecture at the opening event, entitled "Universities and the State."[144]

The minutes of the opening meeting on May 3, 1934, which are preserved in the Nietzsche Archive in Weimar, as well as contemporary reports in the *Thüringische Staatszeitung* of May 4, 1934, and in the *Frankfurter Zeitung* of May 5, 1934, are evidence for Uexküll's participation. In the public part of the meeting, Frank and Rosenberg gave opening speeches to the many invited political representatives. In his speech, Frank formulated the ambition of this "battle committee of National Socialism" that had garnered so much acclaim in the press:[145] "The National Socialist concept of the state will be rebuilt by us upon the foundation of the unity and purity of German humandom [Menschentum], formulated and realized in law and in the leader principle [Führerprinzip]."[146] He predicts that the committee's work will result in the enabling of "the legal development of the National Socialist state to proceed from the intellectual realization of the necessities of the German Volk, and not tolerating an independent legal system in the sense of liberalism."[147] And further: "The foundation for our lawmaking should be the natural-law necessities of Germandom."[148] From Frank's lecture, it would seem that he sees the committee, and its work of legitimizing the future race laws, as a first step toward a new system of law, even if it is possible that not all of the committee members would have agreed. In particular, the committee was to draft a new concept of the total

144 From the Emges file in the archive of the Academy for German Law, German Federal Archives (GSA 72/1588), quoted in ibid. I thank Miriam Wildenauer for providing me with a transcript of this letter.

145 Anonymous, "Thüringische Staatszeitung vom 4.5.1934," in Schubert, *Akademie für Deutsches Recht*, 54.

146 Hans Frank, "Ansprache von Hans Frank," in Schubert, *Akademie für Deutsches Recht*, 48; similarly, *Frankfurter Zeitung*, May 5, 1934, also quoted in Farías, *Heidegger and Nazism*, 271.

147 Hans Frank, "Ansprache von Hans Frank," in Schubert, *Akademie für Deutsches Recht*, 47.

148 Ibid.

state. This ambition converges neatly with Uexküll's attempts to ingratiate himself by publishing a revised edition of *Staatsbiologie*, and Uexküll's invitation to participate means the committee has gained a biologistic theory of state. Uexküll's intended role on the committee was clearly evident when Emge, following Frank's and Rosenberg's remarks, explained the planned division of the committee into subcommittees. One of these working groups was expected to focus on the relationship between race and life: "The organism concept is to be made fruitful in its significance for the law."[149]

There are no surviving records or newspaper reports of Uexküll's planned lecture. It could nevertheless have been held during a closed conference session.[150] Yet it is worth noting that there is another piece of testimony at odds with these archival files: in her biography of her husband, Gudrun von Uexküll discusses a lecture given by her husband in Weimar on that day, without mentioning the committee. The episode is also often cited in literature on Uexküll as proof of his innocence and naïveté. Gudrun von Uexküll writes that in this lecture, which was held at the Nietzsche Archive upon the invitation of the Academy for German Law, and with the attendance of Elisabeth Förster-Nietzsche, Uexküll criticized the measures that had been recently taken against Jewish university professors:

> But since Uexküll had never participated in events that could even remotely serve the purposes of the Third Reich, he made his commitment conditional on whether he was expected to express an opinion, or whether he was being given 'instructions.' There was no question of instructions,

149 Carl A. Emge, "Ansprache von Prof. Dr. C. A. Emge, Weimar," in Schubert, *Akademie für Deutsches Recht*, 52.

150 See "Niederschrift für die Sitzung vom 3.5.1934," in Schubert, *Akademie für Deutsches Recht*.

> the reply said, but a lecture was requested—entirely at his own discretion.[151]

The surviving letters between Uexküll and Emge prove that this statement is not true, as they contain no queries about instructions or opinions. The initiative for this lecture—whenever it took place—came from Uexküll himself. He did not have to fight for his freedom of speech. And the claim that he protested against the dismissal of Jewish professors is at best half true.

Gudrun von Uexküll also notes in these passages how Hitler had by this time begun to "destroy the constitutional state and democracy,"[152] but she neglects to mention that the destruction of democracy corresponded exactly to the agenda of Uexküll's *Staatsbiologie*, and that devising a new conception of state was the committee's mission. She continues:

> The lectures took place in the evening. [The opening event began at 4 p.m.—F.S.] But when Uexküll had come to the actual topic of his remarks, it became apparent that there was obviously not the slightest intention to even listen to any opinion that deviated from the party line. Soon after the first lines of his introduction, the faces in the audience grew dark. Uexküll nevertheless continued unperturbed: "Nowadays, being able to repay a blow with a fist is considered a criterion of fitness for life. But as the biologist knows, this is true only of the effector organs. An eye hit by a fist can go blind but it cannot strike back. Universities, however, have the task of being the eyes of the state . . ." At this point, Uexküll was abruptly interrupted with the specious reason that he had strayed too far from the evening's program. When Uexküll sought to explain why universities needed to be recognized and protected as "sensory organs of the state," Chairman Frank rose to speak. He indicated that he

151 Gudrun von Uexküll, *Jakob von Uexküll, seine Welt und seine Umwelt*, 174.
152 Ibid.

> did not understand exactly what was being talked about, but that he disapproved and wished to protest. After this incident, Uexküll considered the meeting to be over, as far as he was concerned, and moved to leave. But Alfred Rosenberg asked him to come to the Hotel Elefant for a private conversation. At this meeting, Uexküll suggested to Rosenberg that Rosenberg should take a closer look at Chamberlain, whom Uexküll had once admired. In order to give the party not only a program but also an ethics, Uexküll recommended that Rosenberg read Chamberlain's "Words of Christ." Rosenberg was touched, embarrassed by the moment. In this area, he said, he had come a long way from Chamberlain.[153]

The key point of this quotation is also demonstrably false: even after the inaugural event, Uexküll remained committed to the committee's Nazi agenda (now made clear in its entire scope), positioning his Umwelt theory to fulfill this purpose and even transforming it into a doctrine of the "total state." Moreover, as Mildenberger has shown, in Rosenberg's notes of 1945/46, written down in the context of the Nuremberg trials and published after his execution, Rosenberg names Uexküll, alongside Karl-Ernst von Baer and Adolf von Harnack, as a "pioneering representative of the new Umwelt research."[154]

As Wildenauer has shown, Emge also reported in 1960, from a position largely untroubled by his past, that a dispute had arisen between Uexküll and Rosenberg in connection with the committee's inaugural meeting. This dispute, he indicated, had put an end to the committee. Emge's account, however, is significantly different from that given by Gudrun von Uexküll:

> As we began our work, Alfred Rosenberg appeared and recited his famously puerile stuff. The result was that after

153 Ibid.

154 Alfred Rosenberg, *Letzte Aufzeichnungen: Ideale und Idole der nationalsozialistischen Revolution* (Göttingen: Plesse, 1955), 45. Also cited in Mildenberger, *Umwelt als Vision*, 296.

> the meeting Uexküll called on him in the hotel to point out the impossibility of his views. This was a fierce confrontation between the famous scholar, a man of great scientific eminence from the old cultural class, and a dilettantish homo novus. The encounter dealt a death blow to the working group. It was never able to meet again.[155]

Emge says not a word about an aborted lecture.

It is possible that one or both of the reports are false. Yet they cannot both be accurate. In both cases, there were reasons to make the story appear as positive as possible for the side telling the story. Three things are relevant about Emge's quote in this context. Firstly, according to Emge, it was not Rosenberg who asked Uexküll to talk to him; rather, Uexküll supposedly sought out Rosenberg. Secondly, in Emge's description of the committee, his avoidance of mentioning Heidegger and Schmitt, who were still alive at the time, is tactical. Thirdly and finally—and this is decisive—Emge's statement about the end of the committee is just as false as Gudrun von Uexküll's statement about the great gulf between the Nazis and her husband. Until now, these assertions have frequently been taken as evidence of Uexküll's naïveté. Gudrun von Uexküll's account of this episode is often cited by scholars in order to absolve Uexküll from the suspicion of closeness to the Nazi movement.[156] Yet this obscures the true

155 Carl A. Emge, "Erinnerungen eines Rechtsphilosophen an die Umwege, die sich schließlich doch als Zugänge nach Berlin erwiesen, an die dortige rechtsphilosophische Situation und Ausblicke auf Utopia," in *Studium Berolinense: Aufsätze und Beiträge zu Problemen der Wissenschaft und zur Geschichte der Friedrich-Wilhelms-Universität zu Berlin*, ed. Georg Kotowski, Eduard Neumann, and Hans Leussink (Berlin: De Gruyter, 1960), 75–76, also cited by Wildenauer, "Grundlegendes über den Ausschuss für Rechtsphilosophie der Akademie für Deutsches Recht," pt. 1.

156 The episode is uncritically cited, for example, in Charlotte Helbach, *Die Umweltlehre Jakob von Uexkülls: Ein Beispiel für die Genese von Theorien in der Biologie des 20. Jahrhunderts* (dissertation, RWTH Aachen University, 1999), 93; Mildenberger, *Umwelt als Vision*, 160; Florian Mildenberger and Bernd Herrmann, "Nachwort," in *Umwelt und Innenwelt der Tiere*, 309; Thomas

significance of this episode: the fact that Uexküll was not only invited to give a lecture but was a member of this committee; the reason for his being invited; the steps he took to ingratiate himself with the Nazi movement; and his subsequent commitment to the committee's work. Since Uexküll certainly continued to participated in committee activities in the following months, the claims made by Emge and Gudrun von Uexküll that Uexküll resisted the Nazis have grave implications, in that Hans Frank's invitation for Uexküll to join the committee meant that Uexküll had the opportunity to influence Nazi legal policies, but there is no direct evidence that Uexküll did so. Uexküll's role can nevertheless be reconstructed, at least until mid-1934, through additional letters and the lecture that was announced here and published several months later.

3.4 Organs of the Total State

The contradictory indications given by Emge and Gudrun von Uexküll, alongside the surviving documentation, produce an inconsistent picture that invites speculation. It can be considered beyond doubt that there was a conflict on May 3, 1934, because the statements in Uexküll's lecture—published a short time later under the title "Die Universitäten als Sinnesorgane des Staates" ("Universities as the sensory organs of the state") in the *Ärzteblatt für Sachsen, Provinz Sachsen, Anhalt und Thüringen* (*Medical gazette*

Potthast, "Lebensführung (in) der Dialektik von Innenwelt und Umwelt: Jakob von Uexküll, seine philosophische Rezeption und die Transformation des Begriffs 'Funktionskreis' in der Ökologie," in *Das Leben führen? Das Konzept Lebensführung zwischen Technikphilosophie und Lebensphilosophie*, ed. Nicole Karafyllis (Berlin: Edition Sigma, 2014), 198; Brentari, *Jakob von Uexküll*, 38–39; and Juan M. Heredia, "Jakob von Uexküll, an Intellectual History," in *Jakob von Uexküll and Philosophy*. Boria Sax and Peter Klopfer go one step further: "Uexküll does not explicitly support any political agenda. . . . Jakob von Uexküll recognized the danger represented by the Nazis earlier and more clearly than most of his illustrious colleagues"; see Boria Sax and Peter H. Klopfer, "Jakob von Uexküll and the Anticipation of Sociobiology," *Semiotica* 134, nos. 1–4 (2001): 771.

for Saxony, the province of Saxony, Anhalt, and Thuringia)—align only to a limited extent with Frank's and Rosenberg's conceptions of race and law, or with the intended task of the committee. Uexküll's arguments are, however, strongly in agreement with the already nascent transformation into a "total state," something that Frank himself was striving for.

It was in 1931 that Carl Schmitt introduced the concept of the "total state" into Germany's legal philosophy debates, in analogy to Ernst Jünger's "total mobilization." Its apologist purpose was to argue for the unrestricted exercise of state power and the subordination of all individual interests, as opposed to the liberal constitutional state and the freedom of individuals. Schmitt thus describes a state in which the "distinction between state and society, between government and the people," has been torn down: "Now, the state becomes the 'self-organization of society.'"[157] In the "total state," it is thus "no longer possible to distinguish between issues that are political, and as such concern the state, and issues that are social and thus non-political."[158] "Within it, there is no longer any sphere towards which the state could maintain unconditional neutrality in the sense of non-intervention."[159] The total state is thus a state in which everything individual is subordinated to the totality of its scope and every action is integrated into the orientation of the whole.

It is not unlikely that Schmitt's understanding of this term, which was widely discussed by constitutional scholars at the time, played a role in the committee, although Schmitt is not listed as present for any of the meetings.[160] At any rate, Uexküll takes this term—without crediting any sources—and uses it in this

157 Lars Vinx, ed. and trans., *The Guardian of the Constitution: Hans Kelsen and Carl Schmitt on the Limits of Constitutional Law* (Cambridge: Cambridge University Press, 2015), 131–32.

158 Ibid., 79.

159 Ibid.

160 See "Niederschrift für die Sitzung vom 3.5.1934," in Schubert, *Akademie für Deutsches Recht*, 45.

essay, as well as in another letter, thereby making it the foundation of his ruminations and transforming his *Staatsbiologie* into a theory of the total state. Significantly, the revised edition of his book appeared in the same series as the second edition of Carl Schmitt's *Begriff des Politischen* (*The Concept of the Political*) and Ernst Forsthoff's *Der totale Staat* (*The total state*).[161] Uexküll's approach shows that organic holism and totality can be translated into each other despite some points of friction. Uexküll thus makes a biological contribution to Nazi legal philosophy and to the work of this committee. As the editors of the Ärzteblatt write in a short introduction, Uexküll had already advocated for the total state "fourteen years ago, that is, at the time of Weimar's unchecked 'democracy,' or better: 'ochlocracy.'"[162] The fact that Uexküll's text for the opening event ultimately appeared in such an obscure journal raises questions; but the question of whether Uexküll might have turned against the regime in his essay has already been answered by the editors' introduction.

A cry of protest against Nazi policies, as Gudrun von Uexküll suggests, is not what we find in Uexküll's text—on the contrary.[163] Accordingly, it is worth taking a closer look at the essay, which can also be read as a response to Goebbels's hostility. Uexküll's plea for the autonomy of the university as something "connected to the body of the Volk and the state" is explicitly directed against accusations, stemming from an anti-university and anti-intellectual stance, that the institution was alienated from the world, ignorant of practical issues, and prone to hermetic language.

161 The publisher's program on the inside cover of the revised edition refers to these two books. See Carl Schmitt, *Der Begriff des Politischen* (Berlin: Duncker & Humblot, 2009 [1932]), translated by George Schwab as *The Concept of the Political* (Chicago: Chicago University Press, 2009); and Ernst Forsthoff, *Der totale Staat* (Hamburg: Hanseatische Verlagsanstalt, 1933).

162 Uexküll, "Die Universitäten als Sinnesorgane des Staates," 145.

163 The claim by Herrmann and Mildenberger that this essay "diametrically contradicts the Nazi strategies of penetrating all areas of life" is questionable in light of Uexküll's affirmation of the total state. See Florian Mildenberger and Bernd Herrmann, "Nachwort," in *Umwelt und Innenwelt der Tiere*, 309.

The decisive point, however, is that Uexküll locates the source of these attacks not in fascism, but quite to the contrary in the "old democratic way of thinking, all too familiar to us, which is always able to see in the state only a homogeneous mush of men."[164] It is thus not Nazism that threatens the university, but liberal democracy. The university trains the state's "receptor workers" ("Merkarbeiter") just as the factory trains its "effector workers" ("Wirkarbeiter"). Only in the interweaving of receptor and effector workers could the Nazi total state arise, Uexküll argues, as a state possible only in Germany, to "represent a living unity built up of organs working together."[165] What is crucial here is that both Uexküll and Schmitt explicitly position this total state in opposition to democracy, because in it everything is in its place and democracy's "mush of men" gives way to a holistic order combining the Volk and the state into a unity subordinating all individuality to the whole.[166] The total state would therefore only become possible if one were to completely detach oneself from "democratic ways of thinking."[167]

For Uexküll, the state is "total"—in contrast to Schmitt—only if it is organic and thus includes universities as sensory organs. Uexküll thereby furnishes Schmitt's idea of "self-organization"—which Schmitt himself put in quotation marks[168]—with a concrete biological meaning. In addition, he supplements the estate-based order described in *Staatsbiologie* with yet another "place," namely that of the universities, without which the total state would remain blind. Uexküll criticizes the attacks on the universities—likely also with the purges that had taken place at the University of Hamburg in mind—as a threat to this very "totality of the state" formed by an organic whole.[169]

164 Uexküll, "Die Universitäten als Sinnesorgane des Staates," 145.
165 Ibid., 146.
166 Ibid., 145.
167 Ibid.
168 Vinx, *The Guardian of the Constitution*, 131.
169 Uexküll, "Die Universitäten als Sinnesorgane des Staates," 146.

It is at this point in the essay that one finds the passage whose notion was repeated by Gudrun von Uexküll: "It takes very little muscle power to knock out an eye; the eye cannot defend itself, but will simply go blind. Likewise, it costs no effort to destroy the universities; they will not fight back. But the state will become blind."[170] Uexküll's answer to the Nazis' attacks on German universities was thus not to defend these institutions because of their importance for society or in the name of academic freedom, but on the grounds that as sensory organs they were part of a total state that would lose its sight without them. The real danger for him lay in the egalitarianism of democracy. One could continue this thought by saying that the attacks of the Nazis were wrong only because the Nazis were attacking the wrong target—and thus turning against their actual interests. Uexküll shared the intention of creating an antidemocratic total state. Universities, too, were expected to subordinate themselves to this demand.

Immediately after the opening event, i.e., before the text was published, Emge asked all participants to answer several questions on legal philosophy as a basis for further work at the second meeting of the committee, mentioning here the importance of "the German" in matters of law ("des Deutschen," referring to Germanness or German qualities). Neither Heidegger, Schmitt, nor Rosenberg sent an answer, but Uexküll did. This willingness to reply hardly suggests any resistance on Uexküll's part, let alone some abrupt end to the committee. Moreover, in Uexküll's detailed response, he makes it clear that the committee's work toward a new legal philosophy should be anchored in Umwelt theory:

> As a nature researcher, my task can only be a matter of researching the natural laws of the state as a living entity [Lebensgesetze des Staates] and their practical

170 Ibid.

> application—but never of decreeing laws in the way that suggests itself so easily to the politician and jurist.[171]

Insofar as the state is a planned organism, Uexküll's reticence here follows a consistent logic: in the case of the work before the committee, a biologist can only point to internal problems that stand in the way of natural development, but he cannot influence the state from the outside, for example, by instituting laws. Uexküll emphasizes that for a "genuine everyday justice in the state,"[172] it is necessary that citizens not only refrain from doing injustice, but also from tolerating any known injustice. One could read these lines as an indirect justification of Uexküll's own discomfort with the "cleansing" of the universities undertaken at the time.

But Uexküll starts from this thought to sketch another panorama in which the Umwelten of the various occupations are interlinked to form the whole of the total state. The fight against unemployment—one of the issues, after all, that the Nazi party seized upon in winning the Reichstag election of 1933—is for Uexküll, as a "right to work," part of the theory of state organs. The inhabitants of a state can remain in their place only if they are allowed to practice the occupation for which they have been educated or trained, that is, if they remain faithful to the given functional cycle consisting of receptor organs and effector organs. "The new government of the state regards its first task as curing this grave disease by integrating the workers who have been made superfluous [by industrialization, F.S.] into the human chain at a different place."[173] Even in his rhetorical word choices, Uexküll demonstrates his approval. Only if the total state were to succeed in overcoming unemployment by organically integrating all individuals would it be possible for it to realize Planmäßigkeit:

171 Jakob von Uexküll, "Antwort von Prof. Dr. Jakob von Uexküll vom 9.5.1934," in Schubert, *Akademie für Deutsches Recht*, 61.

172 Ibid.

173 Ibid., 62.

"Deeply rooted in his Umwelt, he [man] draws from it his moral support, his honor, and his rights."[174]

Emge echoes precisely this idea in a report on the committee's work, published in the in-house journal of the Academy for German Law, when he asks: "What is the meaning of 'Bauplan' ['building plan'] in a Volk-organism?"[175] Emge's text is similar to the presentation of the subcommittees that he gave at the opening event. Here, though, the wording has changed: just a few months earlier, he spoke of "the organism idea," but now this has been replaced with Uexküll's concept of the Bauplan.[176] Uexküll's influence on the committee is also evident in the following statement: "With the concept of race, however, those of 'organism' and 'holism' also become significant for the sphere of law."[177]

Uexküll also recorded a list of members attending the committee's second meeting in Berlin on May 26, 1934. At this event, as Wildenauer has reconstructed it, Achim Gercke appeared as a racial research expert appointed by the Ministry of the Interior and gave a lecture on the Nazi party's legal constitution of the German Volksgemeinschaft (or "Volk collectivity") as an "organically conceived, biologically coherent collectivity,"[178] and as the "higher breeding of mankind." Gercke's remarks are not far from biologism in the sense also advocated by Uexküll:

174 Ibid.

175 Carl A. Emge, "Ideen über die Aufgaben der wissenschaftlichen Rechtsphilosophie," in Schubert, *Akademie für Deutsches Recht*, 78.

176 Carl A. Emge, "Ansprache von Prof. Dr. C.A. Emge, Weimar," in Schubert, *Akademie für Deutsches Recht*, 52.

177 Carl A. Emge, "Ideen über die Aufgaben der wissenschaftlichen Rechtsphilosophie," in Schubert, *Akademie für Deutsches Recht*, 78, quotation marks in the original.

178 Achim Gercke, "Vortrag des Sachverständigen des RIM über Rasse auf der Arbeitstagung der AfDR am 26. Mai 1934," *Jahrbuch der Akademie für Deutsches Recht*, vol. 1, 1934: 242; also cited by Wildenauer, "Grundlegendes über den Ausschuss für Rechtsphilosophie der Akademie für Deutsches Recht," section 7.10.

> If one also imports National Socialist thinking into this image of the Volk body, then the National Socialist German Workers' Party would be the brain, the center of the will from which the whole unified will emanates, determining the direction in which this Volk shall now march.[179]

What exactly was discussed at this second meeting after Gercke's lecture is not indicated by extant sources. Uexküll does not appear in Emge's report on the annual meeting of the academy on June 25 and 26, 1934.[180] And with this document, the existing archival material ends, supplemented only by the disputed list of names. Although there is evidence of the committee's activities only up to June 1934, the conflict in Weimar had no immediate consequences for Uexküll. For a few months at least, he continued to be involved with the committee's agenda. The image of Uexküll as a blameless aristocrat can thus no longer be maintained.

3.5 Reception and Revisionism

Uexküll scholarship has often relied on Gudrun von Uexküll's revisionist and hagiographic account of these events in Weimar, reading it as a historical source. There has been no detailed investigation of the archival material, or of the published texts already known before the publication of the archival files, despite the fact that these sources shed a different light on the role of Umwelt theory in the 1930s. Even if Uexküll opposed the expulsion of Jewish university professors, his willingness to participate in a committee whose intentions he must have been aware of indicates his agreement with these aims in principle. This approving stance was precisely what Frank and Emge were able to take from Uexküll's revised edition of *Staatsbiologie*.[181] Emge's plan for

179 Achim Gercke, "Vortrag des Sachverständigen des RIM," 243–44, cited in ibid.

180 See Werner Schubert, "Einleitung," in Schubert, *Akademie für Deutsches Recht*, 13.

181 This reading is further backed by the aforementioned review of *Staatsbiologie* by Ernst Lehmann in the Nazi-aligned journal *Der Biologe*, in which

the subcommittee suggests that this book was the reason that Uexküll was invited to be part of the committee.

Uexküll, it can be argued, not only sought for his conservative and antidemocratic theory a connection to the Nazi movement, or at least to a particular form of it that he hoped would be realized; he also accepted the invitation to actively participate in the collaborative development of a Nazi philosophy of state and of law. He certainly did not aim to influence the higher circles of Nazi leadership. But his attempt to make Umwelt theory compatible with recent developments, and to make his holism politically viable, circuitously led him to precisely this destination. Even if the concrete consequences of his participation in this committee remain unclear, and his aristocratism was incompatible with Nazism as a mass movement, the dominant scholarly interpretations of his role during this period are no longer tenable. There is no evidence whatsoever that Uexküll was placed under surveillance by the Nazis, let alone that he was actually a victim here, as Gudrun von Uexküll suggests.

Uexküll was by no means an "advantage-seeking bit player," as Mildenberger writes.[182] To claim, as Brentari does, that Uexküll turned away from Nazism in the 1930s is simply untenable in light of the findings presented here.[183] Brentari's claim, taken from Gudrun von Uexküll, that Uexküll had been under constant Nazi surveillance since his lecture in Weimar, is very one-sided, at the very least.[184] The fact that other texts also refer to Brentari's account has moreover solidified this revisionist interpretation.[185]

Hitler's policies are interpreted as an implementation of holistic and biological research concepts; see Ernst Lehmann, "Rezension," *Der Biologe* 3 (1934): 25.

182 Mildenberger, "Überlegungen zu Jakob von Uexküll (1864–1944)," 147.

183 See Brentari, *Jakob von Uexküll*, 38–43.

184 See ibid., 42.

185 Most recently, for example, in Schroer, "Jakob von Uexküll," 17, as well as Heredia, "Jakob von Uexküll, an Intellectual History."

Charlotte Helbach states that Uexküll "consistently developed his theory until 1944, without letting adverse political circumstances get in his way."[186] Uexküll's Umwelt theory, Helbach argues with recourse to Gudrun von Uexküll, was characterized by "great tolerance as well as an open, positive stance toward and devotion to nature."[187] And in Brett Buchanan's monograph, which also draws substantially on Uexküll, *Staatsbiologie* is not even listed as one of Uexküll's publications.[188] Numerous biographical accounts ignore this phase of his life.[189] In Kalevi Kull's biographical sketch, for instance, the only remark on the reworked version of *Staatsbiologie* reads: "The chapter on pathology is considerably revised for this edition."[190]

Kaveh Nassirin has rightly argued that the diverse composition of the Committee for Legal Philosophy means Uexküll's membership alone does not establish his complicity.[191] However, Nassirin then follows Brentari's account in referring to Uexküll's letter of protest (as described by Gudrun von Uexküll) to Eva Chamberlain regarding the removal of Jewish professors from the German universities, in addition to the one-sided account of

186 Helbach, "Die Umweltlehre Jakob von Uexkülls," 8.

187 Ibid., 9.

188 Brett Buchanan, *Onto-Ethologies: The Animal Environments of Uexküll, Heidegger, Merleau-Ponty, and Deleuze* (New York: SUNY Press, 2008), 12.

189 Examples are Florian Höfer, *Die Notwendigkeit der Kommunikation: Die Missachtung eines Phänomens bei Jakob von Uexküll* (dissertation, University of Bonn, 2007), 12; Heinz Penzlin, "Jakob von Uexküll legte die Grundlagen zu seiner Umweltlehre," *Biologie in unserer Zeit* 39, no. 5 (2009): 349–52; Franz M. Wuketits, *Außenseiter in der Wissenschaft: Pioniere, Wegweiser, Reformer* (Berlin: Springer, 2015), 196–201. An explicit reference to Uexküll's entanglements, however, is found in other scholarship, such as Inga Pollmann, "Invisible Worlds, Visible: Uexküll's Umwelt, Film, and Film Theory," *Critical Inquiry* 39, no. 3 (2013): 784; Leander Scholz, *Die Menge der Menschen: Eine Figur der politischen Ökologie* (Berlin: Kadmos, 2019); Espahangizi, *Wissenschaft im Glas*, 30; as well as Julian Jochmaring, "Im gläsernen Gehäuse."

190 Kalevi Kull, "Jakob von Uexküll: An Introduction," *Semiotica* 134, no. 1/4 (2001): 30.

191 See Nassirin, "Martin Heidegger und die 'Rechtsphilosophie' der NS-Zeit."

events in Weimar (which Brentari mistakenly moves to 1936),[192] to prove that Uexküll, too, had been a blameless member of the committee. Nassirin fails to consider the passages from *Staatsbiologie* that pander to Nazism, the antisemitic and racist quotes from his letters to Chamberlain, and the transformation of *Staatsbiologie* into a doctrine of the total state.

In recent research on Uexküll, there is talk of an "alleged link to Nazi ideology" that supposedly "tainted" him, besmirching his biologist's lab coat.[193] These formulations reverse the direction of suspicion: what is suspicious is now not so much Uexküll's Umwelt theory itself but rather the speculation about a connection to Nazism. Brentari's biographical account is thus used to whitewash Uexküll's lab coat, making it cleaner than it ever was; but that account is now historically untenable. The sources examined here make certainties out of the "ambivalences" noted by Michelini regarding the interpretation of Uexküll's commitment to Nazism.

This example shows that the complex and scattered situation of the source materials makes a precise reappraisal necessary, even if the dearth of sources means much will have to remain unknown and no certainty about the exact events will emerge. What is clear, however, is that Uexküll's remarks are not simply regrettable aberrations or incidental adjuncts to an otherwise unproblematic body of work. To repeat the point: the structural conservatism of Umwelt theory grounds Uexküll's rejection of democracy and results in an identitarian logic in which everything is in its place according to the principle of Planmäßigkeit, and in

192 See Brentari, *Jakob von Uexküll*, 41.

193 Francesca Michelini, "Introduction: A Foray into Uexküll's Heritage," in *Jakob von Uexküll and Philosophy*, 1. In this quote, both the extent of Uexküll's antisemitism (already known at the time of the publication of this book co-edited by Michelini) and his support for Nazism in the revised edition of *Staatsbiologie* are presented as mere conjecture and thus downplayed. These accounts even ignore the easily researchable fact that Uexküll signed the 1933 pledge of German professors to Hitler.

which no mixing should be allowed. It is precisely these internal lines of connection that will be the subject of the two subsequent chapters.

For a further reappraisal of Umwelt theory, it is thus important to vigorously argue against the prevailing impression in Uexküllian studies that his role in the 1930s has already been clarified. As the archival documents prove, Uexküll belongs to the milieu offering at least the theoretical foundation for the Nazi reconstruction of the state and the law—and even if he was perhaps opposed to the details, he did not have objections to the aims of destroying democracy and liberalism, and ultimately Darwinism and mechanism, too. Uexküll justified this position not only politically but by reference to the holistic framework of his Umwelt theory, which in turn proved easy to translate into a doctrine of the total state.

The fact that Uexküll has nonetheless never been thoroughly investigated, apart from the exceptions mentioned above,[194] is due not only to the biography written by his wife. Uexküll fit too well (and still does) into an ecological-holistic worldview that feeds on a seemingly, even seductively progressive notion of multiplicity in which everything is connected to everything else.

4. Conservative Ecology

The task of further investigating Uexküll's entanglements becomes particularly urgent given that the conservative holism of the interwar period is of interest not only for politically uninvolved historians of science. As early as 1977, Alain de Benoist, mastermind of the French *Nouvelle Droite*, referred several times to Uexküll in his anthology of right-wing thought *Vu de droite*

194 Especially E. Scheerer, "Organische Weltanschauung und Ganzheitspsychologie," in *Psychologie im Nationalsozialismus*; Harrington, *Reenchanted Science*; Stella und Kleisner, "Uexküllian Umwelt as Science and as Ideology"; Geoffrey Winthrop-Young, "Afterword."

(*View from the Right*), and especially to both editions of *Staatsbiologie*.[195] Such positions are currently being reclaimed politically in Germany as part of a return to a Conservative Ecology on the part of the New Right and the identitarian movement.[196] Drawing on Armin Mohler, Conservative Ecology sees itself as part of the so-called Conservative Revolution, taking up its antimodernism and antidemocratism, along with a propagation of agrarian organizational models and an understanding of the Volk as tied to "blood and soil."[197] A systematic articulation of its goals can be found in a 600-page volume written by Michael Beleites (a former GDR civil rights activist who is now close to the German right-wing movement PEGIDA) and published in 2015 with a second edition in 2020.[198] Beleites refers in numerous passage to Uexküll, and as an analysis of this 2015 book will now show, it is especially in his political demands for a "libertarian alternative to democracy" that he is clearly allied to Uexküll's *Staatsbiologie*.[199]

195 Alain de Benoist, *View from the Right, Volume 1: Heritage and Ideas* (London: Arkos, 2017) and Alain de Benoist, *View from the Right, Volume 2: Systems and Debates* (London: Arkos, 2018), 64.

196 The following remarks are limited to the German-speaking context, although analogous observations can be made for other countries—especially the United States.

197 See Armin Mohler, *Die konservative Revolution in Deutschland 1918–1932: Ein Handbuch* (Darmstadt: Wissenschaftliche Buchgesellschaft, 1989), 79 and 313. For an overview of "Conservative Ecology," see the contributions in Thomas Jahn and Peter Wehling, eds., *Ökologie von rechts: Nationalismus und Umweltschutz bei der neuen Rechten und den "Republikanern"* (Frankfurt am Main: Campus Verlag, 1991); oekom e.V., eds., *Ökologie von rechts: Braune Umweltschützer auf Stimmenfang* (Munich: Oekom Verlag, 2012); and Kilian Behrens et al., "Ökologie von rechts – Teil 1," *Antifaschistisches Pressearchiv und Bildungszentrum*, last accessed May 3, 2021, https://www.apabiz.de/2019/oekologie-von-rechts-teil-1/.

198 On Beleites and PEGIDA, see Michael Beleites, "Vorwort," in Sebastian Hennig, *PEGIDA: Spaziergänge über den Horizont* (Neustadt: Arnshaugk Verlag, 2015), 11–22.

199 Michael Beleites, *Umweltresonanz: Grundzüge einer organismischen Biologie* (Treuenbriezen: Telesma, 2014), 598.

Beleites repeatedly takes up Uexküll's demand to reverse biology's supposed estrangement from life.[200] Just what is to be understood by such a project becomes obvious in how Beleites adopts Uexküll's conceptions of Planmäßigkeit and being "fitted into" something (and thus also his criticism of Darwin's theory of natural selection).[201] Beleites employs these concepts to explain why certain types can only survive in certain Umwelten,[202] or that an Umwelt is quasi an integral part of any respective organism or species.[203] He advocates for an ethnopluralism typical of the New Right, which he calls "organismic." According to this so-called pluralism, the Volk is a supraindividual category of biology, which corresponds to a natural, precisely "organismic" order only if each Volk is in its place and does not mix with others. Innate characteristics mean that individual human beings belong only in their own Volk. "Human racial diversity is an intraspecific biodiversity . . . a diversity that should be treated with reverence and preserved."[204] This leads to political conclusions—the final chapter is titled "Political Ecology as a 'Logic of Salvation'"—similar to those of *Staatsbiologie*. Here, this biologism results in culturally conservative demands for a return to agrarian organizational models and for population reduction measures, while also presenting tribal hierarchies as proper to human beings.

Like Uexküll, Beleites opposes in particular the social Darwinism propagated by the Nazis, with its "unnatural conceptions of life and conceptions of nature that have lost their connection to life."[205] Though he begins his book with the question of how the

200 Ibid., 227 and 431.

201 Ibid., 266 and 456.

202 Ibid., 456.

203 Ibid., 388–89. Beleites frequently refers to the Gaia concept formulated by Lynn Margulis and James Lovelock, while neglecting its genesis in cybernetics.

204 Ibid., 582. On vitalist ideologies of the New Right, see Chetan Bhatt, "White Extinction: Metaphysical Elements of Contemporary Western Fascism," *Theory, Culture & Society* 38, no. 1 (2021): 27–52.

205 Beleites, *Umweltresonanz*, 580.

Nazi crimes could have been possible, Beleites concludes by elaborating the movement's biological ideology in a way that distinguishes between natural selection theory and the "race issue." Beleites's position is that while Nazism conflated the two, he himself rejects the former. In the latter, however, he finds the basis for an organismic biology according to the maxim: "Nature can change, but it cannot be changed."[206] Beleites accuses liberalism of negating the race issue in favor of an unrestricted principle of natural selection, with the result that competition and equality are adopted as social principles, thereby preventing a truly ecological order: "Competition is the opposite principle of organismic integration."[207]

Like Uexküll, Beleites resists any valuation of different "races" in favor of their universal equivalence. He rejects the Nazi attempt to achieve biologically motivated artificial selection, analyzing instead the "naturally given geographical variation of human beings without the ulterior motive (or even the ostensible intention) of existential struggles between races within the same species."[208] He explicitly defends his position against the idea that an emphasis on racial diversity implies a devaluation of certain races, while reintroducing a hierarchy that is locally relativistic in a sense analogous to Uexküll's arguments because of the way in which species are bound to a certain geography: Beleites argues that the biological constitution of races means they can live in organismic harmony with nature only when they are in their proper (geographic) place.

> If people have developed and maintain a sense of identity with the geographic origin and 'color' of their population, this should not be discredited as a 'blood-and-soil' ideology. The point is that people of a 'population' usually have the need to

206 Ibid.
207 Ibid., 588.
208 Ibid., 582.

> live both in their ancestral homeland and among those who are like themselves.[209]

The aim is to prevent the "geographical decoupling of the genetic constitution, and an all-round divergence of the specific variation zones of human beings."[210]

The consequence of breaking away from these foundations, and of mixing with "races" that are not in the right place, is "irreversible degeneration."[211] And with this conclusion, the threat of certain races living in the wrong place or coexisting with races that are in the wrong place then follows as a biological fact. Beleites sets the foundation for this outcome when he writes that "xenophobia . . . is not generally irrational or short-sighted."[212] In words that could have come from *Staatsbiologie*, his organismic biology extends this idea to include a theory of health and healing for a society suffering from parasites: "We have learned that property and responsibility belong together, but that income gained without performing any real work and speculative transactions are a form of structural parasitism that undermines the functioning of society as a total organism."[213] His subsequent question about a "libertarian alternative to democracy" reveals that he conceives of this organicism as a form of political conservatism.[214] Liberty in this sense does not mean self-determination, but "placing one's life within the context of a meaningful whole."[215]

Beleites systematically develops Conservative Ecology to situate it in the tradition of conservative ecological thought. It has little in

209 Ibid., 605.
210 Ibid., 606.
211 Michael Beleites, "Wir haben gelernt: Sachsen 2030 – Ein Zukunftsmanifest," *Tumult* Frühjahr (2014), 91.
212 Beleites, *Umweltresonanz*, 606.
213 Beleites, "Wir haben gelernt," 91.
214 Beleites, *Umweltresonanz*, 598.
215 Ibid., 593.

common with the scientific findings of academic ecology, understanding itself instead as a worldview. In this context, ecology must always include a theory of the Volk's living spaces as well. This makes Beleites one of the chief figures of a movement whose most important publications include the magazine *Umwelt & Aktiv*, which has been singled out in reports issued by the German Federal Office for the Protection of the Constitution as a right-wing extremist organization, along with its successor magazine *Die Kehre* (The turn) and the online platform *Sezession*. Unlike Beleites, the texts published in these venues rarely refer directly to Uexküll, but the following examples show that they invoke similar patterns of argumentation. Again and again, the authors refer to holistic lines of thought and follow an identitarian logic that classifies all human beings on the basis of their membership in groups, races, or landscapes.[216]

The protagonists of Conservative Ecology see themselves in a tradition that ties the living conditions of a racially defined Volk to its "blood and soil," thereby taking the notion of life in harmony with nature and touting it as the life of a Volk purified of anything foreign. They refer to authors such as Ernst Moritz Arndt (1767–1860), Wilhelm Heinrich Riehl (1823–1897), Ernst Rudorff (1840–1916), Paul Schultze-Naumburg (1869–1949), Ludwig Klages (1872–1956), Oswald Spengler (1880–1936), and Martin Heidegger (1889–1976). Building on these arguments, they posit that it was precisely the harshness of Nordic nature that led to the emergence of a superior race (and, Benoist claims, to the emergence of "ecology" itself).[217] In their view, the German

216 For a critique of the right-wing interpretation of ecology, see Markus Steinmayr, "Fridays for Yesterday: Ein Kommentar zur politischen Ökologie," *Merkur* 74, no. 855 (2020): 20–30, as well as Florian Sprenger, "Zur rechten Ökologie-Zeitschrift *Die Kehre*," *Pop-Zeitschrift*, last updated August 3, 2020, https://pop-zeitschrift.de/2020/08/03/zur-rechten-oekologie-zeitschrift-die-kehreautorvon-florian-sprenger-autordatum3-8-2020-datum/.

217 Alain de Benoist, *Mein Leben: Wege eines Denkens* (Berlin: JF Edition, 2014), 325.

Umwelt consequently needs special protection. Nature becomes normatively charged, standing for a social order and state order that is to be striven for. The romantic combination of naturalism and nationalism comes into play here, with all of its anti-Enlightenment implications.

4.1 "Ecology Is Right-Wing"

This aspiration is accompanied by attempts to reframe the social function of ecology as a discourse. Today, ecological thinking seems left-wing and liberal. But this hasn't always been the case, and if the New Right has its way, it won't be for much longer. "Ecology is . . . antiemancipatory and counterprogressive,"[218] Götz Kubitschek writes, for example. Or "Ecology is Right-Wing,"[219] as Norbert Borrmann, the architect and art historian who died in 2016, titled a text of his own from 2013 in the New Right magazine *Sezession*.[220] The commitment to tradition and homeland that characterizes far-right thought is linked by Borrmann to a nature that is always simultaneously a homeland. Nature thus becomes a living space passed down through time, one that not only shapes a Volk's existential conditions but also cannot be imagined without the Volk that inhabits it.[221] And it is only when a Volk lives

218 Götz Kubitschek, "Entortung und Masse sind per se destruktiv, nivellierend, unorganisch, unökologisch: Interview mit Götz Kubitschek," *Die Kehre* 4 (2020), 31.

219 Norbert Borrmann, "Ökologie ist rechts," *Sezession* 56 (2013): 4–7. Thom Dieke makes a similar argument in "Der Ökologische Komplex: Möglichkeiten für die deutsche Rechte," last accessed May 4, 2021, https://gegenstrom.org/der-oekologische-komplex-moeglichkeiten-fuer-die-deutsche-rechte/.

220 On the importance of magazines and online platforms for the New Right, see Moritz Neuffer and Morton Paul, "'Rechte Hefte': Rightwing Magazines in Germany after 1945," *Eurozine*, last updated November 4, 2018, last accessed May 4, 2021, https://www.eurozine.com/rechte-hefte-rightwing-magazines-germany-1945/.

221 This amalgamation of *Naturschutz* and *Heimatschutz*—of nature protection and homeland protection—pervades right-wing texts in general, but in terms of ecological theory, is specific to the German-language approach (where *Heimat* means both "homeland" and biological "habitat"). In English-language ecology, the connection between nature and "homeland" is hardly

in harmony with the nature surrounding it that it can develop its full potential. The innate characteristics of different Völker mean, however, that not every Volk can achieve this harmony. And it is this exclusionary, holistic idea of harmony that Conservative Ecology seeks to preserve—a harmony that can only exist when a Volk lives in the space that is properly its own (or that it has taken, if necessary, and reshaped for itself). "Rootedness with one's ancestral soil" is declared a political principle,[222] one standing in a direct line of tradition to the "blood and soil" ideology of the early twentieth century.

Philip Stein, cofounder of the right-wing campaign project Ein Prozent (One Percent), similarly spoke at a conference organized by the discontinued ecomagazine *Umwelt & Aktiv*, focusing on ecology as a "question of the future of the European Völker."[223] Stein explicitly equates ecology with organicism, and identifies the attendant worldview as the cornerstone of a right-wing resistance against Western liberalism. What is called for, Stein writes in an "Ecomanifest from the right," is a new "right-wing ecological radicalism."[224] This would understand "changes in the Umwelt" as primarily an effect of migration. Ein Prozent is meanwhile also attempting to use the issue of ecology to reach the bourgeois

present at all, which is not to say that English-language discourse does not also have forms of "Conservative Ecology." Ecofascism is important to the alt-right movement, too. See Janet Biehl and Peter Staudenmaier, *Ecofascism Revisited: Lessons from the German Experience* (Porsgrunn: New Compass Press, 1995/2011). This amalgamation is the result of a selective and narrow reading of the history of ecological theory, a reading that ignores in particular the approaches of the postwar period that were shaped by the ecosystem concept, or else delegates these later approaches to a purely technical image of nature, an image that no longer has any relation to "homeland" and has thus been ostensibly lost.

222 Borrmann, "Ökologie ist rechts," 6.

223 Philip Stein, "Das organische Welt und die ökologische Revolution," last accessed January 19, 2021, https://www.youtube.com/watch?v=-bUTKgmV9x8, 17:37.

224 Philip Stein, "Ökomanifest von rechts," *Sezession*, last update September 22, 2014, last accessed October 10, 2020, https://sezession.de/46543/oekomanifest-von-rechts.

center and secure "interpretational control of this term," by establishing ethnonationalist rural communes, hijacking trade unions, and supporting the identitarian movement.[225]

In this tradition, Heimat or "homeland" appears as the anchoring of a Volk in a Lebensraum or "living space," both biologically and culturally—that is to say, in an Umgebung that gives a Volk its place. A Volk is thus determined not only by the land and a culture, by "blood and soil," but also by its Umwelt.[226] The ways in which Uexküllian theory can be used by this movement is obvious, especially since he has been explicitly understood, via Mohler, as part of the Conservative Revolution. As early as 1915, for instance, Uexküll wrote: "Each Volk can only be the creator of its own state, if this state is to become the living structure of the Volk."[227] Every human being—and this is the starting point that Uexküll shares with the "conservative ecologists" as well as the early proponents of "Heimatschutz" and "Lebensreform" (literally "life reform," a social reform movement beginning in the late nineteenth century that propagated a "natural" way of life)—has a fixed place not only in the hierarchies of culture but also in the living spaces of its own Volk. In both Conservative Ecology and in Uexküll, no Volk can be separated from its Lebensraum without losing its means of survival. In this sense, Conservative Ecology is dedicated not only to nature, but also to the culture that arises from it and has its place in it, and it is in this sense that it understands itself as holistic: "Not only the diversity of species but also the diversity of cultures and thus ultimately a diversity of homelands" must be preserved.[228] Preservation of individual types of humans, and not just of animals, is the right-wing version of this conservationism, which often deliberately neglects to spell out the political consequences of its premises.

225 Stein, "Das organische Welt und die ökologische Revolution," 30:30.

226 On the ideology of blood and soil and the environmental determinism that accompanies it, see Mark Bassin, "Blood or Soil?"

227 Uexküll, "Volk und Staat," 63.

228 Borrmann, "Ökologie ist rechts," 6.

As sociologists Thomas Jahn and Peter Wehling have shown, the protection of nature is understood here as protection against an ostensible over-foreignization, leading to demands for separation and expulsion.[229] For Conservative Ecology, nature conservation and migration policy are closely intertwined. This becomes clear in a special issue of *Die Kehre* on migration, in which the idea of "placelessness" is also taken up in its antiliberal, tacitly antisemitic dimension. The approach followed by all the contributors to this issue is that only the attachment to a given place and its traditions, which would thus foreclose any migration, enables ecological life in harmony with one's own place and one's own blood. Hence only those who live in their place, without mixing with others who are unlike themselves, are capable at all of acting and thinking ecologically: "Unlike the constant wanderer, the person who has taken root in a place will also seek to cultivate it."[230] Building on Paul Schultze-Naumburg's theoretical critique of modernism and industrialization in architecture, Volker Mohr accordingly elaborates the "placelessness of modernism"[231] as an effect of the "tidal wave of the Enlightenment that carried away, into no-man's land, elements that had been previously bound by existing ties."[232] In contrast, an antimodern, conservative understanding of the relationship to nature sees it as a process not of adapting to given circumstances but of self-realization by an autonomous subject, one who is always also part of a Volk and takes on an individual Umwelt. It is precisely this constellation—which is paradigmatic for the Conservative Revolution, but now grounded in biological terms—that exists in Uexküll's Umwelt theory as well.

229 See Thomas Jahn and Peter Wehling, "'Wir sind die nationalen Umweltschützer . . .': Konturen einer Ökologie von rechts in der Bundesrepublik Deutschland," *Soziale Welt* 42, no. 4 (1991): 481.

230 Jonas Schick, "Editorial," *Die Kehre* 4 (2020): 1.

231 Volker Mohr, "Ökologie im Spiegel der Ortlosigkeit," *Die Kehre* 4 (2020): 13.

232 Ibid., 8.

Although Conservative Ecology sees itself more in the tradition of Heimatschutz from the first third of the twentieth century, it also finds Nazi thought to be a fertile source of ideas: "The Third Reich was not just brown [the identifying color of Nazism]; because of its biologically oriented worldview, it was also the first modern industrial state to be green."[233] What Borrmann forgets to mention in his subsequent enumeration of the achievements of Nazi Naturschutz policy is that its underlying concepts always rested on the idea that a Volk can only live in one Lebensraum and that all other Völker must accordingly disappear from it.

From this far-right perspective, a left-wing ecology that supposedly only focuses on environmental protection, or *Umweltschutz*, without grasping the Umwelt as the Lebensraum of a Volk, must seem absurd. It contradicts the notion of holism that binds nature to culture, a Volk to a space, and identity to an Umwelt. With this strategy, the New Right is trying to wrest the issue of nature conservation from the Greens, a party described by the Institute for State Policy (Institut für Staatspolitik, a New Right think tank) as a "corrosive force of emancipation."[234] As "freeloaders with an image of human beings that is contrary to nature,"[235] the Greens are presented as having claimed the field of ecology without any awareness of the right-wing tradition that also exists behind it.[236] The authors of the magazine *Die*

233 Borrmann, "Ökologie ist rechts," 7.

234 See Institut für Staatspolitik, *Die Grünen: Die zersetzende Kraft der Emanzipation* (Steigra: Verein für Staatspolitik, 2013).

235 Borrmann, "Ökologie ist rechts," 7.

236 However, the political movement that led to the founding of the Green Party was in fact characterized by right-wing ecological thinking, especially at its outset. A series of studies have meticulously elaborated how it was precisely during the founding phase of the Green Party that figures such as Herbert Gruhl, August Haussleiter, Baldur Springmann, and Rudolf Bahro followed a path to Conservative Ecology. Peter Bierl has provided an exemplary analysis of this connection with Werner Georg Haverbeck—a member of the Nazi party, the SS, and the SA, and after the war an anthroposophist, member of the Green Party, and professor for social

Kehre, for example, oppose an "instrumentalization of nature for emancipation efforts" and take the side of nature conservation (Naturschutz) against that of environmental protection (Umweltschutz), which they see as technologically focused and liberal.[237] They equate the latter with industrial interventions into the very nature that is supposed to be protected. According to a manifesto written by sociologist Jost Bauch and published by the Herbert Gruhl Society, Conservative Ecology exposes "notions of noninstrumental technology (without exploitation of nature) as unrealistic wishful thinking."[238] Conservative Ecology aims instead "to rein in technical rationality through stable social institutions [meaning families, F.S.] in such a way that it does not become the sole determining logic for the human-nature relationship."[239]

The "nature" found in the pure and right-wing nature conservation of such ecologies, which replaces the "nature" found in climate protection discourses, is described (for example by Michael Beleites in *Die Kehre*) as untouched, antitechnical, and natural.[240] As Peter Bierl has pointed out, even as early as 1900, the destruction of nature denounced by "Heimatzschutz" and "Lebensreform" proponents was not blamed on capitalist overexploitation but was instead ascribed to a "disease of civilization."[241] This assumption bundles together racist, anti-

science at the University of Applied Sciences in Bielefeld. For Haverbeck, "human subspecies . . . are assigned to a respective ecosystem just as plants and animals are"; see Peter Bierl, *Grüne Braune: Umwelt-, Tier- und Heimatschutz von Rechts* (Münster: Unrast, 2010), 17. Biel argues that Haverbeck sees *Umweltschutz* as *Völkerschutz*.

237 Jonas Schick, "Die Kehre," last updated April 28, 2020, last accessed October 10, 2020, https://die-kehre.de/2020/04/28/die-kehre/.

238 Jost Bauch, "Gibt es eine konservative Ökologie?,"*Herbert-Gruhl-Gesellschaft*, last accessed October 10, 2020, http://herbert-gruhl.de/gibt-es-eine-konservative-oekologie/.

239 Ibid.

240 See Michael Beleites, "Die menschengemachte Überhitzung: Zur Entropie der Industriegesellschaft," *Die Kehre*, no. 1 (2020).

241 Bierl, *Grüne Braune*, 5.

semitic, neo-Malthusian, and ecological positions, enabling today's Conservative Ecology to connect with the conservative and ethnonationalist movements of the interwar period, in addition to the holistic ecologies that were as amenable then as they are now. From this point of view, Naturschutz is only possible as Heimatschutz, which means assigning the proper space to each Volk. Following this logic, a culture can only survive if it is positioned against the concept of nature propagated by the climate protection movement—which has always been technologically focused. For Conservative Ecology, this form of nature has already been uprooted by technology, quite precisely in the sense articulated by Martin Heidegger; and according to the right-wing ecological point of view, the urban culture that develops as its opposite cannot avoid becoming liberal and losing the very ground on which it stands, with the consequence that it will not be able to survive the crisis. To Conservative Ecology, this notion of nature appears to be "placeless," and thus to negate and endanger a form of life that sees itself in harmony with nature. Here, the doubled opposition of nature/technology and culture/technology serves to differentiate a technicized, liberal, and implicitly Jewish culture from one that is rooted in the cultural techniques of agrarianism and must not be intermixed. The supposedly "true" core of ecology invoked here—outside of any discourse or insight produced by academic ecology—thus lies in the preservation of nature as a Lebensraum for a culture that lives in harmony with this nature and resists its mechanized, liberal, urban appropriation. The aim of this movement is to return to a lost harmony in which everything has its place.

The continuities are clear.[242] The reactionary line of tradition in German-language eco-holist discourse did not break off in 1945,

242 On this point, see Oliver Geden, *Rechte Ökologie: Umweltschutz zwischen Emanzipation und Faschismus* (Berlin: Elefanten, 1999); Radkau and Uekötter, *Naturschutz und Nationalsozialismus*; Bierl, *Grüne Braune*; Gudrun Heinrich, Klaus D. Kaiser, and Norbert Wiersbinski, eds., *Naturschutz und Rechtsradikalismus: Gegenwärtige Entwicklungen, Probleme, Abgrenzungen*

 either, and there is a need for further studies to examine even more deeply these various continuities, both in terms of ideas and of protagonists, between postwar holism and the New Right. While Böker died in 1939 and Woltereck and Uexküll in 1944, Meyer-Abich remained a professor in Hamburg until 1958 and Weber was appointed to a professorship in Tübingen in 1951. Friederichs also retained his position, while Thienemann was awarded the German Federal Cross of Merit in 1952. The attitude of these unchallenged holists toward Volk, space, and nature did not change after the war, even if they now chose to use a new, politically unsuspicious language: "The ties of ecological research to nature conservation and landscape management in the Federal Republic of Germany were thus accomplished on the basis of their convergences during the Nazi period, and were not a break with that time."[243]

So one certainly cannot say that the New Right appropriated the ecological sphere without any foundation, thereby "infiltrating" the nature conservation movement. The right-wing occupation of this issue is not purely instrumental, either. Rather, the historical continuities are linked by an unbroken line focusing less on right-wing appropriation than on ecology itself. With holistic thinking in particular, its tendencies to lean rightward are clear, and today's political calculations are inevitably entangled with these lines of tradition. It would be avoiding the crux of the matter to simply detach ecological thinking from right-wing

und Steuerungsmöglichkeiten (Bonn: Bundesamt für Naturschutz, 2015). According to Kurt Jax, this continuity is the reason that "ecosystem" as a concept was adopted so late in German-language ecology; see Kurt Jax, "Holocoen and Ecosystem: On the Origin and Historical Consequences of Two Concepts," *Journal of the History of Biology* 31, no. 1 (1998): 113–42.

243 Thomas Potthast, "Wissenschaftliche Ökologie und Naturschutz," in *Naturschutz und Nationalsozialismus*, 250. As Janet Biehl has pointed out, the emergence of ecological thought is infused with reactionary politics as far back as Ernst Haeckel, even if, contrary to Biehl's arguments, Haeckel did not contribute to ecological research; see Biehl and Staudenmaier, *Ecofascism Revisited*, 8.

aspirations and see this discourse as a kind of neutral knowledge that becomes political only insofar as it is employed to support certain positions. Ecology has never been innocent, pure, or natural. It is therefore not surprising that, whether in the in 1970s or the present day, the reactionary movement for Naturschutz and Heimatschutz has been able to connect to parts of the ecomovement whose members do not consider themselves right-wing at all. The topical relevance of ecofascism lies in its attempt to hijack ecological protest movements. The fact that this can be done with such ease is not surprising in light of history.

Such appropriations detach ecology from the ideological conflicts between mechanistic and holistic approaches that were dominant when it emerged, leveling out differences to produce a narrow interpretation of the term. Ecology is becoming synonymous with holism. The starting point for any critique of how ecology and capitalism are connected—a tack shared by left-wing positions[244]—is thus immediately supplemented by a "correct" definition of ecology: an ecology that draws borders and restores the whole. The implication is that we should all return to the one form of ecology that obeys a metaphysics of the whole, an ecology that raises that holistic vision above its individual components, and that understands that a Volk cannot be separated from its Lebensraum without depriving it of its basis for living—or for surviving. These ideas hark back to the ecological approaches that had their heyday in the interwar period—and that were not coincidentally aligned with Nazi ideologies, indeed that actively sought out this proximity, albeit mostly without success. To Conservative Ecology, conservatism consequently appears to be "the only political orientation that makes ecology possible and from which it also springs," because it alone is able

244 See, for example, Jason W. Moore, *Capitalism in the Web of Life: Ecology and the Accumulation of Capital* (London: Verso, 2015); and Andreas Malm, *Fossil Capital: The Rise of Steam Power and the Roots of Global Warming* (London: Verso, 2015).

 to preserve, to recognize borders and limits, and to "identify what is unavailable."[245] The proximity of holism, ecology, and fascism reflects not only how they have been received but an intellectual kinship that any critical history of knowledge and of science must address.

It is more than doubtful whether such a Conservative Ecology is capable of using ecological knowledge to logically reconcile nature's controllability and formability with nature's accelerating destruction. It is certainly possible to agree with the claim that the technicist orientation of ecological thought—as found, for example, in the continuation of ecocybernetic principles in geoengineering or in the discourse on resilience—is regressive insofar as it subjugates its object (whether it be nature or the individual subject) with technomessianic zeal. But it would be reactionary—and intentionally so—to take this as the reason for a "turn," as the magazine *Die Kehre* proclaims in its very name, that would retreat from (inter)mixing to some pure core.

Conservative Ecology, like Umwelt theory, is propelled by certainties and clear borders that it uses to counteract jumbled multiplicity and relationality—and for the critical thinker, this raises the question of what a different ecology might look like, one that cannot so easily be appropriated in this way. In particular, the latest wave of cultural studies research into ecological thought would need to address this issue and investigate the promises of order (or even disorder) that have historically developed in ecology discussions. In any case: the holist promise of order that places the whole above its parts and seeks unity through the functional interchangeability of "Volk, Reich, and Führer" in the organic totality of the Nazi state not only has a place in history—but in the present, too, with its contemporary return.

245 Bauch, "Gibt es eine konservative Ökologie?"

[3]

Uexküll as a Whole: On the Totality of Planmäßigkeit

Gottfried Schnödl

Jakob von Uexküll is often presented as pioneering a multiperspectival, fundamentally relativistic and constructivist conception of the relationship between organism and nature, but this stands in clear contradiction to his political activism and his antisemitism—and also to his theory. There are too many points, and quite significant ones, at which Uexküll has to address another level beyond the specific Umwelten under discussion in order to make his Umwelt theory comprehensible, and to even formulate it in the first place (*Umwelt*, pl. *Umwelten*, literally "around-world," refers not only to the environment, but in this context particularly to an organism's receptor world and effector world, its "Merkwelt" and "Wirkwelt"). This more general level is defined by the principles of *Umgebung* ("surrounding[s]," which will be the focus of the next chapter) and *Planmäßigkeit* ("conformity with a plan," indicating a purposiveness, systematicity, or planned quality). As will be shown, Planmäßigkeit is both capillary and ubiquitous. It functions not only within individual Innenwelt-Umwelt bubbles, but in "nature" itself (*Innenwelt* means "inner world," here as the Uexküllian counterpart to Umwelt).

Planmäßigkeit pervades Uexküll's entire theory, giving it its logical foundation. It forms the basis for both its "subjectivism" or relativism *and* for its determinism—and thus for its politically problematic nature as well.

The following seeks to illuminate this conceptual interrelationship, thus detailing the significance of Planmäßigkeit for the central thesis of the present book, i.e., for the fact that Uexküll's right-wing worldview is not simply the private matter of a biologist but deeply rooted in his Umwelt theory. This worldview pervades the theory as a whole, and not just certain parts of it. In this regard, the present chapter will pursue a two-pronged argument, seeking to first illustrate and articulate the holism of Umwelt theory before then elucidating its political implications and the concrete political connections that result from this holistic complex.

But first, this analysis begins by demarcating its approach from readings of Umwelt theory that try to comprehend it as inherently disjointed. Besides missing the theoretical point of Umwelt theory, such readings also fail to get at its politically problematic nature. The second subchapter will examine how Planmäßigkeit is integral to Uexküll's Umwelt theory as a necessary prerequisite that demands its characteristic merging of epistemological and ontological levels, subjectivity and holism, monadism and totality, and autonomy and determinism. As will be made clear in the third subchapter, this holism of Umwelt theory, virtually built into its structure, means that even the subjectivism and biocentrism that have been so often asserted in more recent scholarship on Uexküll can never be thought of without the aspect of totality. Uexküll's Umwelten, which are subjectivist only in a specific sense, are to be understood as complementary to his overarching holism of nature, not as a counterweight. As will be shown in the fourth subchapter, such ideas began with Goethe's conceptions of holism along with other developments seen in late nineteenth-century biology and aesthetics. It is against this background that the merging of epistemological and ontological levels, subjectivity and holism, monadism and totality, and autonomy and determinism seen in more recent readings as irresolvable or self-contradictory actually proves to logically continue and adapt established lines of thought. And as will be shown by the final subchapter, it is precisely this ability to combine contradictory elements that justifies Uexküll's identification with the "Conservative Revolution." In the Conservative Revolution as well, the line between autonomy and determinism, and between political dominion and natural order, was largely erased, with Nazism, too, adopting the intellectual arguments of such an erasure. In the context of this self-contradictory "revolution" so concerned with preservation, it makes sense that Umwelt theory would fit in so well, precisely on the strength of its holistic foundations, which also means: fitting in as a whole.

1. Fissures in the Whole, Holism in the Parts

While research on Uexküll largely ignores the significance of Umgebung (as the next chapter will show), it does sometimes discuss and acknowledge the concept of Planmäßigkeit. But it is precisely when Planmäßigkeit appears on the level of "nature as a whole" that it is often simply conjured away. From Adolf Portmann's 1956 contention that this is not an explanatory notion but a "great, dark riddle,"[1] to Juan Manuel Heredia's 2020 description of a "tension between an epistemological level and a metaphysical one,"[2] many scholars have presented Uexküll's Planmäßigkeit of nature as problematic, using this to frame him as a metaphysician or a Romantic and thereby ascribing those aspects of his writings that have been identified as politically

1 Adolf Portmann, "Vorwort: Ein Wegbereiter der neuen Biologie," in Jakob von Uexküll and Georg Kriszat, *Streifzüge durch die Umwelten von Tieren und Menschen: Ein Bilderbuch unsichtbarer Welten; Bedeutungslehre* (Hamburg: Rowohlt, 1956), 16.

2 Juan Manuel Heredia, "Jakob von Uexküll, an Intellectual History," in *Jakob von Uexküll and Philosophy: Life, Environments, Anthropology*, ed. Francesca Michelini and Kristian Köchy (London: Routledge, 2020), 26.

 problematic to precisely these aspects.[3] This misunderstanding of Planmäßigkeit as a separable aspect of Umwelt theory is the underlying reason for a reading of Uexküll that is seen often in the literature.

"Thus, Uexküll is divided"[4]—according to this strain of analysis, there is a fissure running through his work. This fissure is used to divide the aspects of his theory that are to be favored (according to one's own tastes) from those that are to be pushed to one side as too metaphysical, too anachronistic, too conservative, or even insufficiently combative—a view sometimes seen in early readings of Uexküll during the Nazi era.[5]

Such interpretations would initially seem to be supported by several aspects. Uexküll's theory actually does seem to be riven by a natural fracture line. Its different Umwelten stand side by side and unconnected, self-contained, and thus closed off from one another. This separateness is also perpetuated on the epistemological level, in the gap between the Umwelten and their observers. Uexküll postulates an inescapable coupling between the Umwelt (the world that a specific organism perceives and in which it dwells, moves, and acts) and the "Bauplan" ("building plan," the constitution of that same organism as a bundle of abilities for activities such as perception, locomotion, etc.). There is no separation between these two components, not even temporarily, and thus no need for adaptation either. Instead, Uexküll assumes that an organism's mental conception of the

3 To cite just one example, Di Paolo identifies a "radical end" and a "conservative end" in Uexküll's work, and relates these two poles to different epistemological models. See Ezequiel A. Di Paolo, "Afterword: A Future for Jakob von Uexküll," in *Jakob von Uexküll and Philosophy*, 253.

4 Dorion Sagan, "Introduction: Umwelt after Uexküll," in Jakob von Uexküll, *A Foray into the Worlds of Animals and Humans, with A Theory of Meaning*, trans. Joseph D. O'Neil (Minneapolis: University of Minnesota Press, 2010), 7.

5 In 1942, for example, Hermann Weber criticized Uexküll's overly harmonistic theory for neglecting the concept of selection, which was ostensibly what Germany needed in order to survive the mortal struggle it faced. See Hermann Weber, "Organismus und Umwelt," *Der Biologe* 11 (1942): 62.

world ("Merkwelt" or "receptor world") and the possibilities of its own activities ("Wirkwelt" or "effector world") are always in perfect congruence. As a result, one cannot speak of different degrees of adaptation—as does his nemesis Charles Darwin—but "only of an equally perfect state of being 'fitted into' different Umwelten."[6] This being "fitted into" (*Einpassung*) is utterly inescapable. It is far more deterministic than Darwin's adaptation (*Anpassung*) precisely because it does not allow any gaps between an organism and nature in which transformations could take place, but instead postulates a complete closure between an organism and its Umwelt. With his concept of being "fitted into," Uexküll rejects the idea of positioning the individual in opposition to an external nature. Organism and nature already meet inside the respective Umwelt, and exclusively so.

This idea also defines the epistemological side of the concept. Uexküll insists that "in every world . . . what is seen is the only thing that can be seen,"[7] meaning there is a congruence between the potential and the actual. To him, the Umwelt is a "prison" whose "walls . . . will not give way until the end of our days"[8]—and on this level too, the preexistent coupling of Innenwelt and Umwelt results in a separation from all externals. For Uexküll, the human being is also subject to this logic of a closed internality, with the resultant separation of the external. Despite all our technologies, instruments, and machines, he argues, other Umwelten have never been opened up to human beings but have remained entirely adherent to the logic of the congruence between organism and Umwelt, Bauplan, and activity: "When we

6 Jakob von Uexküll, *Umwelt und Innenwelt der Tiere* (Berlin: Springer, 1909), 89.

7 Jakob von Uexküll, "Wie sehen wir die Natur und wie sieht sie sich selber?," pts. 1–3, *Die Naturwissenschaften* 10, no. 12 (March 24, 1922): 265–71; no. 13 (March 31, 1922): 296–301; no. 14 (April 7, 1922): 268. See also the similar wording of Maturana and Varela, who were demonstrably influenced by Uexküll: "We don't see what we don't see." Quote from Humberto Maturana and Francisco Varela, *Der Baum der Erkenntnis: Die biologischen Wurzeln des menschlichen Erkennens* (Bern: Scherz, 1987), 23.

8 Uexküll, "Wie sehen wir die Natur," 265.

manufacture our tools, they, in their Bauart [design, literally 'build type'], are always tied to our human receptive capacity. They cannot be made finer than allowed by the smallness and number of places that our receptor world accommodates."[9] It is therefore unsurprising that Friedrich Brock (one of his students) proposed the term "monad" in reference to Uexküll's Umwelten ("organism-Umwelt monads") as early as 1934; that Harald Lassen wrote about Uexküll's monadism in 1939; that Leo Spitzer (probably independently of the other two) referred to Uexküll's monads a few years later; and that ever since then, this characterization has been repeatedly seen in discussions of Uexküll's Umwelten and their holistic character.[10]

It is from this monadic closure of the "bubble" that the ostensibly central problem of Umwelt theory arises—a problem already noted by Uexküll himself and frequently raised in scholarship since then: the question of what conditions might open up the possibility of observing Umwelten that are not one's own.[11] If, as Uexküll emphasizes, "the standpoint of the animal *alone* must become the decisive one,"[12] but this standpoint

9 Ibid., 270.

10 Friedrich Brock, "Jakob Johann von Uexküll zum 70. Geburtstag," *Sudhoffs Archiv* 27 (1934): 193–203; Harald Lassen, "Leibniz'sche Gedanken in der Uexküll'schen Umweltlehre," *Acta biotheoretica* A5 (1939–41): 41–50; Leo Spitzer, "Milieu and Ambience: An Essay on Historical Semantics," pts. 1 and 2, *Philosophy and Phenomenological Research* 3, no. 1 (September 1942): 1–42; no. 2 (December 1942): 212n3. For examples of later references noting Uexküll's monadism, see Sagan "Introduction: Umwelt after Uexküll," 21; Geoffrey Winthrop-Young, "Afterword: Bubbles and Webs; A Backdoor Stroll through the Readings of Uexküll," in Uexküll, *Foray*, 242; Tobias Cheung, "Cobweb Stories: Jakob von Uexküll and the Stone of Werder," *Place and Location: Studies in Environmental Aesthetics and Semiotics* V (2006): 237–41. This monadism of Uexküll's should not be taken as a deliberate adoption of a philosophical concept—it is very unlikely that Uexküll ever read Leibniz. See Lassen, "Leibniz'sche Gedanken," 47.

11 See for example Uexküll, *Umwelt und Innenwelt der Tiere*, 248–53; Anne Harrington, *Reenchanted Science: Holism in German Culture from Wilhelm II to Hitler* (Princeton: Princeton University Press, 1999), 46–47.

12 Uexküll, *Umwelt und Innenwelt der Tiere*, 6, italics added.

is seen as a radically privative one,[13] and this same privation is also understood to be binding on humans,[14] then how should the observation, indeed the scientific investigation, of other Umwelten be possible? The radical linkage (being both fundamental and inescapable) between a specific Innenwelt and *its* Umwelt on the one hand, and the radical separation between different Innenwelt-Umwelt "functional cycles" ("Funktionskreisen") on the other, are mutually dependent. This is where scholars like Winthrop-Young believe that "somehow, the reconnect with nature appears to be linked to a social disconnect."[15] Florian Höfer argues similarly, pointing to a noticeable gap in Uexküll's theory where one would actually expect analyses on the problem of communication and intersubjectivity.[16] Such interpretations suggest that with Uexküll, the view *into* one's own Umwelt and the gaze *upon* another one are mutually exclusive. The irresolvable internal contradiction of observation makes Uexküll's Umwelt theory a precarious one.

For many commentators, this internal contradiction is where the aforementioned fissure begins. Dorian Sagan, for example, distinguishes a neo-Kantian and allegedly anachronistic Uexküll, one who embraces "a transcendental dimension beyond space

13 Uexküll's Umwelten are not simply species-specific; they are also radically different from individual to individual. The Umwelt of a "spirited dog" is thus different from that of a "timid dog." See Uexküll, *Foray*, 106.

14 The Umwelt of a "Mr. Meyer" consists of only "Meyer things," that of a "Mr. Schulz" of only "Schulz things." These two Umwelten would be just as impossible to convey as the Umwelten of dogs and dragonflies, for example. See Jakob von Uexküll, "Zum Verständnis der Umweltlehre," *Deutsche Rundschau* 256 (1938): 64.

15 Winthrop-Young, "Afterword: Bubbles and Webs," 217.

16 Florian Höfer, "Die Notwendigkeit der Kommunikation: Die Missachtung eines Phänomens bei Jakob von Uexküll" (dissertation, University of Bonn, 2007). The gap is reminiscent of that between (on the one hand) the attempt to bring humans closer to nature, or more specifically, to the animal world, and (on the other) the closely related splitting of humanity into distinct, ostensibly identity-based groups or "races." On this point, see Kevin Liggieri, *"Anthropotechnik": Zur Geschichte eines umstrittenen Begriffs* (Konstanz: Konstanz University Press, 2020), 87.

and time," from a progressive Uexküll who seeks to catalog the "details of animal behavior" and thereby deduce "the reality of their perceptual life-worlds."[17] Maximilian Haas argues that what Uexküll "biologically demands" (namely taking the perspective of the animals), he at the same time "epistemologically precludes" (through the monadic closing off of not only animal Umwelten, but also the Umwelt of the researcher), and assumes that this "gap . . . cannot be logically closed."[18] And this is precisely where Helmuth Plessner saw the need to introduce a new concept. Plessner's "Mitwelten" ("shared worlds"), later also taken up by Klaus Michael Meyer-Abich, were intended not least to fill the gap between the different Umwelt monads, and also between them and the researcher's observation, as left behind by Uexküll's model of biology.[19] With other authors too, the observer problem is generally present in one way or another when it comes to discussing Uexküll's work. This is the starting point for fundamental debates on whether Uexküll's biology is actually a biocentric framework or one that is still anthropocentric; whether his theory is relativist constructivist or transcendental, implicitly dualistic and metaphysical or committed to immanence; and whether his biology is subjectivist or harmonistic.

Even lines of argumentation that would locate the problematic in Uexküll's theory not in his holism or the associated determinism (as do Plessner, Portmann, and Sagan above) but rather in his subjectivism (which is ostensibly contrary to this holism) implicitly build on this fissure. For example, there were attempts in the late 1930s and early 1940s by scholars such as August Thienemann

17 Sagan, "Introduction: Umwelt after Uexküll," 7.

18 Maximilian Haas, *Tiere auf der Bühne: Eine ästhetische Ökologie der Performanz* (Berlin: Kadmos, 2018), 167.

19 On Plessner's reading of Uexküll, see most recently Hans Peter Krüger, "Closed Environment and Open World: On the Significance of Uexküll's Biology for Helmuth Plessner's Natural Philosophy," in Michelini and Köchy, *Jakob von Uexküll and Philosophy*, 90. See also Klaus Michael Meyer-Abich, *Wege zum Frieden mit der Natur: Praktische Naturphilosophie für die Umweltpolitik* (Munich: Carl Hanser, 1984).

and Karl Friederichs to make Uexküll's concept of the Umwelt synonymous with "ecology," "biotope," and even "milieu."[20] Marco Stella and Karel Kleisner highlight the one-sidedness of such attempts: "It is quite clear that such ecological theories adopt from Uexküll's sense of Umwelt mainly its holistic element, and neglect its subjectivism."[21] And Bernd Herrmann, too, in summing up the 1943 attempt by Friederichs (a zoologist, colonial official, and from 1934 a member of the Nazi Opferring or "donor circle") to define the term "Umwelt," notes that in his emphasis on all the "direct and . . . concretely tangible indirect relationships to the external world," Friederichs misses the term's specifically subjectivist internal aspect.[22] It could be argued that this reading of Uexküll, as undertaken by German biologists during the Nazi era, similarly results in the notion that Uexküll's work is already bifurcated, making it possible for one part to be cleanly separated from the other and then developed on its own.

The point of Uexküll's work is missed not only in emphasizing its holistic over its subjectivist aspect, but already in the separating of these two aspects and setting them in opposition to one another. In fact, it is doubtful that Uexküll would have failed to close this gap or to at least bridge it provisionally through aesthetic or rhetorical means, making it equally doubtful that there really exists a fissure running through his work.[23] "The notion of

20 Marco Stella and Karel Kleisner, "Uexküllian Umwelt as Science and as Ideology: The Light and the Dark Side of a Concept," *Theory in Biosciences* 129, no. 1 (2010): 43. The authors refer to the following primary texts: Karl Friederichs, "Vom Wesen der Ökologie," *Sudhoffs Archiv* 27 (1934): 277–85; Karl Friederichs, *Ökologie als Wissenschaft von der Natur oder biologische Raumforschung* (Leipzig: Barth, 1937); August Thienemann, *Leben und Umwelt* (Leipzig: Barth, 1941).

21 Stella and Kleisner, "Uexküllian Umwelt as Science and as Ideology," 43.

22 Bernd Herrmann, *". . . mein Acker ist die Zeit": Aufsätze zur Umweltgeschichte* (Göttingen: Universitätsverlag Göttingen, 2011), 257n398; quote from Karl Friederichs, "Über den Begriff der 'Umwelt' in der Biologie," *Acta Biotheoretica* 7 (1943): 157.

23 Haas maintains that Uexküll resolved the observer problem only by using aesthetic means, while Bühler argues it was done solely on a rhetorical level.

 Umwelt is destined to join what we usually separate,"[24] writes Merleau-Ponty. This view is already supported by the lack of caution with which Uexküll juxtaposes the two levels described above. While he does occasionally note the conspicuous contradiction that exists in combining the monadistic Umwelten with the observability of the same (which he nonetheless sees as quite unproblematic), this does not become a central problem for him. One might presume that this was the blind spot of a scientist who relied primarily on experiments at first, and whose wife sometimes claimed that he was not particularly fond of theories.[25] One might also presume that Uexküll thought he had got around the problem of observation through certain experimental methodologies and technical approaches.[26] However, considering the late nineteenth-century discursive lines drawn between Umwelt theory and the longer historical developments of holistic biology (which will be examined later), it is more likely that Uexküll saw the contradiction between the monadic character of Umwelten and their observability (which he nonetheless assumed was essentially possible) as *already resolved.*

Even a brief look at the more extreme assertions of the closedness of Umwelt monads already makes this supposition likely.

See Haas, *Tiere auf der Bühne*, 167; Benjamin Bühler, "Das Tier und die Experimentalisierung des Verhaltens: Zur Rhetorik der Umwelt-Lehre Jakob von Uexkülls," in *Wissen: Erzählen*, ed. Arne Höcker, Jeannie Moser, and Philippe Weber (Bielefeld: transkript, 2006): 41–52.

24 Maurice Merleau-Ponty, *Nature: Course Notes from the Collège de France*, comp. Dominique Séglard, trans. Robert Vallier (Evanston: Northwestern University Press, 2003), 173.

25 Uexküll considered these as "cheap as blackberries." See Gudrun von Uexküll, *Jakob von Uexküll, seine Welt und seine Umwelt* (Hamburg: Wegner, 1964), 37.

26 For example, through the use of a special training wagon, which was intended to bring the guide dog's Umwelt at least partially in harmony with that of the human, as will be shown in the next chapter. Or through the use of film to visually demonstrate Planmäßigkeit's production of effects; on this, see Katja Kynast, "Kinematografie als Medium der Umweltforschung Jakob von Uexkülls," *Kunsttexte.de* 4 (2010): 1–14.

It is striking that Uexküll's monadism, i.e., the idea that one's Innenwelt is inescapably restricted to one's own Umwelt, is often described at the same time through a wide-angle, totalizing lens, with a view to the greater whole. This is already made clear by the text providing the above-cited quotations on the impenetrability of Umwelt bubbles, with mention of the prison-like quality of Umwelten. The actual goal of Uexküll's essay "Wie sehen wir die Natur und wie sieht sie sich selber?" (How do we see nature and how does it see itself?) is to elucidate the concept of a nature that is itself presented as a subject, a nature in which *all* Umwelten merge. This can also be seen in Uexküll's adoption of the principle of "Anschaulichkeit" (literally "seeable-ness," "openness to view," or "visualizability") in the representation of biological frameworks,[27] which demonstrates a tendency toward expanding to a wide-angle, totalizing view, for example in his book *Staatsbiologie*, where he calls for nothing less than a comprehensive and complete mapping of those functional cycles that he believes makes up the state.[28] And this can even be seen in the seemingly minor detail that among the organisms listed in Uexküll's *Innenwelt and Umwelt der Tiere*, there is no entry for "human": in its place is one for "the observer."[29] In these examples, the categorical

27 Writing in the *Dictionary of Untranslatables*, Catherine Chevalley notes that since the 1930s this German term has "presented a typical case of untranslatability." Chevalley traces the history of the term from its original derivation from Kantian "Anschauung," or "intuition," to its modification in the natural sciences of the late nineteenth century and specifically in the physics of the 1920s. Pointing to Kant's influence on "all the work done by German mathematicians, physicists, and physiologists of the second half of the nineteenth century," she writes, "*Anschaulichkeit* designates what is translated inaccurately in French as the *caractère intuitif* or in English by the 'visualizability' or 'clarity' of a physical theory, but it in fact refers to the possibility of giving phenomena and objects a 'spatiotemporal representation,' that is, an image in ordinary space and time." Catherine Chevalley, "Anschaulichkeit" in *Dictionary of Untranslatables*, ed. Barbara Cassin, trans. Steven Randall et al. (Princeton: Princeton University Press, 2014), 37.

28 Jakob von Uexküll, *Staatsbiologie: Anatomie, Physiologie, Pathologie des Staates* (Berlin: Paetel, 1920), 55.

29 Uexküll, *Umwelt und Innenwelt der Tiere*, 248–53.

 distinctions between observer and observed, between Umwelt and "nature as a whole," and between the human organism and the state organism, seem to be erased.

This occurs through the introduction of something bigger. But this takes place without changing the category or determining principle, and that is precisely Uexküll's point. His scaling up is not an attempt to jump between levels but is instead accomplished *horizontally,* on a total level where the observer—to whom all of living nature is completely observable—can be invoked *alongside* the completely closed functional cycle of the *Rhizostoma pulmo* jellyfish.[30]

It is on this total level that the observer problem evaporates and the apparent fissure in Uexküll's work closes up. Umwelt monadism and nature holism do not represent opposing conceptions from which one side can simply be taken alone, as if (for example) subjectivism or biocentrism could be taken without total holism. They are nothing other than two manifestations of a *single* principle: Planmäßigkeit. Uexküll's solution is holism and not plurality, even where he talks about the manifoldness of Umwelten and their innumerable "subjects."

The observation problem is undeniably important for understanding Uexküll's work. Readings of Uexküll that try to divide Umwelt theory into opposing parts along the fault line of this problem do have a certain logic on their side. However, they miss the point of the holistic harmonization that permeates Umwelt theory, and thus they miss its political point. What is even more important than the observation problem is thus its solution. The key here is Planmäßigkeit, as the central pillar of Umwelt theory. Uexküll builds upon it even before refining it into a terminological concept; it is through Planmäßigkeit that Umwelt theory itself becomes a complete whole.

30 See table of contexts at ibid., 261.

2. Planmäßigkeit and Totality

As Walter Gebhard notes, a major force behind many conceptions of "nature" in the late nineteenth and early twentieth centuries, especially in the German-speaking world, was "totality consciousness." A central characteristic of this consciousness is the recognition of the whole not only in the greater thing that subsumes the parts but also in these parts themselves. Holisticness-as-totality thus becomes a principle that can be introduced at any level, no matter which is under discussion. This idea defines the parts not only relative to a greater superordinate but already internally within themselves. "The 'part' is thought of as 'the whole in the small' or 'the small whole.'"[31]

Uexküll's Planmäßigkeit fits into this totality consciousness. A look at its genesis makes it clear that Uexküll is establishing here a principle that is as fundamental as it is ubiquitous, one that can be applied across the entire breadth of this "flattened" level where jellyfish cavort alongside inquiring observers. Planmäßigkeit achieves this central position in Uexküll's biology only if it is no longer seen as something derived or extrapolated, as a product or consequence, but instead as quite simply the fundamental and primary principle of all living entities. There are essentially two preconditions for this to apply, both of which are to be framed in a largely negative sense. First, in order for it to be universally existent, Planmäßigkeit cannot be reified. And second, so that it cannot be reified and limited to certain functional cycles, but instead be understood as fundamental, it must be understood as always existing and producing effects in every interior.

Tendencies toward such an interpretation emerged early on. Uexküll first begins by introducing the term "Bauplan." This

31 Walter Gebhard, *"Der Zusammenhang der Dinge": Weltgleichnis und Naturverklärung im Totalitätsbewußtsein des 19. Jahrhunderts* (Tübingen: Max Niemeyer, 1984), 7.

appears in his 1905 book *Leitfaden in das Studium der experimentellen Biologie der Wassertiere* (Guide to the study of the experimental biology of aquatic animals), in a chapter on "the reflex," a section devoted to what is here called the "central problem of biology."[32] In turn, the term "Planmäßigkeit" is used by Uexküll as early as 1908, in a published essay.[33] Brentari has noted that in the second edition of *Umwelt und Innenwelt der Tiere* (Umwelt and the inner world of animals), the chapter on the reflex has been replaced by one on the "functional cycle," which Uexküll sees as a structure of Planmäßigkeit.[34] The development of the terms "Bauplan" and "Planmäßigkeit" are therefore both connected to Uexküll's consideration of the reflex as a starting point for redefining the relationship between the organism and its external context. There is one characteristic of reflex reactions that remains relevant here: the interactions being studied do not happen with a random spontaneity or even consciously but are instead subject to an inevitability. However, what would seem more important than this continuity is the shift undertaken by Uexküll when his interest in the inside/outside interface moved to inside of the Umwelt-Innenwelt bubble, as evidenced at the latest with his analysis of the functional cycle in *Umwelt und Innenwelt der Tiere*.

When Uexküll later claimed that by end of the nineteenth century he had already devoted himself to researching Planmäßigkeit,[35] despite having conceptualized the term only later, then this might have simply been an all-too-obvious attempt at retrospectively smoothing over his lifework's trajectory.[36] However, there actually

32 Uexküll, *Leitfaden in das Studium der experimentellen Biologie der Wassertiere* (Wiesbaden: Bergmann, 1905), 8.

33 Jakob von Uexküll, "Die neuen Fragen in der experimentellen Biologie," *Rivista di szienzia* 4, no. 2 (1908): 72–86.

34 Carlo Brentari, *Jakob von Uexküll: The Discovery of the Umwelt between Biosemiotics and Theoretical Biology* (Dordrecht: Springer, 2015), 97–98.

35 Gudrun von Uexküll, *Jakob von Uexküll, seine Welt und seine Umwelt*, 39.

36 Mildenberger argues that Uexküll was still completely devoted to a mechanistic paradigm at the time. See Florian Georg Mildenberger, *Umwelt als*

are certain aspects demonstrating that his research interests, right from the start, rested upon at least two characteristics of Planmäßigkeit that are of particular interest here: its nonmateriality and its internality.

Uexküll's path to Planmäßigkeit began even before its conceptual formulation, with studies of organisms that were of enormous importance for German-speaking biologists from the last third of the nineteenth century onwards, namely lower marine animals.[37] As early as his university days in Dorpat (today's Tartu, Estonia), he was already participating in Baltic Sea expeditions and developing a particular interest in invertebrates. His focus on organisms lacking a centralized nervous system continued in the physiological and behavioral research he conducted during the 1890s at the experimental biology station in Naples. It impressed him that even without a centralized nervous system, the organism's logical structure and self-repeating biological processes were preserved. The seemingly obvious conclusion was that these processes cannot be localized and therefore cannot be materially based.[38]

Uexküll's early investigations were inspired not least by the research of his mentor Wilhelm Kühne, for whom Uexküll worked in Heidelberg from 1888 to 1890.[39] Kühne was focused on enzymes as triggers of specific processes within organisms—a research area that Uexküll had already come into contact with as a biology student in Tartu. It was during this early phase of his work as a biologist—and thus before his terminological conceptualization of "Bauplan" and "Planmäßigkeit"—that Uexküll's focus already turned to an organism's involuntary inner workings, leaving interactions with external phenomena to the physicists

Vision: Leben und Werk Jakob von Uexkülls (1864–1944) (Wiesbaden: Steiner, 2007), 57.

37 Ibid.

38 Uexküll tried to resolve this problem through the use of film. See Kynast, "Kinematografie."

39 On Kühne's influence, see Harrington, *Reenchanted Science*, 39.

and physiologists. This laid the groundwork for the attraction he would soon display to Hans Driesch's notion of "entelechy." In this context, it is hardly surprising that Uexküll later developed an enthusiasm for investigations into Herbert Spencer Jennings's conception of regulatory capabilities.[40] A comparison with Karl Ernst von Baer's notion of "goal-directedness" ("Zielstrebigkeit"), which was just as important as Driesch's entelechy in shaping Uexküll's thinking, also makes it clear how much importance Uexküll ascribes to internal processes in particular. While von Baer was interested in the relationships between a living organism and external objects or processes, Uexküll focused on the internal relationship within a given Innenwelt-Umwelt bubble.[41]

With the phenomena under discussion, their internality and their nonmateriality are mutually dependent. Despite all the differences between the ideas of Driesch and Jennings, it was clear to them as well as to Uexküll that the principle creating these relationships, and thereby order in the living world, was not to be found in material phenomena.[42] But it is only in the manifested form of a specific "finished" Bauplan that this principle becomes *anschaulich* (literally "seeable," where "to see" also

40 Jennings describes this regulatory capability of living entities not as something that emerges from specific, materially anchored centers and that works through a physiologically predetermined hierarchical structure, but as one that materializes such centers and structures, and thus the entire organism—an analysis that accords entirely with Uexküll's views. On Uexküll's interest in Jennings's research, see for example Jakob von Uexküll, *Bausteine zu einer biologischen Weltanschauung* (Munich: Bruckmann, 1913), 161–62.

41 Charlotte Helbach, "Die Umweltlehre Jakob von Uexkülls: Ein Beispiel für die Genese von Theorien in der Biologie des 20. Jahrhunderts" (dissertation, RWTH Aachen University, 1999), 39.

42 On how Uexküll distinguished his own approach from that of Driesch, see ibid., 46–47; Mildenberger, *Umwelt als Vision*, 143 among others. On Jennings, who wanted to position himself as a purely objective researcher, and his own reservations in regards to an Umwelt theory that would go beyond such an objectivism, see ibid., 83.

means "to clearly intuit," referring here to the representability of a phenomenon in a spatiotemporal framework)—and it is precisely this demand for *Anschaulichkeit*, borrowed from Goethe, that Uexküll already defines as a central task of biology by 1902.[43] Furthermore, Uexküll does try to trace out the effects of Planmäßigkeit in its real, materially expressed formations, right down to the smallest detail. In later texts, for example, he writes about the impulses by which genes instruct protoplasmic cells to take on certain forms and processes and expresses the hope of one day "capturing the formational development process in a test tube."[44] But this certainly does not mean that the starting point of such processes has to be materially fixed and bound to a certain substance. On the contrary, Uexküll emphasizes that "for the correct formation of an animal, there is a second factor beyond the genes, namely the plan,"[45] and with this, something that is firmly to be understood as an "extramaterial law."[46] Charlotte Helbach is therefore undoubtedly right when she writes that "the sequence of Planmäßigkeit, plan, impulse system, gene, and protoplasm does not change if the middle term is assigned to the material column. The role of Planmäßigkeit as the life-determining factor remains untouched here."[47] This dual characterization of Planmäßigkeit as nonmaterial and internal enables Uexküll to see it as ubiquitous and fundamental. At the base of all living entities is not a particular substance but a plan, one that defines relationships and structures.

43 Uexküll, *Bausteine*, 55–66. Uexküll's first turning toward "Anschauung" (or "intuition" in the Kantian tradition) can already be found in Jakob von Uexküll, "Psychologie und Biologie in ihrer Stellung zur Tierseele," *Ergebnisse der Physiologie, II. Abteilung: Biophysik und Psychophysik* 1 (1902): 218.

44 Jakob von Uexküll, *Kompositionslehre der Natur: Biologie als undogmatische Naturwissenschaft; Ausgewählte Schriften*, ed. Thure von Uexküll (Frankfurt am Main: Propyläen, 1980), 178–79.

45 Uexküll, *Bausteine*, 172.

46 Ibid., 175.

47 Helbach, "Die Umweltlehre Jakob von Uexkülls," 42.

For Uexküll, Planmäßigkeit thus represents an internal and fundamental relational principle that is abstracted—and even emancipated—from material phenomena: "the primary factor is the relationship."[48] He sees this relational principle as life itself, and by placing it above all else, he negates both "psychism and materialism," along with the dualism of such a distinction. In this dualism, as his book's editor Felix Gross writes, "the phenomenon of life must serve only to mediate between the psyche and the physique as the sole primary phenomena, and to bridge the enormous chasm that yawns between them," but with Uexküll's biology, this "phenomenon of life"—and thus the mediating relational principle—is now to "take on a central position" itself.[49]

It is thus the nonmateriality and internality of Planmäßigkeit that enables Uexküll to understand it as such a fundamental and ubiquitous relational principle. This understanding is necessary not only for exploring Planmäßigkeit through concrete investigations of its effects in specific Umwelten, but also for theorizing it above and beyond all such concrete experimental efforts. By 1945, Wilhelm Szilasi was already speculating that Planmäßigkeit was the ultimate principle of nature, equally as applicable "to the whole field of being as to the special being of living entities."[50] According to Höfer, Uexküll knows no other principle of nature.[51] And Uexküll himself states that Planmäßigkeit has to be reckoned with both on the microlevel of individual Innenwelt-Umwelt couplings, i.e., the actual functional cycles, and on the macrolevel of "nature":

> All functional cycles are built according to the same principle. In them I see the active natural plans that must be regarded as elementary factors of the universe. The entire universe, which consists of nothing but Umwelten, is held together by

48 Jakob von Uexküll, *Biologische Briefe an eine Dame* (Berlin: Paetel, 1920), 76.

49 Felix Gross, "Einleitung," in Uexküll, *Bausteine*, 10.

50 Wilhelm Szilasi, *Wissenschaft als Philosophie* (Zurich: Europa-Verlag, 1945), 70.

51 Höfer, *Die Notwendigkeit der Kommunikation*, 114.

> functional cycles, and compounded into a unity according to an overall plan, a unity we call nature.[52]

Planmäßigkeit is therefore not only what binds the respective Innenwelten to their Umwelten, but also what organizes the resulting bubbles in relation to one another. As a logical parallel to what is already known from the microlevel of the individual Umwelten, namely that receptor processes (*Merkprozesse*) are congruent with effector processes (*Wirkprozesse*), a principle is thereby established that is both ontological and epistemological. As a "universal, superordinate connecting principle,"[53] Planmäßigkeit regulates the internal relationships of the subjective Umwelt units (i.e., all processes between Innenwelt and Umwelt, thus regulating the respective "subject" itself). At the same time, it also makes it possible for these very relationships to be observed. The observability of other Umwelten is based on the existence of a higher level that is *likewise* defined by the selfsame principle of Planmäßigkeit. This conceptual merging is another one whose roots are already found in Uexküll's early writings. In his 1905 book *Leitfaden in das Studium der experimentellen Biologie der Wassertiere*, Uexküll not only introduces the term "Bauplan" but also uses the word "planmäßig" ("conforming to plan"), although not yet as a scientific concept in the strict sense. It first appears here in his characterization of science as a "planmäßig-ordered experience," where it is used to describing the process of scientific observation, and also points to a closeness between "planmäßig" observation and the observed "Baupläne" (pl. of Bauplan).[54] With this, Planmäßigkeit is understood as not only the principle of nature that biology has to describe but also the principle that gives this biology its methodological

52 Jakob von Uexküll, *Theoretische Biologie*, 2nd ed. (Berlin: Springer, 1928), 220. Unlike the 1920 first edition, the 1928 second edition (with its revised and expanded text) was not translated for publication in English.

53 Höfer, *Die Notwendigkeit der Kommunikation*, 115.

54 Uexküll, *Leitfaden*, v.

 foundation. Uexküll is concerned with "discerning and explaining nature, both in and *through* its plans."[55]

The idea cited above that the irresolvable internal contradiction of Uexküll's Umwelt theory "cannot logically be closed"[56] is therefore only valid as long as one fails to comprehend that the observation of other Umwelten does not require an escaping from the monadic enclosure but is to be found in another "larger" monadic enclosure that itself is also subject to the same Planmäßigkeit. Uexküll does not shift from a monadic to a dualistic structure but instead scales up this monadic structure to embrace nature as a whole. What at first glance seems to be a contradiction between the impossibility of transcending one's own Umwelt on the one hand, and Uexküll's numerous descriptions of other Umwelten on the other, is actually explained as an effect of Planmäßigkeit, which has always provided for both order and observability, regardless of the scaling level.[57]

Planmäßigkeit thus appears wherever Uexküll draws connections, tries to describe relationships, and establishes coherences. Nothing can lie beyond it, since it already exists inside everything. As such a total and internalized principle, it determines Uexküll's "subjective" biology.[58]

3. Planmäßigkeit and Subjectivity

Uexküll subordinates his biology to one and only one epistemological premise: "*All reality is subjective appearance.* This must

55 Helbach, "Die Umweltlehre Jakob von Uexkülls," 59, italics added.

56 Haas, *Tiere auf der Bühne*, 167.

57 See, for instance, Andreas Weber's critical view regarding the autonomy and autopoiesis that Uexküll ascribes to living entities: "What Uexküll's biology postulated is ironically the opposite of a harmonious, unified biological worldview." Andreas Weber, *Die Natur als Bedeutung* (Würzburg: Königshausen & Neumann, 2003), 78.

58 Uexküll, *Bausteine*, 143.

constitute the great, fundamental admission even of biology."[59] But this statement does not actually contradict the central importance assigned to Planmäßigkeit by Uexküll as described above; instead, it can be seen as further evidence of the idea. What Uexküll meant by this subjectivity can be adequately understood only by discarding the previously mentioned assumption of a dichotomy between holism and subjectivism.[60] The conception of Planmäßigkeit outlined in the previous subchapter leaves no room for a subjectivity that could in any way be placed in opposition to it. Instead, subjectivity attains its strong position within Umwelt theory only insofar as it is seen *as* Planmäßigkeit.[61] A closer look at this specific subjectivity will, on the one hand, demonstrate the structural holism that pervades Uexküll's Umwelt theory, and on the other, lead to its political point. Since subjectivity can only appear as Planmäßigkeit, the subject's dominion over its Umwelt cannot be understood as some sort of autonomous spontaneity either, but only as a determinism "conforming to plan." This naturalization of dominion, which is intrinsic to Planmäßigkeit and determines its political component, will be presented in more detail in the last subchapter. But first, the conceptualization of subjectivity *as* Planmäßigkeit will be outlined in contrast to the ideas of two other authors: Charles Darwin and Immanuel Kant.

3.1 Holistically with and against Darwin

In Darwin's conception, the theory of evolution is a history of difference production, which must always start with the concrete individual organism and its position relative to an externality,

59 Jakob von Uexküll, *Theoretical Biology*, trans. Doris L. Mackinnon (New York: Harcourt, Brace & Company, 1926), xv, italics in original. This translation is based on the 1920 first edition of Uexküll's *Theoretische Biologie*.

60 See for example, once again, Stella and Kleisner, "Uexküllian Umwelt as Science and as Ideology," 43 and 50.

61 Esposito, "Kantian Ticks, Uexküllian Melodies," 37.

be it a competitor or the natural conditions.[62] This "liberal individualist" reading of evolution theory was often ignored during the late nineteenth century among Darwin's German-speaking admirers, and was largely swept under the rug.[63] For example, Ernst Haeckel, who in the late 1860s began presenting himself as *the* leading Darwinist of the German-speaking world, misses Darwin's point when he completely conjures away the oppositionality of the external in Darwin's theory, trying to read it primarily as evidence for the seamless interconnectivity of all of nature—a possible but by no means obligatory consequence of Darwin's analysis, and one that Darwin himself sees, but to which he attaches very little importance.[64] In contrast to Darwin, Haeckel casts evolution as a history built on types, the history of

62 "Hence I look at individual differences, though of small interest to the systematist, as of the highest importance for us, as being the first steps towards such slight varieties as are barely thought worth recording in works on natural history. And I look at varieties which are in any degree more distinct and permanent, as steps towards more strongly-marked and permanent varieties; and at the latter, as leading to sub-species, and then to species." See Charles Darwin, *The Origin of Species by Means of Natural Selection, or the Preservation of Favoured Races in the Struggle for Life*, 6th ed. (London: John Murray, 1876; Cambridge: Cambridge University Press, 2009), 41–42.

63 Bowler has shown that numerous attempts at a new biology during the late nineteenth century often mentioned Darwin's name only for strategic reasons, without actually building upon his theory or even seriously addressing it. See Peter Bowler, *The Eclipse of Darwinism: Anti-Darwinian Evolution Theories in the Decades around 1900* (Baltimore, MD: John Hopkins University Press, 1983); Peter Bowler, *The Non-Darwinian Revolution: Reinterpreting a Historical Myth* (Baltimore, MD: John Hopkins University Press, 1988). For a closer look at Haeckel's reading of Darwin, see (among others) Robert Richards, *The Tragic Sense of Life: Ernst Haeckel and the Struggle over Evolutionary Thought* (Chicago: University of Chicago Press, 2008).

64 Darwin writes that, based on the fact that all organisms "have much in common," we must "admit that all the organic beings which have ever lived on this earth may be descended from some one primordial form." But such a conclusion would not advance science, since "this inference is chiefly grounded on analogy, and it is immaterial whether or not it be accepted." See Darwin, *Origin of Species*, 425.

a totality that develops in and out of itself, and thus one that is *not* confronted with external oppositionalities.[65]

While still a young university student quite interested in Darwin, Uexküll was offered an interpretation of evolution theory that was shaped by Haeckel and cleansed of this aspect. As Mildenberger has shown, figures such as Julius von Kennel, a professor at Dorpat, followed Haeckel's reading of Darwin in believing that one "can disregard the importance of individual processes . . . [and] construct kinships between all animal species."[66] Just as Uexküll's early flirtation with Darwinism did not start with Darwin himself but with Haeckel's interpretation of Darwin—thus overlooking the importance of the oppositionality of the external—so did his later and all the more aggressive anti-Darwinism primarily target Haeckel, whose reductionism he attacked while ignoring his holism (especially where he transformed and further developed it in essential aspects).[67] Thus, like Haeckel and many other German-speaking biologists of the time, Uexküll rejected what he disqualified as a "planless" and chaotic thinking in differences,[68] something that was essential for Darwin himself. Even as a young Darwinist, Uexküll implicitly rejected Darwin's thinking in

65 Despite his enthusiasm for Darwin's alleged pioneering of a "continuous chain" concept that would encompass all organisms, Haeckel does not actually follow what Darwin proposes regarding this chain of living entities. Here, and using Darwin to argue against Darwin, the assumption of a "primordial organism" (see Ernst Haeckel, *Die Radiolarien [Rhizopoda radiaria]: Eine Monographie mit einem Atlas von fünf und dreissig Kupfertafeln*, 2 vols. [Berlin: Georg Reimer, 1862], 1:232, n) is derived from Haeckel's belief in the existence of a "historically continuous developmental interrelationship" (see Jürgen Sandmann, "Ernst Haeckels Entwicklungslehre als Teil seiner biologistischen Weltanschauung," in *Die Evolution von Rezeptionstheorien im 19. Jahrhundert*, ed. Eve-Marie Engels [Frankfurt am Main: Suhrkamp, 1995], 330), and not from Darwin's conception of *how* the interrelationships between living entities could be explained (see Haeckel, *Die Radiolarien*, 1:232, n).

66 Mildenberger, *Umwelt als Vision*, 34.

67 See for example Uexküll, *Bausteine*, 17–34.

68 See for example ibid., 19–34.

 differences—a rejection that would then become explicit in his later years as an overt anti-Darwinist.

In contrast to Darwin, Uexküll does not see an individual organism asserting itself against competitors or nature, and conversely, does not see nature standing in opposition to it. If, as Hans-Jörg Rheinberger states, Darwin's evolution is to be understood as a process in which "development is no longer thought of as the 'interior' of a nature seen as an immanent yet overarching subject,"[69] then Uexküll's conception results from a reversal of that statement: for him, the immanent yet overarching subject is located both in the individual Umwelt bubbles and in nature as a whole. The merging of subjectivity and Planmäßigkeit mentioned at the beginning of this subchapter thus appears as an alternative to Darwin's biology, with its focus on the importance of minute differences and oppositionalities. This is not least due to the other discursive context from which this merging arises—as will be shown in the next subchapter. For now, it should simply be noted that Uexküll's handling of Darwin is shaped by his rejection of an oppositionality between subject and nature.

3.2 Immanently with and against Kant

A very similar disinclination toward thinking in categorical contradictions also characterizes Uexküll's treatment of the thinker he repeatedly cites as the philosophical basis for his "subjective" biology. Immanuel Kant's ideas were to facilitate the formulation of Uexküll's biology on "a peculiar theoretical basis of its own, which is in no way deducible from the fundamental concepts of physics and chemistry."[70]

Uexküll certainly does not consider himself a philosopher and states that he is only attempting to apply well-known

69 Hans-Jörg Rheinberger, "Entwicklung als 'Prozess ohne Subjekt,'" in *Rekurrenzen: Texte zu Althusser*, ed. Hans-Jörg Rheinberger (Berlin: Suhrkamp, 2014), 106.

70 Uexküll, *Theoretical Biology*, xiii.

philosophical concepts to the field of biology; at most, he sees himself as simply extending them by applying them to biology.[71] Such an appropriation of Kant for the purposes of science was anything but unusual in Uexküll's time. With examples ranging from the reductionism of Hermann von Helmholtz and Rudolf Virchow to the biological development mechanics of Wilhelm Roux[72] and the neovitalism of Hans Driesch,[73] many concepts from the practice and theory of the natural sciences borrowed from Kant's work. Even Anton Dohrn, the head of the zoological station in Naples where Uexküll and so many others conducted research, tried to draw a connection between Kant and various biological theories, specifically the theory of evolution.[74] It is therefore unsurprising that Uexküll, who had already read Kant as a youth in secondary school as was customary at the time,[75] writes in 1905 of the "three great critical works of Kant, which are not a philosophical system, but contain a scientific consideration of the laws that govern the life of the human soul."[76]

Despite the countless references to Kant in Uexküll's work and the undoubtedly great influence that Kant's philosophy had on Uexküll's biology, it should be noted that the latter did not find its "guiding philosophy" in Kant, as Brett Buchanan claims.[77] Rather,

71 Ibid., 9.

72 Mildenberger, *Umwelt als Vision*, 47.

73 See for example Hans Driesch, "Kant und das Ganze," *Kant-Studien* 29 (1924): 365–76.

74 Mildenberger, *Umwelt als Vision*, 48.

75 Brentari, *Jakob von Uexküll*, 22.

76 Uexküll, *Leitfaden*, 130.

77 Brett Buchanan, *Onto-Ethologies: The Animal Environments of Uexküll, Heidegger, Merleau-Ponty, and Deleuze* (New York: University of New York Press, 2008), 13. See also similar analyses from, among others, Brentari, *Jakob von Uexküll*, esp. chap. 4; Haas, *Tiere auf der Bühne*, 63 and 65; Kalevi Kull, "Jakob von Uexküll: An Introduction," *Semiotica* 134, no. 1/4 (2001), 8 among others; Francesca Michelini, "Introduction: A Foray into Uexküll's Heritage," in Michelini and Köchy, *Jakob von Uexküll and Philosophy*, 3; Sagan, "Introduction: Umwelt after Uexküll," 11; Helene Weiss, "Aristotle's Theology and Uexküll's Theory of Living Nature," *Classical Quarterly* 42, no. 1/2 (1948), 49.

 as will be shown in the next subchapter, the theoretical backbone of Umwelt theory is supplied by other lines of thought, including some that are clearly anti-Kantian. Uexküll fundamentally transforms Kant's theses and concepts to make them compatible with, and subservient to, his biology.[78] It is precisely this transformation of Kant's philosophy that demonstrates (by negative example) the importance of the holistic lines of thought that shaped Uexküll's biology. Uexküll drops anything in Kant's philosophy that cannot be brought into accord with them.

This even applies to the most basic starting points. Where Kant points to cognition (*Erkenntnis*), Uexküll points to *Merken* and *Wirken* (the active reception of stimuli and the active production of effects).[79] However, these are tied to the specific Bauplan. Just as Hermann von Helmholtz before him, whom he held in high esteem, Uexküll also grounds every organism's cognitional world in its corporeality (even if this is seen as simply the expression of a "deeper" nonmaterial Bauplan). For example, the sensory organs determine what is accessible to perception. But this also applies to space and time, the "principles of pure cognition" that come even before these categories in Kantian thought. This means—to single out one of many examples from a research effort concerned with "first securing the Umwelt of each animal"[80]—that even something seemingly as fundamental as space cannot be treated as a transcendental category. According to Uexküll (borrowing from von Baer and in contrast to Kant), space exists in the form of innumerable *representations* of space that can be traced back to particular organic Baupläne

78 Merleau-Ponty was one of the first to emphasize the difference between Umwelt theory and Kant's philosophy (Merleau-Ponty, *Nature*, 177–78). Further examples of this can be found in Aldona Pobojewska, "Die Subjektlehre Jakob von Uexkülls," *Sudhoffs Archiv* 77, no. 1 (1993): 54–71; Helbach, "Die Umweltlehre Jakob von Uexkülls"; Esposito, "Kantian Ticks, Uexküllian Melodies"; and Morten Tønnessen, "Umwelt Transitions: Uexküll and Environmental Change," *Biosemiotics* 2 (2009): 47–64.

79 Pobojewska, "Die Subjektlehre Jakob von Uexkülls," 70.

80 Uexküll, *Umwelt und Innenwelt der Tiere*, 6.

and their associated action patterns (i.e., the specific modes of Wirken). With Uexküll, then, space is not to be seen as a *transcendental* enabling condition for perception and cognition; instead, particular representations of space emerge as products of the different physiological forms of living organisms, which are in turn the expressions of different Baupläne: "The Bauplan of every living entity is not only expressed in the structure of its body, but also in the relationships between the body and the world surrounding it."[81] These spaces, which are ethologically and physiologically privative and not subjective as seen for example in transcendental idealism, are no longer located in an empty external world but on a higher level of the same structure. This is made clear by Uexküll's comment (which will come up again from a different angle in the next chapter) on Albert Einstein's theory of relativity: "But Einstein has now destroyed this unified imaginary space by taking away its center. A space cannot exist without a center, and if you give it multiple centers, then you split it into multiple spaces. This means we're going back to subjective spaces."[82]

Esposito is thus certainly not going too far when he says that the position occupied by the subject in Kant's philosophy is taken instead by Planmäßigkeit in Uexküll's framework.[83] Uexküll himself is clear here, such as when he writes that the Bauplan "creates first the subject, and with it, its Umwelt."[84] Considering the importance that Uexküll assigns (especially in his later writings) to the living organism's current disposition and situation, this

81 Uexküll, ibid., 4. On this, see also Luca Guidetti, "The Space of the Living Beings: Umwelt and Space in Jakob von Uexküll," in *The Changing Faces of Space*, ed. Maria Teresa Cantena and Felice Masi (Cham: Springer, 2017), 3–18, on von Baer see 3–6.

82 Letter to Adolf von Harnack, September 10, 1928, quoted in Jutta Schmidt, "Jakob von Uexküll und Houston Stewart Chamberlain: Ein Briefwechsel in Auszügen," *Medizinhistorisches Journal* 10, no. 2 (1975): 122.

83 Esposito, "Kantian Ticks, Uexküllian Melodies," 37.

84 Jakob von Uexküll, "Biologie oder Physiologie" (1933), in *Kompositionslehre der Natur*, 124.

 tendency could be defined even more precisely: Merken and Wirken are doubly determined by Planmäßigkeit. On the one hand, this principle manifests as a Bauplan and finds expression in physiological characteristics, thereby preconditioning the organism's specific behavioral forms and the production of its Umwelt. And on the other hand, each Umwelt is attuned to a Planmäßigkeit that also arranges it situationally to other Umwelten, thereby once again dictating the organism's specific Merken and Wirken, and thus its Umwelt and its particular subjectivity.

But contrary to Esposito, who still sees Uexküll's biology as transcendental despite acknowledging its merging of subjectivity through Planmäßigkeit,[85] it must be stated that such a reframing of Kant's notion of cognition does necessarily imply a fundamental shift. Such a shift has been asserted by authors such as Ernst Cassirer, Karl Lorenz, and Carl Friedrich von Weizsäcker, and has been interpreted as either an excessive fulfillment or profound undermining of the Kantian model.[86] For the argument presented here, the main point of this shift is that with Uexküll's particular take on the organism's cognition of the world, any Kantian notion of transcendence, or even of the universal, has been driven out. With Uexküll, cognition is not a product of transcendental categories that are equally common to all beings capable of cognition (i.e., humans) but is instead a bundle of abilities that are individually and situationally different, depending on a being's disposition. It is also not the product of a transcendent praxis reaching out to an externality but instead remains perpetually limited to the inside of a bubble, although one whose extent could well encompass nature as a whole. Instead of a universalism built upon categories and limited to humans, Uexküll presents a particular form of something that

85 Esposito, "Kantian Ticks, Uexküllian Melodies," 40. Also see, for example, Haas, *Tiere auf der Bühne*, 176.

86 Helbach, "Die Umweltlehre Jakob von Uexkülls," 65, 108, and 130–31.

Kant actually rejected: a "natural teleology," one in which nature itself "guarantees that all elements are fitted in."[87]

Therefore, the *broadening* of Kant to nonhuman, animal life,[88] which has been so often highlighted in recent scholarship on Uexküll, also represents an anti-Kantian *narrowing* of each organism's nature as determined by Planmäßigkeit, which last but not least also necessitates a negation of the capacity for cognition. Kant's Enlightenment impulse is thus suspended. While Kant says that unlike the animal, which "is already fully equipped through instinct," the human "must arrange the plan of his own behavior,"[89] thereby opening up the possibility of reason, Uexküll has animals and humans completely merged into their own respective Umwelten.

Kant's inquiry is focused on the possibility of cognizing reality, and its foundation lies in the transcendental working (i.e., Wirken) of the conditions of the possibility of cognition that are unequivocally granted to every human individual. In contrast, Uexküll's Merken and Wirken cannot be abstracted from the relationship between the Innenwelt and the Umwelt, a relationship that already *is* subjectivity (and not simply a designator for its enablement).[90] With Uexküll, the subject appears "as a unit: its body and experience are viewed together."[91] The Innenwelt *and* the Umwelt, in a perpetual interaction that can never be broken off, make up Uexküll's subject, which he sees as "a higher unit of the most exquisite harmony."[92] For him, subjects are beings who are "organized as wholes and who automatically build an Umwelt with which they are correlated."[93] Uexküll's "subject"

87 Weber, *Die Natur als Bedeutung*, 87.

88 See (among others) Buchanan, *Onto-Ethologies*, 13.

89 *The Educational Theory of Immanuel Kant*, trans. and ed. Edward Franklin Buchner (Philadelphia: J. B. Lippincott, 1904), 102–3.

90 Esposito, "Kantian Ticks, Uexküllian Melodies," 41.

91 Helbach, "Die Umweltlehre Jakob von Uexkülls," 31.

92 Uexküll, *Bausteine*, 204.

93 Bühler, "Das Tier und die Experimentalisierung," 41–52.

thus represents the nexus of Innenwelt, Umwelt, and behavior pattern, appearing in the wider "plan" only as an already existing whole;[94] this is precisely how the concept of the subject is entirely congruent with that of Planmäßigkeit. It is Bernd Herrmann who sums up what could perhaps be best described as Uexküll's "holistic subjectivity." Herrmann finds in the "formula of 'human and Umwelt' . . . a category error"; even the combining of two nouns with a coordinating "and" would presuppose a separation that Uexküll did not accept and therefore did not convey.[95]

This means that Aldona Pobojewska is correct in stating that "Uexküll has largely reinterpreted the Kantian conception *before* he begins to develop it further in biology."[96] Looking ahead at the next subsection, one could say more precisely that this reinterpretation is based on certain lines of thought inspired by Goethe (and thus already departing from Kant) that developed in the biology of the second half of the nineteenth century. In contrast to Kant, but in continuation of concepts such as Goethe's God-Nature (to which Uexküll explicitly and repeatedly refers) and Haeckel's self-awareness of nature,[97] Uexküll's subjectivity is not necessarily tied to consciousness. An autonomous Merken and Wirken is enough for establishing an organism's individual Umwelt.[98] With Uexküll's merging of subjectivity and plan, this separation of consciousness and subjectivity becomes inescapable. It is already anchored in the conceptualizing of a "Planmäßigkeit" that takes as its starting point the reflex (as previously described), a phenomenon that is by definition unconscious. This turning away from consciousness is precisely what causes Kant's conscious and *self-conscious* subject to dissolve into its relationship with that which it is perceiving and acting upon.

94 As Uexküll writes in *Kompositionslehre der Natur*, 140, "the subject and Umwelt thus form a whole."

95 Herrmann, *Mein Acker ist die Zeit*, 234n363.

96 Pobojewska, "Die Subjektlehre Jakob von Uexkülls," 58, italics added.

97 See for example Uexküll, *Foray*, 192; Uexküll, *Bausteine*, 122.

98 The basis of this shift is to be found in Uexküll's separation of plan and consciousness. On this, see for example Uexküll, *Bausteine*, 175 and 176.

Where Kant places fundamental importance on the separation between the understanding with its objects (i.e., appearances) and actual reality, this differentiation (between understanding and the senses, between true things and real ones) collapses into itself with Uexküll, who (in contrast to Helmholtz) does not draw upon some unknowable external reality of things.[99]

As Ludwig Feuerbach noted, holistically unbounding the "subject" is only the flip side of abandoning the notion of oppositional externality. In this, he sees a clear disruption of Kantian philosophy. The corresponding passage helps clarify what is happening with Uexküll's reshaping of Kant, not only in relation to the subject but also more generally in terms of epistemology:

> If we therefore eliminate this contradiction [between intellect and senses, between truth and reality], we have the philosophy of identity . . . where the subject is no longer limited and conditioned by something existing apart from it and contradicting its essence. But the subject which has nothing more outside itself and consequently no more limits within itself, is no longer a 'finite' subject—no longer *the* ego to which an object is counterposed; it is the Absolute Being whose theological or popular expression is the word 'God.'[100]

This line of thought is also found in Uexküll. Every single Umwelt, and not just "nature," is seen as a boundless whole that exists in identity to itself. The elimination of the external from this immanently understood "Umwelt" means that subjectivity (which merges with Planmäßigkeit) is elevated to a totalizing category entirely free from oppositionality while also being reified into a closed bubble.[101]

99 See Buchanan, *Onto-Ethologies*, 13–14; Helbach, "Die Umweltlehre Jakob von Uexkülls," 58.

100 Ludwig Feuerbach, *The Fiery Brook: Selected Writings*, trans. Zawar Hanfi (London: Verso, 2012), 208.

101 Herrmann characterizes Uexküll's Umwelt as a "relational concept" that "cannot be reified" (see Herrmann, *Mein Acker ist die Zeit*, 257), but it should be countered that the relationality described above simply represents the

Uexküll thereby removes subjectivity from its oppositional relationship with the external, be it with competitors and with continually life-threatening nature (as with Darwin) or with the externality of real things (as with Kant). He also ties it inextricably to the principle of ubiquitous Planmäßigkeit. With this change also comes a shift in focus. Uexküll's Umwelt theory is not aimed at understanding the relationships between inside and outside but rather at fathoming what are always internal relationships. Within this shift, there is already a conservative tendency. Uexküll remains ensconced in the internal, in "what one has" and "what one is." The unsettling question of adaptation (*Anpassung*) is thus replaced by the certainty of Planmäßigkeit's being "fitted into" (*Einpassung*), the question of what is needed to enable cognition by the certainty of Planmäßigkeit's Merken. Such inner certainties also underpin Uexküll's more overtly political texts; it is not by accident that these criminalize what is pathological, meaning any deviation or departure from what is "natural." According to Umwelt theory, it is not possible for danger to come from without; it must come from within. Uexküll sees danger in the degeneration of the natural state, understood as natural Planmäßigkeit. Uexküll's antisemitic descriptions of Jews as parasites and his reactionary notions of a static estate-based society as described in *Staatsbiologie* (see previous chapter) have their roots in his particular conception of subjectivity. This will be explored more deeply in the final subchapter. But first, it is necessary to take a closer look at the roots of Planmäßigkeit itself.

other side of the monadic enclosure. This enables a reification of the living precisely by allowing the living organism, including all its activities and behaviors, to be understood as being entirely what it already is. Contrast this, for example, to Plessner's "positionality of the excentric form," which has also been invoked against Uexküll, although the concept is only related to the human being. See Helmuth Plessner, *The Levels of Organic Life and the Human: Introduction to Philosophical Anthropology*, trans. Millay Hyatt (New York: Fordham University Press, 2019), 267–322.

4. Planmäßigkeit and the Holistic Tradition

Like his conception of Planmäßigkeit, Uexküll's conception of subjectivity can hardly be traced back to Darwin or Kant. As this subchapter will demonstrate, Uexküll's subjectivity instead continues the German tradition of biological holism,[102] particularly the strand beginning with Goethe. It was with the German Empire's founding in 1871 that Goethe's writings on natural philosophy underwent a new boom that lasted into the 1930s and 1940s, a period that also resulted in several profound reinterpretations that will be returned to momentarily. These also strengthened holism's tendency to develop into a conservative and sometimes far-right worldview, although this certainly does not mean that German-speaking biology's entire holistic tradition can be assigned to the right.[103] But one can plainly identify certain longstanding and broadly developed strands in which the holistic view is combined with an emphasis on conservative preservation and a naturalization of dominion. Uexküll's Umwelt theory can be assigned to such a strand.

The potency of this tradition lies in its potential for harmoniously dissolving categorical oppositions and for naturalizing this dissolution. Problems disappear into the whole. The aforementioned question of how monadically closed-off Umwelten can be made observable, even though each observing entity can only access its own similarly closed-off Umwelt, is already resolved in this tradition. Uexküll's Umwelt theory builds upon such solutions. What may appear to be irresolvable or self-contradictory for later readers of Umwelt theory actually proves to be a logically consistent continuation and adaptation of established lines of holistic thought.

102 On the characterization of this holistic tradition as German (referring to the broader German-speaking region, and not just the territory of the German Empire itself), see Harrington, *Reenchanted Science*, xxi.

103 Harrington also highlights the politically pluralistic character of this tradition, see ibid., xxi.

The shift in the focus of Planmäßigekeit sketched above to what is internal and nonmaterial, along with the associated merger of Planmäßigkeit and subjectivity, was closely tied to the search for order and structure, especially in what is disordered, centerless, and amorphous. This search was what drove the late nineteenth century's German-language marine biology, and which played no small role in cementing the importance it had in shaping the epistemological foundations of ecology and "Umgebungswissen" (the "study of surroundings").[104] As Wessely notes, Uexküll himself refers to this fact in 1913 when he writes that "the greatest strides in fertilization and gestation studies of the last twenty years" had been thanks "almost exclusively to sea creatures."[105] Uexküll's own early research efforts took place entirely within the field of marine biology. As a result, the problems driving marine biology inevitably became his own. But the solutions he formulated here would also have a fundamental influence on his Umwelt theory. They revolve around questions of how form develops and more generally around questions of order.

But biology's established methods for approaching these questions were difficult to conduct underwater. For the marine biologists of Uexküll's day, it was hard to find even glimmers of an external order, considering the near shapelessness of many marine creatures and the seeming paucity of structure in the milieu itself. The taxonomy of Carl Linnaeus begins with shape, but this could hardly be applied to organisms whose bodies were extremely malleable even when alive, and which then turned all too quickly into lifeless and shapeless lumps of jelly when

104 On the epistemological productiveness of this research, and on the sometimes extreme efforts undertaken by marine biologists around 1900 to collect organisms *along with* their milieu and to look at them *within* it, see Christina Wessely, "Watery Milieus: Marine Biology, Aquariums, and the Limits of Ecological Knowledge circa 1900," *Grey Room* 75, no. 6 (2019): 37–59.

105 Uexküll, *Bausteine*, 120–21, cited in Wessely, "Watery Milieus," 44.

removed from their milieu. As recounted by Anton Dohrn, the founder and director of the marine biological station in Naples:

> It happens often enough that animals of the same species and same locality, when preserved in different ways, can hardly be identified, while others remain completely unidentifiable, and descriptions made of the living animal do not apply to the conserved, so that one does not match the other.[106]

It was not only classical taxonomy but also Charles Darwin's evolutionary biology that had problems with the sea and its inhabitants. While natural barriers (such as rivers, mountain ranges, etc.) favor the diverging development of the terrestrial species that Darwin's theory tries to describe, this does not apply to the sea. Darwin presumes here a milieu that is continuous and unstructured, and so he conjectures far more of what he calls "transitional forms" than he does on land.[107] From the perspectives of both classical taxonomy and evolutionary biology, the sea and its organisms therefore represented an almost primordial disorder, and thus a problem.

Among the concepts and methods used by German-speaking biologists during the late nineteenth century in response to this problem, it is possible to identify two general tendencies, which were in fact continuously entangled. The first tendency sprang from the difficulty of finding no foothold in externalities for explaining particular organic structures, and it met this challenge by postulating an internal principle that gives structure.[108] The second approached the same problem from a different angle: the

106 Anton Dohrn, "Vorwort des Herausgebers," in *Die Ctenophoren des Golfes von Neapel und der Angrenzenden Meeres-Abschnitte*, ed. Carl Chun (Leipzig: Wilhelm Engelmann, 1880), vi.

107 Darwin, *Origin of Species*, 283.

108 See for example Haeckel, *Die Radiolarien*. While Haeckel may claim he wants to follow Darwin (231–32), he does not actually do so, probably because he is unable to explain differences between radiolarian species through differences in food intake, reproduction, etc. (128 among others).

 difficulties of scientifically grasping these organisms (and with them their inner structural principles and then their behavioral ones), and even of adequately studying them at all, were to be sidestepped by deploying new notions of perception and cognition. Both of these tendencies are holistic. The difference lies in the level of focus: one tendency focuses on the organism *as a whole*, while the other focuses on nature *as a whole*, with the explicit inclusion of humans.

Both tendencies can already be identified in the marine research of the mid-nineteenth century, for example with Carl Vogt and Matthias Jacob Schleiden. A few decades later, they can still be seen in the work of influential biologists such as Ernst Haeckel and Karl Möbius—and indeed in the work of Uexküll as well, whose Umwelt theory not only expresses both tendencies in a particularly radical way but also ties them inextricably together. Even if many of these biologists still cite Darwin again and again and still continue the tradition of classical taxonomy, it is also true that they explore other paths as well, particularly in light of the problems mentioned above.

For a consideration of Uexküll and the observer problem that is so central to his theory, what is of particular interest in this research is bioaesthetic attempts to gain access to the lower marine animals by means of a different notion of perception. However, the close interweaving of milieu and organism that can be taken from Dohrn's quotation above does also imply an alienation of human beings, or more precisely, a gap between the milieu of the organism being studied and that of human beings. But it is precisely in the remoteness and autonomy of these life forms that the fascination they elicit is rooted. As early as the mid-nineteenth century, the fact that marine organisms could not be slotted into taxonomic arrangements as easily as flowering plants, for example, was already seen by some as something other than a problem. In fact, whatever refused to fit into the nominalistic system was often seen as an expression of life itself—and as *beautiful* too. In 1848, for example, Carl

Vogt (who was introduced to marine biology by Louis Agassiz and later became a radical democratic member of the Frankfurt Parliament) asked whether it might be possible, “without that systematic dryness, without that endless going into details which attaches to our zoological sciences, to sketch in broad strokes a picture of that luxuriant life” under study.[109] As Christian Kockerbeck has shown, it was not only terra firma that is abandoned here but the traditional taxonomic system as well: the leap into the sea was as enchanting as a leap into life itself, a life that cannot be bound by systems.[110]

The point of the new conception of natural beauty inspired by such views is that this is not to be understood as simply a particular kind of representation, and thus of a perception process that would mediate between what are initially different things. Instead, the conceptual model emerging here is one that blends the complete closing off of organisms in milieus foreign to human beings with the idea of a chaotic life that is basically the same everywhere, a model that is also seen in highly aesthetic terms. Following Kockerbeck, this means that, on the one hand, newly discovered marine organisms are seen as having complete aesthetic self-sufficiency. On the other hand, precisely this ascription becomes the starting point for theories of perception that assume a preexisting connection between humans and these self-sufficiently beautiful organisms, a connection that is explained by the simple fact that both sides of the equation are occupied by living entities.[111] This twofold radicalization of the autonomy of living entities (extending to the sphere of perception) and of their essential similarity and interconnectedness (extending to the idea of an undivided nature that

109 Carl Vogt, *Ocean und Mittelmeer: Reisebriefe*, 2 vols. (Frankfurt am Main: J. Rütten, 1848), 1:15–16.

110 On Vogt’s marine biology research, its implicit critique of zoological taxonomy, and its aesthetic implications, see Christian Kockerbeck, *Die Schönheit des Lebendigen: Ästhetische Naturwahrnehmung im 19. Jahrhundert* (Vienna: Böhlau, 1997), 54–67.

111 Ibid., 50.

 emanates into innumerable forms) achieves a kind of squaring of the ecological circle.

This two-pronged argumentation achieves a radical break from not only the traditional theories of biology, but also those of aesthetics. The postulated self-sufficiency of organisms, which also encompasses a beauty that is understood as "for itself" and not "for others," removes the possibility of a representational logic that was just as necessary for Linnaeus as it was for the choice of a mate in Darwin's theory of sexual selection.[112] It lays the foundation for conceptualizing perception as a process that happens inside a holism.[113]

This development can be seen as the continuation of a holistic tradition. Where the ideas of Linnaeus and Darwin failed to convince, there was a different founding father who attracted the interest of German marine biologists in particular, namely Goethe.[114] With him, the two-pronged approach is already

112 Concerning Linnaeus's visibility-oriented regime and its implementation in representative descriptive language, see Michel Foucault, *The Order of Things* (London: Routledge Classics, 2002), 141–48. In contrast to the ideas described here, the choice of a mate in Darwin's theory of sexual selection is based on a fundamental difference, namely that between bodies and signs. For example, Darwin shows that with some species, the male's potency-indicating characteristics "are only associated *with* strength or potency," meaning that they influence what is only a *choice* and do not trigger some completely predetermined process. Here, the *impression* of beauty is assigned to the animal who is observing, and is described as the effect of a functional process. On this, see Philipp Sarasin, *Darwin und Foucault: Genealogie und Geschichte im Zeitalter der Biologie* (Frankfurt am Main: Suhrkamp, 2009), 272–86, quote on 280.

113 Kockerbeck, *Die Schönheit des Lebendigen*, 51.

114 On this continuity, see Philip C. Ritterbush, *The Art of Organic Forms* (Washington, DC: Smithsonian Institution Press, 1968); Hans Werner Ingensiep, "Metamorphosen der Metamorphosenlehre: Zur Goethe-Rezeption in der Biologie von der Romantik bis in die Gegenwart," in *Goethe und die Verzeitlichung der Natur*, ed. Peter Matussek (Munich: C. H. Beck, 1988), 259–75. For a retrospective view of this continuity, see also Adolf Meyer-Abich, *Biologie der Goethezeit* (Stuttgart: Hippokrates, 1949); Meyer-Abich was a holistic biologist and signatory of the *Vow of Allegiance of the*

apparent, postulating an inner design principle on the one hand, and bringing the observer close to the observed on the other. As a natural philosopher focusing less on form and more on how form *develops*, Goethe proved particularly compatible with the investigations into the specific problems outlined above. One sees this clearly, for instance, in his work on metamorphosis. Goethe is concerned with transformation processes that generate forms and structures from within (similar to Johann Friedrich Blumenbach's concept of the *Bildungstrieb*, or "formative drive").[115]

The structural equivalence between the observer and the observed as outlined above also builds upon Goethe's ideas. Against Linnaeus and "such a fragmented way of dealing with nature," Goethe articulates the goal of "portraying it as alive and active, with its efforts directed from the whole to the parts."[116] Right from the start, this shift implies a change not only in the objects under observation, but also in the relationships existing between them and with the investigative observer. Goethe's holism consequently starts "midway between nature and subject,"[117] namely at the sensory organs. It is precisely here that Goethe postulates a juncture between the observed and the

Professors of the German Universities and High-Schools [sic., Institutions of Higher Education] *to Adolf Hitler and the National Socialistic State.*

115 Johann Wolfgang von Goethe, "Bildungstrieb," from *Hefte zur Morphologie*, vol. 1 (1817–1822), in *Johann Wolfgang Goethe: Sämtliche Werke*, vol. 24 (Frankfurt am Main: Deutscher Klassiker-Verlag, 1987), 451; on Blumenbach and Goethe, see Olaf Breidbach, "Blumenbachs Vorfeld und Umfeld: Wolff und Goethe und auch etwas Hegel," in *Wissenschaft und Natur: Studien zur Aktualität der Philosophiegeschichte; Festschrift für Wolfgang Neuser zum 60. Geburtstag*, ed. Klaus Wiegerling and Wolfgang Lenski (Nordhausen: Bautz, 2011), 149–71.

116 Johann Wolfgang von Goethe, *Scientific Studies*, ed. and trans. Douglas Miller (New York: Suhrkamp, 1988), 19–20.

117 Gunter Mann, Dieter Mollenhauer, and Stefan Peters (eds.), *In der Mitte zwischen Natur und Subjekt: Johann Wolfgang von Goethes Versuch, die Metamorphose der Pflanze zu erklären, 1790–1990* (Frankfurt am Main: Waldemar Kramer, 1990).

observer, one no longer conceived as a leap across some deep chasm of radical difference but as a harmonious structural similarity:

> We will in the end be in a position to conclude that our mind—like our eyes are constructed in total harmony with the objects beheld, and like our ears are built in harmony with the swinging movements of the quivering bodies—stands in harmony with the deep elementary forces of nature; it is capable of imagining them as purely as the objects of the visible world represent themselves in a clear eye.[118]

Similar ideas are seen again and again in the biology and natural philosophy of the late nineteenth century. One such example is presented by the staunch monist Wilhelm Bölsche, who contributed greatly during that period to popularizing this conception of the relationship between man and nature. Drawing upon Goethe and Haeckel, Bölsche postulated that the feeling of beauty can only occur against the backdrop of a relatedness between the observer and the observed. He sees both as part of nature, making them close or equal to one another. And for him, aesthetic enjoyment lies precisely in the recognition of this closeness and structural equivalence. In this context, Bölsche posed the rhetorical question of

> whether that which produces rhythmic stylizations from the unicellular organism onwards, in shaping the body in accord with a kind of crystalline directional force, might not be *identical* with material processes in our human brain,

118 Johann Wolfgang von Goethe, "Reine Begriffe," in *Sämtliche Werke*, vol. 4, bk. 2 (Munich: Beck, 1986), 332–33, quoted and translated in Matthias Kross, "Engineering Phenomena: Wittgenstein and Goethe on Scientific Method," in *Goethe and Wittgenstein: Seeing the World's Unity in its Variety*, ed. Fritz Breithaupt, Richard Raatzsch, and Bettina Kremberg (Frankfurt am Main: Peter Lang, 2003), 31.

ones that appear in our psychology as a tendency to create rhythmic art and find enjoyment in the stylized.[119]

As further reinforced by a significant number of aesthetes and scientists researching perceptual physiology around 1900 (and reiterated in more recent movements toward a "political ecology"),[120] the point here is the reciprocity and self-referencing to be found in the act of perception: the perceiver, in the act of perceiving, perceives the self as part of a universal whole, to which the perceived also belongs. In this context, it is precisely this feeling of universal belongingness that accounts for the enjoyment found in perceiving nature and art alike. With this, the paradigm of a distance between the observer and the observed is nullified, to be substituted by notions of closeness and equivalence that presume and affirm a bond connecting all living entities with one another.

Uexküll often drew upon this tradition, incorporating some of its propositions into his theories.[121] For example, a frequently

119 Wilhelm Bölsche, *Stirb und Werde! Naturwissenschaftliche und kulturelle Plaudereien* (Jena: Diederichs, 1913), 159–60, italics added.

120 This concept is taken up by authors such as Steven Johnson and Jane Bennet, although without mentioning Haeckel, Bölsche, or Uexküll: "Clusters of neurons in a human brain, groupings of buildings in a city, and colonies of slime all have been shown to follow similar organizational rules; each is an instant of what Steven Johnson has called, 'organized complexity.'" See Jane Bennett, *Vibrant Matter: A Political Ecology of Things* (Durham: Duke University Press, 2010), 10, with a note citing Steven Johnson, *Emergence: The Connected Lives of Ants, Brains, Cities, and Software* (New York: Scribner, 2001), 18.

121 So far, this has been demonstrated primarily with regard to Uexküll's recourse to Goethe. See for example Frederick Amrine, "The Music of the Organism: Uexküll, Merleau-Ponty, Zuckerkandl, and Deleuze as Goethean Ecologists in Search of a New Paradigm," *Goethe Yearbook* 22 (2015): 45–72; Winfried Kudszus, "Linguistico-Literary Reflections on the Science of Light: Sensory Emergence in Goethe's *Theory of Colors*; and Jakob von Uexküll's Metaphoricity of Semiosic *Scaffolding*," *Studies about Languages* 26 (2015): 83–109. However, one can also assume connections to more contemporary conceptions of biological holism. The natural history theories of Johannes Peter Müller and Karl Ernst von Baer (both greatly admired by Uexküll)

 quoted stanza from Uexküll's *Theory of Meaning* not only plays upon Goethe's famous lines, but also resonates with the above quotation from Bölsche: "Were the flower not beelike / And were the bee not flowerlike, / The consonance could never work."[122] For erudite German-speaking readers of the period, the allusion was obvious.

Where this framework offers no possibility of concrete communicability, Uexküll fills the gap with the proposition of an always preexistent communication. Similarly to Haeckel and Bölsche, he also presumes a "grandiose unity,"[123] one in which a universal being called "nature" has already abrogated the stark isolation of all beings while stretching a universal bond across what is still seen by some as the "*constitutional differences* of the different Umwelten."[124] It is only with Uexküll's confidence in the existence of an "all-encompassing happening"[125] (an idea most likely taken from the bioholistic tradition) that overcoming the hard breaks between individual Umwelt bubbles becomes possible, and that perceiving the "coherence of the great and

repeatedly refer to Goethe and continue some of his ideas, just like Haeckel does with his biological monism. Uexküll's vehement rejection of Haeckel (see for example Uexküll, *Bausteine*, 35–36 and 109) from the 1890s onwards was certainly not in all aspects, and he still implicitly agreed with Haeckel on precisely the point discussed here, a fact that is likewise explained most likely by Uexküll's membership in this discursive constellation. Thus, even as Uexküll rejects Haeckel's reductionism in particular, he also ignores (as mentioned above) an interpretation that is much closer to his own position, namely one that emphasizes the holistic element in Haeckel's monism. On this element in Haeckel's ideas, see Gebhard, *Der Zusammenhang der Dinge*, and Bernhard Kleeberg, *Theophysis: Ernst Haeckels Philosophie des Naturganzen* (Cologne: Böhlau, 2005).

122 Uexküll, *Foray*, 190.

123 Uexküll, "Wie sehen wir die Natur," 321.

124 Ibid., 265, italics in original. Uexküll also believes he can see a "Bauplan" across nature as a whole, one that thwarts the second law of thermodynamics (likewise rejected by Haeckel) by combining all existing things into a universal *perpetuum mobile*; see ibid., 321.

125 Ibid., 322.

wonderful universal becoming"[126] can be set as biology's goal. The framework for this perceiving is provided by the previously described interplay between parts *inside a whole*: "Together, man and the surrounding nature make up a unity that is harmonious and *planvoll* [literally 'plan-ful'], one in which all parts exist within a purposive interaction."[127] It is precisely this harmonious unity, taken here as a given, that is both the point of Uexküll's Umwelt theory and its political problem, as will be discussed in more detail below.

4.2 Cognition as a Whole

Uexküll's recourse to older lines of holistic thought can also be seen on an even more fundamental level. For example, Uexküll also shares the idea that the form-giving principle strives toward cognition, a notion that did not start with Haeckel's conceptualization of morphology but with Goethe's, as was shown above. Like these authors, who were concerned not with describing given forms but with describing the law behind their formation, Uexküll also focuses on the "non-spatial promoters of spatial processes,"[128] further declaring that "mortal is the structure," but "the structure-creator is . . . indestructible and eternal."[129] Here, the search for the form-giving principle becomes a search for a structure-giving principle that regulates interrelationships like the one between Innenwelt and Umwelt. Uexküll draws on Goethe's conception of *Anschauung*,[130]

126 Uexküll, *Bausteine*, 104.

127 Ibid., 142.

128 Uexküll, *Theoretical Biology*, 203.

129 Uexküll, *Bausteine*, 273. Amrine also finds it "abundantly clear that Uexküll shares Goethe's view that biological forms ultimately have formal or archetypal causes." To support this idea, Amrine cites (among other things) Uexküll's explicit recourse to Goethe's "Urbild" or "primal image" (Amrine, "Music," 50 and 51); see also Uexküll, *Foray*, 159.

130 In Goethe's work, the concept of *Anschaulichkeit* (literally "seeable-ness") signifies much more than simply "visibility" or "intuitability," representing instead an attempt take phenomena that cannot be slotted into the framework of representation and make them self-evident again. On this, see Eva

especially when trying to open the reader's eyes to a seemingly "unseeable"[131] Planmäßigkeit.[132] In his largely implicit departure from Kant as outlined above, Uexküll follows paths similar to those of Goethe.[133] But he also transforms Goethe's holism in a way that became more or less standard in the late nineteenth century: rather than using analogies to draw relationships between different phenomena and fields, he instead postulates a structural equivalence.[134] The turn of the century saw many of Goethe's successors (including monists, organicists, and Uexküll himself) now frowning upon the use of analogy,[135] thereby marking a significant shift in the holistic tradition, even among those claiming unbroken descent from Goethe's natural philosophy and still citing his works. This radicalizing shortcut as applied to the "old school" of holism is what enables the strong immanence of Umwelt theory, which later shaped Uexküll's political texts in particular.

Geulen, "Urpflanze (und Goethes *Hefte zur Morphologie*)," in *Urworte: Zur Geschichte und Funktion erstbegründender Begriffe*, ed. Michael Ott and Tobias Döring (Munich: Fink, 2012), 155.

131 See for example Uexküll, *Bausteine*, 55–66; Jakob von Uexküll, "Vorschläge zu einer subjektbezogenen Nomenklatur in der Biologie," in Uexküll, *Kompositionslehre der Natur*, 133.

132 On Anschauung in Uexküll's work, see Bühler, "Das Tier und die Experimentalisierung," 46–51.

133 As Engelhardt explains, Goethe refuses—despite all his fascination with Kant—to recognize the "gap between mind and nature" that is so fundamental to Kant's transcendental idealism; see Engelhardt, "Der Versuch als Vermittler zwischen Objekt und Subjekt," 24. Uexküll's mostly implicit break with Kant is rooted, as shown, in this same refusal.

134 According to Eva Geulen, Goethe forestalls the total immanence that characterizes numerous subsequent theories by resorting instead to analogy, as a method that is entirely opposed to imposing equivalent sameness and that presumes difference instead of suspending it. See Eva Geulen, *Aus dem Leben der Form: Goethes Morphologie und die Nager* (Berlin: August Verlag, 2016), 96.

135 For example, Uexküll (like many influential organicists of his time) does not see just an analogy between state and organism, but an equivalent sameness: the state is not *like* an organism, it *is* one. See Uexküll, *Staatsbiologie*, 5.

Uexküll's borrowings from the holistic tradition are therefore as diverse as they are far-reaching. They made up the theoretical bedrock from which the concept of Planmäßigkeit arose. Hence the way that Uexküll tries to conceptualize scientific ideas in general, and his own thinking and research specifically, can be described as holistic only in the sense described above. Uexküll understands the science that produces Umwelt theory as being itself a planmäßig abandonment of nature (i.e., one "conforming to plan"). With this, too, he inscribes himself into a holistic tradition. But this is also precisely how he makes his theory impervious to criticism.

As described above, Uexküll understands research itself as a "planmäßig" practice. In doing so, he takes up a line of thought that has been repeatedly pursued since Goethe—including in the field of biology. The aforementioned desire to harmonize the relationship between man and nature, seemingly foreshadowing Uexküll's congruence of Bauplan and Umwelt, represents a turning away, seen since Goethe, from the demand for scientific objectivity. Such a demand requires a strict separation between reality and intellect, making it necessary for the latter to expend "much labor on resolving and again compounding its concepts," as Kant writes.[136] In contrast, Goethe's nature does not require such laborious exertions, offering knowledge "of its own accord" and giving it to an observer who only needs to be "careful in . . . work and observations."[137] This conjecture presupposes not only

136 Immanuel Kant, "On a Recently Prominent Tone of Superiority in Philosophy," in *Theoretical Philosophy after 1781*, ed. Henry Allison and Peter Heath, trans. Gary Hatfield et al. (Cambridge: Cambridge University Press, 2002), 431, German original cited in Martin Jörg Schäfer, *Die Gewalt der Muße: Wechselverhältnisse von Arbeit, Nichtarbeit, Ästhetik* (Zurich: Diaphanes, 2013), 42.

137 Johann Wolfgang von Goethe, "Significant Help Given by an Ingenious Turn of Phrase," in *Scientific Studies*, ed. and trans. Douglas Miller (New York: Suhrkamp, 1988), 41.

a knowledge based on revelations instead of evidence,[138] but also a certain relationship to the object: one that does not need producing in the sense of actively relating two things to one another, but is instead a given; one that may at worst be disturbed through excessive effort, but not advanced.

It may be because of the generally strong influence of Goethe's natural philosophy on the biology of the late nineteenth century that this particular line of thought often recurs there too. For example, Bernhard Kleeberg writes that for Haeckel, it is "not the actions of the subject that are the reason why something can become the object of cognition at all, but rather a correspondence between the structures of the object and those of the subject."[139] As a biologist who frequently refers back to Goethe,[140] Haeckel derives from this idea an epistemology proposing that "the cognition of truth is a *physiological process of nature*."[141]

Like Goethe and Haeckel, Uexküll also rejects a science anchored in objectivity and distance. As Kudszus notes, this demonstrates a turning away from "what both he and Goethe describe as a

138 "Any truth whose basis is not evidence is preferable to that which has evidence as its basis." Johann Wolfgang von Goethe, cited in Hans Blumenberg, *Quellen*, ed. Ulrich von Bülow and Dorit Krusche (Marbach am Neckar: Deutsche Schillergesellschaft, 2009), 38.

139 Bernhard Kleeberg, "Evolutionäre Ästhetik," in *Text und Wissen: Technologische und Anthropologische Aspekte*, ed. Stefan Rieger and Renate Lachmann (Tübingen: G. Narr, 2003), 159.

140 Not only does Haeckel mention Goethe in numerous texts and always affirmatively, he often opens with a quote from Goethe and even uses a Goethe neologism as a book title, as seen in his *Gottnatur (Theophysis): Studien über monistische Religion* (Leipzig: Alfred Kröner, 1914). He also devotes longer passages to discussing Goethe's natural philosophy. Here, it becomes clear that it is especially Goethe's idea of an inner relationship between different natural phenomena, and between human and nature, that Haeckel adopts and expands into his conception of a universal coherence.

141 Ernst Haeckel, *Die Lebenswunder* (Stuttgart: Kröner, 1904), 26.

Newtonian world in which material objectivity reigns,"[142] and thus a turning away from a world that Uexküll, with his previously described "subjectivist" thinking, cannot accept. Uexküll justifies his criticism of modern research into nature with the argument that it has further widened the gap between human views and scientific truths, and thus, one could add, endangered the monadic integrity of his theory's self-contained Umwelt bubbles. While this stance might be related to his own career as a researcher, which was marked by disappointments and relatively late academic recognition, it also fits seamlessly into the model of holistic cognition that had already been put forward by Goethe and later advanced by both Haeckel and Bölsche.[143]

Like their models of cognition, that of Uexküll is both relativistic *and* total at the same time. To Uexküll (as he wrote in 1905), "science is a planmäßig-ordered experience,"[144] and as such, it is also subject to the same principle as every other phenomenon in life—and thus to its "subjectivist" structure as well. This means that even the most rigorous natural science is not engaged with some *objective* "authority of nature," something that, in Uexküll's view, simply does not exist. Rather, each "doctrine" remains tied to a specific Umwelt bubble and thus to a certain subjectivity, as its "authority" consists of nothing other than that of the "investigator, who has himself answered his own question."[145] The result is a profound resistance to the modern paradigm of objectivity: "The framework of our own subjectivity . . . encompasses all processes in nature without exception. Therefore, we can only

142 Kudszus, "Linguistico-Literary Reflections," 106.

143 This has already been demonstrated for both Goethe and Haeckel. See also Bölsche's discussion of a parallelism between psychological and physical phenomena, in Wilhelm Bölsche, *Die naturwissenschaftlichen Grundlagen der Poesie: Prolegomena einer realistischen Ästhetik* (Leipzig: Carl Reissner, 1887), 39ff.

144 Uexküll, *Leitfaden*, v.

145 Uexküll, *Theoretical Biology*, ix. See also Harrington, *Reenchanted Science*, 46, n56.

speak of a relative objectivity."[146] This relativism, misleadingly described by Uexküll as a continuation of Kant's philosophy,[147] does not attempt a remodeling of scientific paradigms in the face of newly acquired knowledge, as happened most prominently around the same time with Albert Einstein. Instead, and in a manner comparable to Oswald Spengler's historical relativism, which also draws upon Goethe, Uexküll argues for a direct connection to an unmediated view of the world, and thus to "nature" itself. This line of thought points to a tradition of natural philosophy going at least as far back as the Romantic era, one that, with its "hypothesis of a self-observation of nature, allowed man's theoretical and aesthetic efforts to be integrated into the process of the natural."[148]

Although Uexküll does concede that scientific paradigms have changed over time and are thus historically contingent,[149] he describes this change as something that happens only superficially. It is in this context that he postulates an unmediated knowing, something that he calls "soul" and sets in opposition to "mere" intellect, similarly to what Ludwig Klages would later do.[150] And it is precisely on this unmediated knowing that Uexküll builds his own theory, thereby withdrawing it from the constantly changing course of scientific discovery and criticism. This is how Uexküll tries, for example, to grasp the totality of the individualized—and thus *internal*—Planmäßigkeit of each human being with the concept of the soul (which is supposedly universally

146 Uexküll, *Bausteine*, 186. On Uexküll's departure from "objectivism," see Weber, *Die Natur als Bedeutung*, 77.

147 In conceding certainty to hard sciences like mathematics and physics, Kant tried to philosophically legitimize them by placing them in accord with transcendental idealism's categories of understanding. Uexküll did not take up this attempt to reconcile philosophy with the hard sciences but instead turned it on its head and cited Kant to do so. See Esposito, "Kantian Ticks, Uexküllian Melodies," 38.

148 Wolfgang Müller-Funk, *Die Rückkehr der Bilder: Beiträge zu einer "romantischen Ökologie"* (Vienna: Böhlau, 1988), 52.

149 Pobojewska, "Die Subjektlehre Jakob von Uexkülls," 56.

150 Ludwig Klages, *Der Geist als Widersacher der Seele* (Leipzig: Barth, 1929).

understood, but is also irrational), and to describe it as the naturally given power of insight within *all* humans. At the same time, he describes this same Planmäßigkeit as the principle that relates all these insights to one another within a naturally given order.[151] Uexküll's relativism therefore does not contradict his central goal of creating or making *anschaulich* (or "seeable") a naturally given universal order but instead represents a different route to this same order.[152] While his insistence on the subjectivity of truths can be understood as a rejection of objectivism, this does not imply a renunciation of the idea of a superior truth, insofar as whatever appears as the researcher's subjective truth (if one assumes the "world-defining power" of Planmäßigkeit)[153] has to be regarded as an expression of nature itself—and thus as the highest truth to be achieved. This practice could be described with a passage from Max Horkheimer (one in which Mildenberger, perhaps not unjustifiably, suspects an implicit critique of Umwelt theory):[154] "Such absolutizing is the other side of the exaggerated relativization of science."[155]

The epistemology embedded within Uexküll's Umwelt theory is thus characterized by a harmonizing merging of relativism

151 In writing about "every human being," Uexküll says that "this soul governs his body, and he presupposes a likewise governing soul in his fellow men, which governs the actions of their body. Accordingly, he will also be inclined to assume that the totality of all objects is likewise governed by a world soul, which he calls God. This is indeed the only reasonable conclusion appropriate to the nature of man, one to which he always returns when he has freed himself from all influences exerted by the words of wisdom from his fellow men." See Uexküll, *Bausteine*, 124.

152 "The goal of all natural science is *order*." See ibid., 35, emphasis in original.

153 Jakob von Uexküll, "Biologische Briefe an eine Dame, Brief 4–12," *Deutsche Rundschau* 179 (1919): 281.

154 Mildenberger, *Umwelt als Vision*, 161.

155 Max Horkheimer, "Materialism and Metaphysics," in *Critical Theory: Selected Essays*, trans. Mathew J. O'Connell (New York: Continuum, 2002), 31. This link between relativism and absolutism is broken by Kant himself (thus emphasizing once again the chasm between transcendental idealism and Uexküll's approach) through his relating of the *noumena* to the reality of the thing-in-itself, which lies outside it.

 and determinism. However, there is no watering down of the two sides in order to achieve a mutual reconciliation; instead, it is precisely as two sides forced together that they are both actually hypostatized. Uexküll's biology is totally relativistic *and* totally deterministic. With this harmonization of conflicting approaches, Uexküll has solved, on the one hand, his epistemological problem. His natural Planmäßigkeit guarantees that in the cognition of every Umwelt, even the narrowest, the universal cognition of "nature" always shines through. On the other hand, Uexküll also tries to address political problems the same way. They too are met with this harmonizing of subjectivism with holistic Planmäßigkeit, this merging of a relativistic approach with a deterministic one.

5. Planmäßigkeit to the Right: On the Deterministic Relativism of Umwelt Theory

> *"But the more you observe, the more you come to believe in a great mysterious control exercised by a great biological reason."*
> *– Ernst Jünger*[156]

The "synthesis . . . of freedom and bonds" is, Thomas Mann notes in 1921, one of the essential characteristics of the Conservative Revolution.[157] What is politically problematic about this worldview is not simply that it would subject the individual to an external force, but that it rejects as unnatural any contradiction between the individual and the so frequently glorified "community" ("Gemeinschaft," literally "commonality"), between sovereign

156 Ernst Jünger, "Der Neue Typ des Deutschen Menschen," in *Stahlhelm-Jahrbuch 1926*, ed. Wilhelm Kleinau (Magdeburg: Stahlhelm-Verlag, 1925), 171.

157 Thomas Mann, *Essays II, 1914–1926* (Frankfurt am Main: S. Fischer, 2002), 1:341.

will and naturalized determinism. This "untenable concept,"[158] in which the idea of a natural social order is forced together with the demand for revolutionary change, is already self-contradictory on a semantic level, thus demanding conceptual approaches that could resolve this self-contradiction. As early as 1957, Kurt Sontheimer noted that the relevant approaches generally derive from "conception[s] of the organism, of holism" as pursued by authors like Othmar Spann, Ernst Jünger, Oswald Spengler, Carl Schmitt, Karl Anton Rohan, and Arthur Moeller van den Bruck.[159] While Harrington is certainly correct in observing that the German holistic tradition does not entirely or inevitably merge into the spectrum ranging from radical conservative to Nazi thought,[160] it is also true that holistic ideas are more the rule, and less the exception, in the thinking of the Conservative Revolution.

Uexküll's affiliation with the Conservative Revolution, which is not often discussed in the literature,[161] is grounded in the fact that his Umwelt theory produces a synthesis in which subjectivity, autonomy, and sovereignty are inextricably bound to Planmäßigkeit, totality, and determinism. "Each is the master of his Umwelt":[162] but this dominion is subject to Planmäßigkeit,

158 Stefan Breuer, *Anatomie der konservativen Revolution* (Darmstadt: Wissenschaftliche Buchgesellschaft Darmstadt, 1995), 4.

159 Kurt Sontheimer, "Antidemokratisches Denken in der Weimarer Republik," *Vierteljahrshefte für Zeitgeschichte* 5/1 (1957): 50. See a more detailed analysis in Kurt Sontheimer, *Antidemokratisches Denken in der Weimarer Republik: Die politischen Ideen des deutschen Nationalismus zwischen 1918 und 1933* (Munich: Nymphenburger Verlagshandlung, 1962).

160 Harrington, *Reenchanted Science*, xxi.

161 Armin Mohler, *Die konservative Revolution in Deutschland 1918–1932* (Darmstadt: Wissenschaftliche Buchgesellschaft, 1989). Mohler refers primarily to Uexküll's *Staatsbiologie* (ibid., 71). Meanwhile, by looking at Uexküll's writings on, and use of, language, Milan Hornacek has demonstrated Uexküll's affiliation with the Conservative Revolution. See Milan Hornacek, *Politik der Sprache in der "konservativen Revolution"* (Dresden: Thelem, 2015). For additional discussion, see for example Mildenberger, *Umwelt als Vision*, and Weber, *Die Natur als Bedeutung*.

162 Jakob von Uexküll, "Weltanschauung und Gewissen," *Deutsche Rundschau*, no. 197 (1923): 266.

 which is not an external but an internal determinant, meaning that it collapses into one with this dominion enjoyed by the "subject." With Uexküll, subjectivity is conceived as absolute—and at the same time naturalized in its own Umwelt, robbed of any spontaneity. It does not in fact represent an act of transcending, as the subject is not relating to something outside itself, but only to its own Umwelt, which it has produced and over which it has dominion. There is nothing transcendent clinging to it. Instead, this subjectivity is nothing other than Planmäßigkeit, and thus something that is always immanent—while also being a principle that is total and ubiquitous.

An investigation of Umwelt theory's political aspect therefore cannot be limited to examining things such as Uexküll's correspondence with Houston Stewart Chamberlain, his aggressive stance against the Weimar Republic, his later pandering to the Nazi regime, or his published articles in journals like *Die Tat*.[163] It was an inescapable aspect of his work even before World War I, although it is only in 1915 that Uexküll's publications begin arguing in more overtly politically terms. And it was not only with the publication of his *Staatsbiologie* that it began to emerge, even if this is where Uexküll first expressed himself more broadly in a truly "biopolitical" way.[164] Certainly, it is only with this text, originally published in 1920, that Uexküll joins the ranks of organicist, radical conservative political theorists, as one who does not see the state as simply *analogous* to an organism (similarly to his compatriot, the Baltic German organicist sociologist Paul von Lilienfeld in his highly influential *Gedanken zur Sozialwissenschaft der Zukunft*) but instead understands it as a

163 Jakob von Uexküll, "Die Stellung des Naturforschers zu Goethes Gott-Natur," *Die Tat: Monatsschrift für die Zukunft deutscher Kultur* 15, no. 2 (1923): 492–506.

164 The concept of biopolitics was coined in 1920 by the organicist political scientist Rudolf Kjellén in his analysis of "life forms," specifically in the case of the "German state." See Rudolf Kjellén, *Grundriss zu einem System der Politik* (Leipzig: S. Hirzel, 1920), 17, n1. For an investigation of the early conceptual and theoretical history of biopolitics, see Roberto Esposito, *Bíos: Biopolitics and Philosophy* (Minneapolis: University of Minnesota Press, 2008).

real organism, thereby naturalizing it and thus its dominion over its members.[165] But it is actually long before *Staatsbiologie* that he manages to square the circle by reconciling freedom and bonds, so that autonomous subjectivity is harmonized with the naturalized, individual-determining "community," i.e., the "Gemeinschaft" that was so central to the thinking of the Conservative Revolution.

The political side of this conceptual development emerges as early as 1913 (before World War I and the Weimar Republic, and thus the phase in which Uexküll publishes more political texts), when Uexküll writes worriedly about a "Volk torn apart from nature," for example.[166] His arguably most political text, *Staatsbiologie*, builds upon the same holistic lines of thought that shaped Umwelt theory from the very beginning. Although he translates them here into political terms, he does so without needing to bend them much. On the one hand, Uexküll sees both the state and the Volk as natural wholes that are subject to Planmäßigkeit, and which Umwelt theory says cannot be anything

165 Uexküll, *Staatsbiologie*, 5. As Paul von Lilienfeld wrote in his *Gedanken über die Sozialwissenschaft der Zukunft, Erster Theil: Die menschliche Gesellschaft als realer Organismus* (Mitau: E. Behre, 1873), 26: "If we had taken all the common assertions, some accepted by science, that point to the coherence and interrelatedness between phenomena in nature and in society as being simply rhetorical ideas, then we would be following in the footsteps of all the economic and political doctrinaires, and all the social metaphysicians." On the late nineteenth century's shift from understanding the state as *analogous* to an organism to understanding it as *being* one, see Sophus Reinert, "Darwin and the Body Politic: A Note on Schäffle, Veblen and the Shift of Biological Metaphor in Economics," in *Albert Schäffle (1821–1903): The Legacy of an Underestimated Economist*, ed. Jürgen Backhaus (Frankfurt am Main: Haag & Herchen, 2010), 129–52, esp. 129–30. For two particularly influential examples of this type of state organicism that appeared around the same time as Uexküll's text, see Othmar Spann, *Der wahre Staat: Vorlesungen über Abbruch und Neubau des Staates* (Leipzig: Quelle & Meyer, 1921); and Carl Schmitt, "Die Staatsphilosophie der Gegenrevolution," *Archiv für Rechts- und Wirtschaftsphilosophie* 16 (1922): 121–31.

166 Uexküll, *Bausteine*, 133. The word "Volk" generally means "people" or "nation," but in this context also means "ethnonation."

other than what they are. But on the other hand, he articulates in the same text a paranoid fear of the corrosion and destruction of order, which leads him to call for Planmäßigkeiten (pl. of Planmäßigkeit) to be supported, defended, and even created, despite the fact that he also presents them as natural and inescapable givens. This contradictory duality can be seen as a variation of the duality behind a "revolution" that strives to achieve what it also claims as an inescapable and naturally given reality. But this is rooted in the much older link between Umwelt monadism and the Planmäßigkeit of nature as a whole, something that was already politically problematic in itself, long before any explicit politicization by Uexküll. Even where it "only" wants to address biological questions, Umwelt theory implies lines of thought that already connect it to the Conservative Revolution. To offer an instructive example, it is not only with respect to the antisocialist criticism, aggressive nationalism, antidemocracy, and naturalization of society to be found in his *Staatsbiologie* that Uexküll coincides with his reader Oswald Spengler, the exemplary "prophet of heroic modernity."[167] The demonstrable conceptual proximity of the two thinkers is in fact already apparent in the harmonization of determinism and relativism that was central not only to the radical conservative thinking of the interwar period but also to Uexküll's Umwelt theory.[168]

167 Heinz Dieter Kittsteiner, "Die Heroische Moderne" (manuscript), posthumous papers, sig. 10, cited in Jannis Wagner, "Spengler in der heroischen Moderne: Zu Heinz Dieter Kittsteiners Spengler-Rezeption," in *Spenglers Nachleben: Studien zu einer verdeckten Wirkungsgeschichte*, ed. Christian Voller, Gottfried Schnödl, and Jannis Wagner (Springe: zu Klampen, 2018), 260.

168 While Mildenberger asserts that Spengler presents an "objectivist interpretation of the world based . . . not [on] biology" and therefore has "hardly any points of contact" with Uexküll (Mildenberger, *Umwelt als Vision*, 114), this assertion must be rejected, already in view of Spengler's doctoral dissertation with its biophilosophical citations, as well as his many references to Goethe's natural philosophy. Furthermore, Spengler's work includes both implicit and explicit references to and borrowings from Uexküll's Umwelt theory.

This chapter continues by first illustrating this harmonization through a comparison with Spengler, thereby demonstrating once again Planmäßigkeit's harmonizing impact, which is most salient in the case of Uexküll's political activism. It will then show how this harmonization is precisely what rendered Umwelt theory vulnerable to Nazism.

5.1 The Umwelt of the Conservative Revolution: Uexküll and Spengler

Some important parallels can be identified between Spengler and Uexküll. In his dissertation (the only text in which he argues his monist-holistic stance with diverse references, instead of relying almost exclusively on Friedrich Nietzsche and Goethe as in his later works), Spengler already sacrifices "the concept of substance" in favor of a "pure, uniform, incessant 'becoming.'"[169] Here, as Anton Koktanek notes, nature goes from a material phenomenon (and one that is oppositional in its very materiality) to a hyperrelational idea, and it is only as such that it has always been able to encompass humans and culture as well, a fact that lays the groundwork for Spengler's later concept of the "cultural organism."[170] This also turns out to anticipate the relativism so central to the "morphological" method of Spengler's *Decline of the West*, i.e., the proposition that all conceivable phenomena (as well as their observation) are culturally contingent—and yet naturally determined. As early as 1904, after his exposure to monistic and bioholistic texts, Spengler was already convinced

169 Oswald Spengler, *Der metaphysische Grundgedanke der Heraklitischen Philosophie*, inaugural doctoral dissertation (Halle: C. A. Kaemmerer, 1904), 19 and 18.

170 Anton Koktanek, *Oswald Spengler in seiner Zeit* (Munich: Beck, 1968), 77. This dematerialization of nature, and thus the negation of its oppositionality, remains fundamental to Spengler's thinking. In writing about *Decline of the West*, Adorno has noted that "nature, with which men have had to struggle in history, is disdainfully pushed aside by Spengler's philosophy." See Theodor W. Adorno, "Spengler after the Decline," in *Prisms*, trans. Samuel Weber and Shierry Weber (Cambridge, MA: MIT Press, 1981), 68.

that "all creations of culture, state, society, customs, and views are products of nature; they are subject to the same conditions of existence as the rest."[171] Like Uexküll, Spengler maintains that cultures and social institutions should be seen as real organisms, and not simply analogous to them.[172] Like Uexküll, Spengler also understands the identity of every organism, no matter what kind or shape, as the expression of a particular formational development principle that emanates from inside to outside, and that is itself nonmaterial. In analogy to Ernst Jünger's thinking, one could speak here of what Werner Hamacher calls "morphontology."[173] Where Uexküll talks about Planmäßigkeit, Spengler talks about "style," which shows itself in all organisms from the lowliest plant to the culture of "the West," in each case demonstrating a form-giving and behavior-defining principle.[174] And like Uexküll, Spengler does not stop at the description of individual "organisms," instead pointing time and again to a greater level, but one that is structurally no different from that of the individual phenomenon. Just as Uexküll's Planmäßigkeit binds "nature as a whole" to every single Umwelt, Spengler's "style" ties the superordinate cultural organism to every phenomenon contained within, no matter how small. What Adorno writes about Spengler's *Decline of the West* could thus be equally said about Uexküll's manifold Umwelten so harmoniously merging into the totality:

171 Spengler, *Der metaphysische Grundgedanke*, 30.

172 "The one and only definition of the being of that which comes to expression in cultural forms is: a culture is an *organism*, an autonomous organic life (emerging, blossoming, dying out). Spengler has provided a consequential and preeminent expression of this manner of seeing the past." See Martin Heidegger, *Ontology—The Hermeneutics of Facticity*, trans. John van Buren (Bloomington: Indiana University Press, 1999), 29, italics in original.

173 Werner Hamacher, "Arbeiten: Durcharbeiten," in *Archäologie der Arbeit*, ed. Dirk Baecker (Berlin: Kadmos, 2002), 173.

174 Oswald Spengler, *The Decline of the West, vol. 1: Form and Actuality*, trans. Charles Francis Atkinson (New York: Alfred A. Knopf, 1926), 108.

> Everything individual, however exotic, becomes a sign of something grandiose, of the civilization, because Spengler's conception of the world is so rigorously governed by his categories that there is no room for anything which does not easily and essentially coincide with them.[175]

At the same time, Spengler sees this naturalism of cultures as the basis for their monadic character (reminiscent of Uexküll's Umwelten), with each culture's specific inner style making it autonomous and distinguishable from others. Again and again, he emphasizes that an individual culture can neither be derived from another nor traced back to something greater outside of it. For him, even the possibility of mutual influence is seen only in rare, exceptional cases. Each culture has its own inner nature, and this is what determines its development, not external influences.

From this it also follows that cognition itself can only be viewed as a product of a particular culture and is thus relative. This is the idea upon which *The Decline of the West* builds its methodology. Spengler states that it is not possible to write an objectively "true" history, but instead, the "thinker . . . has no choice; he thinks as he has to think. Truth in the long run is to him the picture of the world which was born at his birth."[176] As early as 1904, in his dissertation on Heraclitus (which is peppered with biotheoretical and monistic references), Spengler writes of a *natural* system that is *also* a "completely thought-out system of relativism."[177]

This system is compatible with Uexküll's Umwelt theory; Spengler refines the former by drawing on the latter. While Spengler does not yet name Uexküll explicitly in his bestselling *Decline of the West*, the term "Umwelt" (variously translated as the world around, the world that envelops, the external world, etc.) appears

175 Adorno, "Spengler," 121.

176 Spengler, *Decline*, 1:xiii.

177 Spengler, *Der metaphysische Grundgedanke*, 31.

in the German text at numerous points that are central to the argument. And even if Spengler sometimes uses the word to simply mean "Umgebung" ("surrounding[s]")—this blurring is also a problem for Uexküll himself, as will be shown in the next chapter—there are still many passages in which he is clearly invoking Uexküll's Umwelt theory. For example, in the introduction to *Decline of the West,* he states that "man may inwardly possess . . . the world around him" (the German text says "seine Umwelt" or "his Umwelt"). There is a whole subchapter with a major focus on showing that a "world" ("Welt") cannot be described in terms of what it "is," but only in terms of "what it signifies to the being that it envelops" (the last word is a translation of "umgeben," the verbal form of "Umgebung"; the *um*-prefix means "surround," as in "Umwelt," the "around-world"). And there is even a point in *Decline of the West* where Goethe's conception of Anschauung is connected to a theory of Umwelt (in this case translated as "the world about").[178]

Hence Uexküll—who himself did read Spengler[179] and even used a quote from him as a preface to his 1925 essay "Biologie des Staates"[180]—remains unmentioned in *Decline of the West*.[181] But then in 1931, Spengler does cite him by name in *Der Mensch und die Technik* (with a 1932 English version entitled *Man and Technics*), as a way to give scientific justification to a worldview that, so typically for his milieu, vacillates between ideology and

178 Spengler, *Decline*, 1:6, 1:164, and 1:118. The German version uses the term "Umwelt" in ways that are clearly reminiscent of Uexküll. See Oswald Spengler, *Der Untergang des Abendlandes: Umrisse einer Morphologie der Weltgeschichte* (Munich: dtv, 2006), for example at 75, 80, 106, 109, and 172.

179 Mildenberger, *Umwelt als Vision*, 116.

180 Jakob von Uexküll, "Biologie des Staates," *Nationale Erziehung* 6, no. 7/8 (1925): 177.

181 Which, however, says little, and can probably be taken as evidence of Spengler's very consistent practice of banishing almost all references from his writings, which may be traced to his intentionality-oriented conception of knowledge. See Frits Boterman, *Oswald Spengler und sein "Untergang des Abendlandes"* (Cologne: SH-Verlag, 2000), 100. Thanks to Fabian Mauch for pointing this out.

epistemology. In doing so, he chooses not the political texts of Uexküll, such as his already decade-old book *Staatsbiologie*, but instead draws upon the 1913 essay compilation *Bausteine zu einer biologischen Weltanschauung* (Building blocks toward a biological worldview).[182]

In his *Man and Technics*, Spengler delineates a concept he calls "Lebenstaktik" ("tactics of living"), which is not simply about facilitating or even preserving life but is purportedly life itself. Like life itself, this Lebenstaktik is not only purposeless, but also "'without rhyme or reason,' like everything else in actuality."[183] Arguing analogously to Uexküll, Spengler here describes behavior *toward* nature as not only itself naturally given but also as the fundamental and primary phenomenon from which all objective notions of nature must be derived in the first place. This means that the relational principle within the Innenwelt-Umwelt coupling, namely Lebenstaktik in Spengler's case, is life itself. Drawing upon Nietzsche's "will to power" as was typically done among right-wing authors of the interwar period, Spengler presents Lebenstaktik as resulting in fight or flight, depending on the relevant organism's form. It is through such a fight that life really shows itself, according to both Spengler and Uexküll.[184] Here, it is clear that the relativism specific to the Conservative Revolution has nothing to do with showing tolerance toward the unfamiliar but instead assumes the existence of an all-pervading agonality, one that is equally well exemplified by Jünger's statement that "values . . . are therefore relative, but in the sense of a warlike one-sidedness."[185] It is in fighting that life first produces

182 Oswald Spengler, *Man and Technics: A Contribution to a Philosophy of Life*, trans. Charles Francis Atkinson (London: George Allen & Unwin, 1932), 18; also 28, n1 among others for further examples of science references.

183 Spengler, *Man and Technics*, 37.

184 Uexküll, *Bausteine*, 118.

185 Ernst Jünger, *The Worker: Dominion and Form*, ed. Laurence P. Hemming, trans. Bogdan Costea and Laurence P. Hemming (Evanston, IL: Northwestern University Press, 2017), 52. See also Ernst Jünger, "Der Pazifismus," *Die Standarte (Sonderbeilage des Stahlhelm)* (November 15, 1925), 2: "All living

the distinction between object and subject—something that Uexküll already noted as a product secondary to the relevant organism's Merken and Wirken (i.e., its active reception of stimuli and active production of effects), and not their precursor. Relying upon physiological characteristics like Uexküll does,[186] Spengler assigns a specific form of this Merken and Wirken to beasts of prey, with humans as their highest representative.[187] Here, predators and humans are distinguished above all by their special view of the world—or as Uexküll might put it, by a special "Weltanschauung" (literally "world-viewing," combining the aspects of Umwelt and Anschauung)—which provides the foundation for a specific form of relating to the world: "But this act of fixation by two eyes disposed forward and parallel is equivalent to the birth *of the world* . . . as a picture . . . The world-picture is the environment [Umwelt] as *commanded* by the eyes."[188]

Therefore, what appears as nature, externality, or object is completely subsumed into something that is itself naturally given, unconscious, and immutable, be it Lebenstaktik or Merken and Wirken. With both Spengler and Uexküll, the human being's sovereign dominion over nature (here in the form of the human's *own* Umwelt) collapses into one with the naturally given determination of human nature (through Lebenstaktik and/or Planmäßigkeit). This is the idea that underlies the initially puzzling simultaneity of determinism and relativism already apparent in *Decline of the West*, an idea that shimmers at the end of *Man and Technics* in the marriage of heroism and fatalism that is so

entities are different and this already sets them in warlike opposition to one another." On the one hand, the difference with Uexküll's harmonistic worldview is bridged by the common basic assumption of self-contained, monadic life units. On the other, it is collapsed wherever Uexküll sees oppositionality, particularly in the form of social oppositionality as encountered in his concept of state pathology.

186 Spengler, *Man and Technics*, 24.

187 Ibid., 19.

188 Ibid., 24, italics in original.

characteristic of heroic modernity. Spengler closes his book by gazing upon

> that Roman soldier whose bones were found in front of a door in Pompeii, who, during the eruption of Vesuvius, died at his post because they forgot to relieve him. That is greatness. That is what it means to be a thoroughbred. The honourable end is the one thing that can *not* be taken from a man.[189]

The soldier's Umwelt determines that he will not abandon his post; Spengler suggests that for the Roman, who is called a hero for this very reason, the possibility does not even enter his head. His heroism and his clearly defined, narrow horizons are two sides of the same coin. This line of thought, so reminiscent of Uexküll's Umwelt bubbles (in which there are only "Schulz things" for Mr. Schulz and only "Meyer things" for Mr. Meyer, and thus only the corresponding possibilities for action),[190] strongly shapes Spengler's thinking. Contained within it is a harmonization of determinism and relativistic subjectivism, which can be seen as laying the groundwork for the antidemocratic and anti-revolutionary tendencies that would naturalize every existing dominion, tendencies that characterize the writings of both authors. The parallels between them, as shown above in terms of the relationship between human and nature, or human and Umwelt, also continue into the sphere of the political.

For Spengler, like for Uexküll, this naturalization of society means that differences between persons or groups are not to be seen as oppositions but as the *immanent* segmentation of a *single* social form.[191] As soon as oppositions emerge, both authors scale up and jump to the next higher level: with Spengler, for example, the contrast between worker and leader is to be seen as the contrast

189 Ibid., 104, italics in original.

190 Uexküll, "Zum Verständnis der Umweltlehre," 64.

191 Spengler, *Decline*, 47.

between an organism's hand and its brain, and not as a class conflict or a relationship of dominion. This means that revolutions do not arise from social contradictions that have become intolerable enough to trigger a backlash, but solely because "authority was in process of dissolution,"[192] that is, because of an internal transformation on the metalevel (here the state level). Spengler thus points to the same relationship that Uexküll illustrates with his comparison of a state minister and a sewer cleaner, in which he makes a hard distinction between them (as representing two self-contained Umwelten that cannot be compared), while simultaneously tying them together (in the metaorganism of "the state") like the legs and back of a metaphorical chair that are "carved of the same wood."[193] What Uexküll the biologist calls a pathology of the state, Spengler sees (with an argumentation that is just as immanent) as the decay of authority due to an internal lack of strength.

The concept of "blood and soil" ("Blut und Boden"), which Spengler cites and thereby popularizes in *Decline of the West*, builds upon this line of thought. In this pairing, the inner immutable essence is tied to the ancestral Umwelt, and in a naturalized way. It should come as no surprise that, even during Uexküll's lifetime, "blood and soil" was linked to his Umwelt theory by several authors, among them the already mentioned Karl Friederichs, August Thienemann, and Hermann Weber.[194]

192 Oswald Spengler, *The Hour of Decision, Part One: Germany and World-Historical Evolution*, trans. Charles Francis Atkinson (London: George Allen & Unwin, 1934), 36.

193 Uexküll, *Staatsbiologie*, 46.

194 Stella and Kleisner, "Uexküllian Umwelt as Science and as Ideology," 42. Stella and Kleisner cite authors including Friedrichs, "Vom Wesen der Ökologie"; Thienemann, *Leben und Umwelt*; and Hermann Weber, "Organismus und Umwelt," *Der Biologe*, no. 11 (1942): 57–68, especially 57.

As this chapter has shown, Uexküll's Umwelt theory combines two sides that would appear mutually exclusive at first glance: an all-connecting, total nature, and a multiplicity of solipsistic Umwelt bubbles. It is in the union of these two sides that complete determinacy merges with absolute dominion over one's own Umwelt. Like Spengler's "destiny," Uexküll's "Planmäßigkeit" functions as a uniting framework in which the contradictory duality of "freedom and bonds" (so important for the Conservative Revolution),[195] like that of relativistic subject autonomy and holistic determinism, is expressed as a unity, with the way this linkage contradicts itself being naturalized as well. Uexküll's holistic practice of harmonizing such contradictions is significant not least because of its relationship to Nazi ideology, which itself resorts to holistic lines of thought at certain points in order to resolve its contradictions.[196] It is the resolution of the contradictions between ostensibly autonomous subjects and a greater or "higher" order that is significant here.[197] Particularly with regard to their conceptions of deterministic relativism, there are clear lines of continuity that can be drawn between the Conservative Revolution, Uexküll's Umwelt theory, and Nazism.

195 Mann, *Essays II*, 1:341.

196 For example, the aforementioned Uexküllian and Spenglerian notions that a culture or "Volksgemeinschaft" (i.e., a Volk as a collective community) cannot be threatened by a factor from without, but only by a "pathology" or "dissolution" from within, can be compared to Hitler's statement that "men do not perish as a result of lost wars, but by the loss of that force of resistance which is contained only in pure blood." See Adolf Hitler, *Mein Kampf*, trans. Ralph Manheim (Boston: Houghton Mifflin, 1943), 296. More generally on the adoption of bioholistic concepts by Nazism, see Harrington, *Reenchanted Science*, 175–212; Margrit Bensch, "Rassismus als kulturelle Entwicklungstheorie: Formen biologischen Denkens im Sozialdarwinismus" (dissertation, Technical University of Berlin, 2009). The following will look at the connections between holism and certain parts of Nazi ideology, particularly in regards to conceptions of leadership and the "total state."

197 See Bensch, "Rassismus als kulturelle Entwicklungstheorie," 162–67 and 170–73.

The latter continues such conceptions through ideas like the "total state" and the "Führerprinzip" ("leader principle"), thereby drawing upon models from the Conservative Revolution. For instance, Rohan's 1930 interpretation of ideal leadership, specifically as one that demands "not spineless subordination of followership under the *potestas patris* of the leader, but instead devoted submission to the man who has been recognized as the strongest realization of the brother leader,"[198] is later transformed into the Nazi Führerprinzip. This also adopts the notion of harmonizing the individual's will with the leader's will, a goal that Rohan aims to achieve by establishing a "deeper national community" (the "nationale Gemeinschaft").[199] In practice, this harmonization often lands on one side of the equation, so that the will of the leader, expressed as an order, is to be treated as the absolute and final authority, without any need for surveying the will of the people at all.[200] Nonetheless, this idea of a harmonization between the will of the leader and that of each and every individual is often expounded in Nazism, forming the basis of the Führerprinzip at least in theory. The "leadership" of Nazism, which is rigorously differentiated from "dictatorship," is to be achieved (to cite Paul Ritterbusch, a legal scholar and Nazi functionary) "neither through a compromise between opposing elements, nor through the dictatorship of one over the others," and "cannot be conceptually derived at all from a pluralistic concept of social existence."[201] Instead, leadership is to be based on a concord between the leader and those he leads, as both prerequisite and goal.

198 Karl Anton Rohan, *Umbruch der Zeit 1923–1930* (Berlin: Stilke, 1930), 60.

199 Ibid., 62.

200 See Ernst Rudolf Huber, "Verfassungsrecht des großdeutschen Reichs," in *Grundzüge der Rechts- und Wirtschaftswissenschaft: Reihe A (Rechtswissenschaft)*, ed. Georg Dahm and Ernst Rudolf Huber (Hamburg: Hanseatische Verlagsanstalt Hamburg, 1939), 230.

201 Paul Ritterbusch, *Demokratie und Diktatur: Über Wesen und Wirklichkeit des westeuropäischen Parteienstaats* (Berlin: Deutscher Rechtsverlag, 1939), 67.

This same conception of how the individual and the political rulership relate to one another (or at least ought to) also underlies the Nazi idea of the state. This "total state" (as discussed in the previous chapter in reference to Carl Schmitt) also builds on the holistic concept of a congruence "between issues that are political, and as such concern the state, and issues that are social and thus non-political."[202] Uexküll's likewise aforementioned adoption of the total state as a concept is therefore no mere opportunism. Instead, it shows that these basic stances regarding the relationship between state and society, or state and Volk, are compatible with one another. Here, a state order that is both considered ideal and presented as natural does not result from a coerced or violent subordination of all individuals or society as a whole to the state or political leadership, but from a harmonious merging into the state holism and/or the will of the leader, absorbing all individuals, social affairs, and social phenomena.

Moreover, it is certainly not just with the revised edition of 1933 that Uexküll incorporates this idea into his *Staatsbiologie*. In fact, it can already be found in the first edition from 1920. This text compares the relationship between the individual and the state to that of colorful "woolen threads" within an "embroidery pattern."[203] With Uexküll, the conflict of interests arising between the individual and the state is resolved by the "conscience" ("Gewissen") and thus a power which is in turn subject to the "omnipresent Planmäßigkeit of nature." The existence of this "conscience" is also taken as evidence that every individual "embodies a natural plan"—and is thus an elemental component in the same Planmäßigkeit that also defines the state.[204] Both have their roots in the "overall character of the Volk," one that not

202 Lars Vinx, ed. and trans., *The Guardian of the Constitution: Hans Kelsen and Carl Schmitt on the Limits of Constitutional Law* (Cambridge: Cambridge University Press, 2015), 132–33.

203 Uexküll, *Staatsbiologie*, 28.

204 Ibid., 30 and 31.

only imparts "characteristic traits" to the individuals belonging to it but also "imprints itself on the state."[205] The harmonization of determinism and subjectivism thus finds support in a biological understanding of the Volk as early as 1920.

With Uexküll, as with Rohan and later with Nazism, the leadership of such a holistic state is not seen as a dictatorship built on coercion and violence, but as a leadership demonstrating the will of the Volk and representing the natural order of the state. Political dominion is expressed here as a naturalized relationship between the leader and those he leads, which at the same time implies an equally naturalized self-understanding for all those involved—this is where Uexküll talks about a "conscience." Any attempts at negotiating or questioning would contradict the postulated naturalness of this relationship. As early as 1920, and as a logical consequence of his Umwelt theory, Uexküll also states that this harmonization of dominion and natural order, of centralized leadership and the "conscience" of the individual, would be destroyed if the monarch were to be subordinated to the "decision-making of some collective body." In doing so, he anticipated by nearly twenty years the concept of "Führergewalt" ("leader's authority") as defined by Nazi constitutional scholar Ernst Rudolf Huber.[206]

Uexküll's Umwelt theory therefore overlaps with several ideas from the Conservative Revolution and from Nazism: not in prioritizing what is deterministic above what is subjectivist, but in the harmonious collapsing of the two. The aforementioned proposition from Stella and Kleisner—that the inclusion of Umwelt theory in the right-wing and Nazi discourse would necessitate a turn against its implicit "subjectivist" side in favor of its ostensibly separate "holistic" side[207]—is based on the assumption

205 Ibid., 52.

206 Ibid., 23; see same idea in Huber, "Verfassungsrecht des großdeutschen Reichs," 230.

207 Stella and Kleisner, "Uexküllian Umwelt as Science and as Ideology," 43.

that the "subject" can play no role in totalitarian systems.[208] But considering the significance of concepts like the Führerprinzip and the "total state" in particular, this assumption becomes quite doubtful.

Nor does it adequately explain Uexküll's relationship to Nazism. As detailed in the previous chapter, his attempts to ingratiate himself with the Nazis from 1933 onwards did not in fact require him to reshape his fundamental thinking in terms of its harmonization of subjectivism and determinism. In fact, such an ingratiation would be a logical consequence of this thinking. Hence it is not only for reasons of opportunism that Uexküll joins the Nazi movement (where he was not always welcome, either). And in turn, this opportunism does not necessarily manifest itself in an overemphasis on the "holistic" side at the expense of the "subjectivist" one, but rather in an even stronger emphasis on how both sides collapse into one. The 1933 edition of *Staatsbiologie* differs from the 1920 version mainly in discussing the *German* state instead of simply "the state" in the abstract sense.[209] With this reframing, however, Uexküll simply presents an obvious ramification of a subjectivist monistic idea that had been established long before: if the baker, the state minister, and the sewer cleaner each have a different Umwelt, then so does the German and the foreigner. In Uexküll's "subjective" holism, one always takes the position that is natural to oneself. But as shown above, this relativistic approach certainly does not prevent the formulation of overarching universal truths. If the necessity

208 Ibid., 50.

209 Jakob von Uexküll, *Staatsbiologie: Anatomie, Physiologie, Pathologie des Staates*, 2nd ed. (Hamburg: Hanseatische Verlagsanstalt, 1933). A very similar shift can also be seen with Spengler and his 1933 publication of *Jahre der Entscheidung* (published in English the following year as *Hour of Decision*): instead of writing about "the West" (and seven other cultures) as he did a decade and a half earlier, he now writes about "Germany and world-historical evolution." While this book is certainly not simply supportive of Nazism, it does demonstrate a clear shift in perspective similar to that seen between the two editions of Uexküll's *Staatsbiologie*.

of speaking only from one's own position (which itself is determined by a specific Bauplan and disposition in accordance with Planmäßigkeit) also applies to the researcher, then a *Staatsbiologie* focused on the very state where the researcher lives, and among whose nominal Volk he counts himself, is even more logical than simply discussing the state in the abstract, as was done in the book's 1920 edition. Narrowing the state to the German state does not make it less total—on the contrary. Uexküll's move toward Nazism therefore in no way contradicts Umwelt theory but in fact can be explained by the holistic thinking that underlies the theory.

Considering the lines of continuity outlined above, Uexküll's Umwelt theory can thus be seen as part of the Conservative Revolution and placed in proximity to certain Nazi ideologemes. This categorization does not come from certain separable aspects of Umwelt theory but from Planmäßigkeit in general and the important role it plays in harmonizing contradictions and naturalizing relationships. It arises from the principle that merges Umwelt monads with "nature," the observer with the observed, methods with their objects, and subjectivism with determinism. Therefore, it is not simply because of the ways in which right-wing thinkers "appropriate" Umwelt theory that it becomes politically problematic. Instead, this problematic character is already rooted in the harmonistic ideas of Planmäßigkeit, which permeate Umwelt theory and likewise make it a whole.

[4]

Umwelten and their Surrounding(s)

Florian Sprenger

In the center of an *Umwelt*, in the sense developed by Jakob von Uexküll, is a subject, be it an animal or a human being ("Umwelt," literally "around-world," refers not only to the environment, but here particularly to an organism's receptor world and effector world, its "Merkwelt" and "Wirkwelt"). As a biological creature, each subject creates a unique Umwelt of its own as the world in which it lives. And as the previous chapter has shown, Uexküll understands this act of creation, in a markedly idiosyncratic appropriation of Kant's transcendental philosophy, as the production of fundamental, constitutional forms. This generating is transcendental only in the sense that the subject creates objects according to its own rules by projecting categories of cognition onto what it intuits. But whereas Kant means to discover these categories through a critique of knowledge, Uexküll grounds them in biology. For both men, however, objects exist in relation to a subject that can itself be grasped only in relation to objects. Subject and object form a dyad in which one part cannot be thought of without the other. The sensory organs of each living entity determine both the scope of its respective Umwelt and the knowability of the objects from which this Umwelt is formed. This is all that a living entity has at its disposal. Seen from the outside, an Umwelt is thus not a space but something that gives a living entity its place by giving it a "surrounding-world," an "Um-Welt."

As the first chapter demonstrated, this promise of order underlies Uexküll's antisemitism and his reshaping of *Staatsbiologie*, a biology of the state, into a theory of the "total state." While the focus in chapter 1 was on reconstructing the historical constellation that existed in 1934, this chapter will now pursue the epistemological consequences of this idea.

For Uexküll, a subject's Umwelt is also part of an external world or surrounding—an *Umgebung* in German, meaning literally that which is given and which "gives around," the giving and the givenness of this surrounding. In Uexküll's account, the surrounding encompasses everything that is independent of the subjects who are each at the center of a respective Umwelt.[1] The spatiality of this surrounding lies in the way it gives a specific place to the diversity of Umwelten (pl. of Umwelt) and thus locates them in the world. These Umwelten never merge into their surrounding, because they cannot exceed it—because Uexküll binds, via what he calls a functional cycle (*Funktionskreis*), the elements from a surrounding that become part of an Umwelt to the very spaces of this surrounding. Umwelten, however, are not just spatial relations. They are also selective: an Umwelt is what is relevant to a living entity in its surrounding, while for a surrounding, there

1 This distinction between *Umwelt* and *Umgebung* can be understood as a response to the problem of organicist philosophies, such as those advocated at the same time by John Scott Haldane or Lawrence B. Henderson. These understand the whole to mean the interlacing of organism and environment, which raises the question of how to demarcate an animal's environment from the rest of the universe. It is precisely this question, left unanswered by organicism, that Uexküll is able to circumvent with his distinction. See Florian Sprenger, *Epistemologien des Umgebens Zur Geschichte, Ökologie und Biopolitik künstlicher Environments* (Bielefeld: Transcript, 2019), 119–66.

is no criterion of relevance.[2] In this sense, furnishing an Umwelt with a place does not mean assigning a specific space to a living entity, but rather that its place is located within a structure of *Planmäßigkeit* ("conformity with a plan," indicating a purposiveness, systematicity, or planned quality). This Planmäßigkeit determines how a living entity is "fitted into" its surrounding and thus also what is relevant for it, that is to say, what becomes part of its Umwelt. For Uexküll, meaning exists only within an Umwelt, which is related to a subject as a "distinct representational construct residing in the individual's mind," but not in its surrounding.[3] Because an Umwelt always corresponds to a living entity's functional cycles and the scope of what is perceived by its sensory organs, it can include everything in a surrounding that is important for the living entity—but nothing that is irrelevant. The surrounding in this sense is the set of all objects that can potentially be part of one or more Umwelten. *Umwelt*, then, as a concept is not primarily spatial but epistemological. Instead of an extraction from a surrounding, it is the creation of a world of relevance out of a given surrounding that distinguishes the living, a world whose objects "owe their construction to the subject."[4]

According to this "epistemological autism," every living entity has access only to its own Umwelt.[5] Uexküll nevertheless presupposes that there is *one* surrounding that is independent of all subjectivity and possesses a spatial extension that remains independent of the subject's perspective. The subjectivist concept of Umwelt, whose roots, as the previous chapter showed, lie in nineteenth-century biology and aesthetics, is closely

2 See, for instance, Georg Toepfer, "Umwelt," in *Historisches Wörterbuch der Biologie*, vol. 3, ed. Georg Toepfer (Stuttgart: Metzler, 2011), 573.

3 Martin Fultot and Michael T. Turvey, "Von Uexküll's Theory of Meaning and Gibson's Organism-Environment Reciprocity," *Ecological Psychology* 31, no. 4 (2019): 292. Biosemiotics builds on this sign-like character of the Umwelt.

4 Jakob von Uexküll, *Theoretical Biology*, trans. D. L. Mackinnon (Edinburgh: Edinburgh Press, 1926), xv.

5 Kijan M. Espahangizi, "Wissenschaft im Glas: Eine historische Ökologie moderner Laborforschung" (dissertation, ETH Zürich, 2010), 30.

 intertwined with this spatial concept of a surrounding, albeit in a relationship of tension. Building on this idea, what follows elaborates on these tensions.

The Umwelt does not merge into spatiality (in that case, it would be a surrounding), because it always comprises only a certain perspective on space; nor is the surrounding subjective, because in that case it would be an Umwelt. The two are nonetheless linked, because a surrounding enables the exploring of Umwelten, while each Umwelt is encompassed by a surrounding that gives it its place. What Uexküll calls Planmäßigkeit creates an order among all Umwelten in such a way that they obey a superordinate harmony as parts of a whole. This harmony, Leander Scholz points out, is not fed by a cosmology in which a greater order dominates the whole, but by the constitution of the Umwelten themselves: "The source and bearer of order is the individual subjective life itself."[6] Uexküll does not break through this logic with any form of transcendence. But he does scale it so that the state, and even nature, can be understood as subjective forms of life.

In giving a place to that which they surround, these two conceptions, Umwelt and Umgebung, are different in the spatial relations they imply. The Umwelt furnishes the subject that creates it with a place in the center; and the Umgebung furnishes, qua Planmäßigkeit, Umwelten with their place in the world. Comparable to an objective reality, Uexküll's spatial Umgebung includes what lies outside the Umwelten, along with all of their components. This assumption of an Umgebung that surrounds the Umwelten has two functions within Uexküll's method. First, it relates the multiplicity of Umwelten, i.e., the multiplicity of subjective worlds of experience, to the unity of the world determined by Planmäßigkeit, in which everything has its innate place. And

6 Leander Scholz, *Die Menge der Menschen: Eine Figur der politischen Ökologie* (Berlin: Kadmos, 2019), 99. As Scholz shows, Uexküll thus ontologizes Kant's transcendentalism (see ibid., 101).

secondly, it explains how a researcher, who as a living entity has access solely to his own Umwelt, can explore the Umwelten of other living entities and communicate information about them.[7] If Umwelt and Umgebung, then, are both theoretically entangled and epistemologically exclusive, the question arises: What is the Umwelt of an Umgebung, and what is the Umgebung of an Umwelt? This chapter will argue that this relationship is both an epistemological key to Umwelt theory and an irresolvable aporia, to be elaborated here once again from a different perspective.

Despite Uexküll's sometimes contradictory statements, this charged relationship between Umwelt and Umgebung forms the core of Uexküll's examination of different observer positions, subject models, and knowledge paradigms. Until now, its tension has not been systematically examined. On the contrary, a look at many texts that build on Uexküll's thought reveals that they fail to recognize the contradictions of Umwelt theory and thus hide its holistic dimension, which rejects any change and is structurally and politically conservative.

In order to work out the problematic implications of Umwelt theory, not only politically but also epistemologically, this chapter will also deconstruct the aporias of Umwelt theory, starting from the tension between Umwelt and Umgebung. The inconsistency of the simultaneous entanglement and separation of the categorically different concepts of Umwelt and Umgebung appears in a few places in Uexküll's work, but they turn out to be central in a number of ways, including in his reception. Not least, they allow us to see the metaphysical and biopolitical

7 Geoffrey Winthrop-Young has described this as the "hermeneutic dilemma of Romanticism": "The price for the increased ability to express subjective inwardness is the growing inability to successfully communicate it to others." See Geoffrey Winthrop-Young, "Afterword; Bubbles and Webs: A Backdoor Stroll through the Readings of Uexküll," in *A Foray into the Worlds of Animals and Humans: With a Theory of Meaning*, ed. Geoffrey Winthrop-Young, trans. Joseph D. O'Neil (Minneapolis: University of Minnesota Press, 2010), 217–8.

 implications of the epistemology of surrounding(s) that characterizes Umwelt theory.

1. Concepts of Surrounding(s)

Historically, Uexküll's concept of Umwelt belongs to a number of terms for surroundings that rose to prominence in the first decades of the twentieth century as key concepts in the international discussion of life sciences, and which should not be equated with each other, even though they were often used to address similar issues. These terms, which include "milieu" and "environment," in addition to "Umwelt," each denote specific kinds of relating, since a surrounding (an "Umgebung") cannot be thought of without something it surrounds.[8] In each case, they imply specific epistemologies of surrounding(s) that determine the ways in which one side is entangled with the other and the causal interactions that mediate between them. The differences between the three most prominent such terms and their historical semantics are more revealing than their continuities.[9] And because of these differences, the terms cannot be translated into each other, even though they are often used interchangeably. An *environment* is not a *milieu* is not an *Umwelt*.

8 On the relationship between these terms, see Florian Sprenger, "Zwischen Umwelt und milieu: Zur Begriffsgeschichte von environment in der Evolutionstheorie," *Forum interdisziplinäre Begriffsgeschichte* 3, no. 2 (2014), http://www.zfl-berlin.org/tl_files/zfl/downloads/publikationen/forum_begriffsgeschichte/ZfL_FIB_3_2014_2_Sprenger.pdf.

9 In this respect, it is noteworthy that even the research literature on Uexküll rarely differentiates between possible translations. In a large-scale monograph on the history of the concept in Uexküll, Heidegger, Merleau-Ponty, and Deleuze, for instance, Brett Buchanan writes that Umwelt is "a term that more literally means 'surrounding world' or 'environment.'" See Brett Buchanan, *Onto-Ethologies: The Animal Environments of Uexküll, Heidegger, Merleau-Ponty, and Deleuze* (New York: University of New York Press, 2008), 7. *Umwelt* is also used synonymously with *milieu* in the German translation of Deleuze and Guattari's *Mille Plateaux*; see Gilles Deleuze and Félix Guattari, *Tausend Plateaus: Kapitalismus und Schizophrenie* (Berlin: Merve, 1992), 75.

The differences between the three terms and their historical semantics reveal the epistemological relations they convey and thus, in contrast, the specific characteristics of Umwelt as a concept. Umwelt is characterized more strongly than *environment* and even more strongly than *milieu* by a centering that fixes and binds what is surrounded to its surrounding. In the center of the Umwelt is the living entity that creates this Umwelt through the relationship of "Merkwelt" and "Wirkwelt," or "receptor world" and "effector world." What forms the Umwelt depends on this center that the Umwelt envelops like a bubble.[10] It is from this center that a living entity grasps its own world, as a world in which everything is related to this center, while everything outside the Umwelt remains unreachable as its surrounding. In this duplication of the subjective center of an Umwelt and the spatial starting point of a surrounding, the world of the subject is closed because its horizon is conditioned by the organs of the living entity, while the surrounding encompasses everything and has no center.

The tension between the potential openness of the surrounding (on the one hand) and the centeredness of the Umwelt on the internal central living entity (on the other), which determines what can become part of the Umwelt, is what defines Umwelt as a concept. A *milieu*, by contrast, as the historian of science Georges Canguilhem argues, resembles "the representation of an indefinitely extendible line or plane, at once continuous and homogeneous, and with neither definite shape nor privileged position."[11] In the research to which Canguilhem points, ranging from Jean-Baptiste de Lamarck to Auguste Comte to Hippolyte Taine, *milieu* is described as an extension without a center, whereas in an Umwelt all extension emanates from the center. An *environment* is similarly characterized by a center point, represented frequently in ecological diagrams as a circle around

10 Uexküll, *Foray*, 43.

11 Georges Canguilhem, *Knowledge of Life*, trans. Stefanos Geroulanos and Daniela Ginsburg (New York: Fordham University Press, 2008), 103.

 the organism it surrounds.[12] Like an *environment*, an Umwelt, too, has a central point, which suggests the distinction between a something external that surrounds and something internal that is surrounded.

Uexküll writes about his use of Umwelt and its untranslatability into other terms for surroundings as early as 1912:

> The word quickly caught on—but the concept did not. The word 'Umwelt' is now being applied to the specific surrounding of a living entity in the same sense as was done earlier with the word 'milieu.' As a result, its actual meaning has been lost.[13]

The political dimension of this rejection of the term *milieu* has been highlighted by the science historian Wolf Feuerhahn, who has shown that Umwelt is not a translation of *milieu*, as a term that was already being used in biology as early as the eighteenth century, but rather an explicit countermodel.[14] For Uexküll, a living entity has a formative, generative power within its own Umwelt. This assumption implies a freedom that also distinguishes his concept from other terms for surroundings. For him, the living entity generates its Umwelt instead of being determined by its surrounding, as in the case of a *milieu*: "No one is a product of his milieu—everyone is master of his

12 See Florian Sprenger, "Zirkulationen des Kreises: Von der Regulation zur Adaption," *Zeitschrift für Medienwissenschaft* 23 (2020): 41–54.

13 Jakob von Uexküll, "Die Merkwelten der Tiere," *Deutsche Revue* 37, no. 9 (1912): 352. In his 1907 essay "Die Umrisse einer kommenden Weltanschauung," Uexküll still speaks of milieu shortly before coining his concept of Umwelt; see Jakob von Uexküll, "Die Umrisse einer kommenden Weltanschauung," *Neue Rundschau* 18, no. 1 (1907): 641–61.

14 See Wolf Feuerhahn, "Du milieu à l'Umwelt: Enjeux d'un changement terminologique," *Revue philosophique de la France et de l'étranger* 134, no. 4 (2009): 419–38 and Marco Stella and Karel Kleisner, "Uexküllian Umwelt as Science and as Ideology: The Light and the Dark Side of a Concept," *Theory in Biosciences* 129, no. 1 (2010): 39–51.

Umwelt."[15] At points like these, as Feuerhahn points out, Uexküll's anti-Darwinism is mixed with his criticism of the concept of *milieu*, which accords external factors more importance than internal, innate characteristics. In its Umwelt, the organism is autonomous, not heteronomously controlled by external conditions, with which it exists, rather, in a balanced relationship.

Freedom over and by means of an Umwelt—as a surrounding world strictly opposed to both the supposed determination of the French *milieu* and to Darwinism—has a political dimension for the antidemocratic aristocrat Uexküll: A strong, self-determined subject acting with its biological creative power—and, in the case of human beings, with their own individual will—exists for Uexküll only in the German Umwelt, precisely because, among other reasons, this power and this will themselves represent nothing other than Planmäßigkeit and, consequently, the principle of nature par excellence. In contrast, a *milieu* imposes its structural constraints on the internal. For Uexküll, the weak, externally determined subjects of the French *milieu* lose themselves in being determined from the outside, in liberalism and in democracy.[16] The autonomy of living entities—and especially, but not only, of human beings—within their Umwelt serves as a means for them to assert a sovereignty of their own, while also being given a fixed and unchanging place in the world corresponding to their biological features. Here, as the previous chapter has shown, "subjective" freedom coincides with determinism according to principles of Planmäßigkeit. This means that, for Uexküll, no biological science can be built upon the concept of milieu, because it

15 Jakob von Uexküll, "Weltanschauung und Gewissen," *Deutsche Rundschau*, no. 197 (1923): 266. I cannot elaborate here on this overly simplistic reading of the term *milieu*. See also Uexküll's essay "Biologie in der Mausefalle," which deals with the differences between *Umwelt, Wohnwelt* (*living-world; the world in which something lives*), *Umgebung, and milieu*, without coming to any significant differentiation. See Jakob von Uexküll, "Biologie in der Mausefalle," *Zeitschrift für die gesamte Naturwissenschaft* 2 (1936/37): 213–22.

16 I have not been able to find any statements made by Uexküll about the term *environment*.

imposes a determination that makes its study impossible. Caught in such a conception, the researcher as a subject cannot free himself from this determination and recognize the *milieu* as his own surrounding. Uexküll himself is forced to justify, via laborious detours, his assumption that an Umwelt can be studied: this assumption requires the scientist to step out of his own Umwelt and observe, not subjectively but objectively, other Umwelten from the perspective of their surrounding, while at the same time acting in a strong sense as a subject. For the term *milieu*, by contrast, Uexküll does not see any such strong observer position.

2. Sets of Surroundings

One fruitful way of understanding Uexküll's theory of Umwelt, in terms of a relationship of surrounding(s), is set theory. Read thus, we can posit a superset of all objects as a surrounding and multiple subsets of objects that, depending on the respective living entity, make up an Umwelt of objects that serve as "Merkmale," or receptor cues, for that particular organism (*Merkmal*, pl. *Merkmale*, generally means "feature," but relates here more specifically to the Uexküllian conception of *Merken*, the active reception of stimuli). Viewed from an outside perspective, the closed subsets can overlap or even be identical, but there is no direct access between the two. The question that thus appears implicitly in a number of places in Uexküll's work, without ever being explicitly discussed, is whether there is an observer who can observe the superset of all objects and thus also describe the subsets in their relation to the respective organism—inasmuch as he (once again, the gendering of this observer as male is Uexküll's) has access to various subsets as part of the superset, which is to say, the surrounding. If there were no superset, but only subsets, then the observer could compare Umwelten only by switching from one subset to the other. But Uexküll considers this to be impossible.[17] If there were a superset, by contrast, the observer could gain access to the *Merkwelt* and *Wirkwelt*, the receptor world and effector world, of other living entities, i.e., to other subsets, via the overlap of the objects in his Umwelt with objects in other Umwelten. In Uexküll's writings there is evidence for both assertions: for the categorical closedness of a

17 The fact that Niklas Luhmann's definition of Umwelt corresponds more to how "environment" is generally understood than to Uexküll's model is related to the fact that Luhmann's references all operate with "environment" as a concept—though this is a thesis that I can only suggest here without further elaboration. Luhmann takes recourse to an ecological-cybernetic understanding of environment, based on Uexküll, that is formulated by Heinz von Foerster, Humberto Maturana, and Francisco Varela, and to Talcott Parson's organizational-theoretical concept, which was articulated at Harvard in the context of the Pareto Circle. These two genealogies allow us to tie Luhmann's concept of Umwelt more closely to the English term "environment" than to Uexküll's term "Umwelt." It is true that Luhmann explicitly draws from Uexküll in further developing the distinction between Umwelt and Umgebung. The Umwelt in this context is the system seen from the perspective of the system, and the Umgebung is what an external observer of the system recognizes: "Jakob von Uexküll showed an early awareness of the fact that the environment of an animal is not that which we would describe as its surrounding or milieu. We can see more (or perhaps fewer) and other things than the ones an animal can perceive and process. Hence, two concepts of environment must be distinguished." (Niklas Luhmann, *Introduction to Systems Theory*, trans. Peter Gilgen (Cambridge: Polity Press, 2013), 57). But Uexküll's distinction is not as clear as Luhmann's, because Uexküll's has no conception of a self-referential figure of the observer, causing difficulties in his theory for this position. A number of ideas—Ludwig von Bertalanffy's systems theory, the concept of the ecosystem, and cybernetics—lie between Uexküll and Luhmann, all of which contributed to the consolidation of the observer. Luhmann's solution to the problem of the Umgebung of the Umwelt, that is to say, of the Umwelt and its surrounding, is to introduce the observer: the observer of the observation can be distinguished into the observing subject and the medium in which the observation takes place. For the first-order observer, the Umwelt is observable as Umwelt (which in turn is part of the second-order observer's Umwelt). The Umgebung of the Umwelt is therefore what appears to the second-order observer as the world. Observers of any number of orders can be added, but one has no access to the world outside the Umwelt. For Luhmann, the world marks the epistemological limit of all Umwelten, while for Uexküll it represents their metaphysical unity.

 multiplicity of Umwelten; and for the possibility of comparison by means of the surrounding.

As shown above, the external surrounding of the external world includes all "objective" things that can be part of an Umwelt at all, even if Umwelten do not merge into the spaces of the surrounding because they are subjectively constituted. But who could have access to the surrounding of these Umwelten, if every living entity, and thus also the observer, has access only to his own Umwelt? At the crux of Uexküll's theory lies the question of the reality of the external world and the conditions of cognition, especially of scientific cognition. Unlike in philosophy, the biologist Uexküll wants to explore Umwelten through experiments; but he faces the methodological obstacle that the observer he has introduced can cognize only those things in the Umwelt of other living entities that are part of his own Umwelt, that appear as an effector cue or receptor cue, depending on his organs. Uexküll's Umwelt theory is forced to confront this limit again and again. Both options—the breaking off of relations between surrounded and surrounding, and the multiplication of such relations—are important for Uexküll despite the contradictions they entail. We find arguments, for instance, both for an unquestionable relativity of all points of view and for an unquestionable reality of the outside world. This emphasis on radical subjectivity is complemented by attempts to break out of this perspective in order to gain access to the Umwelten of other living entities, notwithstanding all the objections this provokes. Crucially, Uexküll needs the external world for his argument in order to demonstrate his scientific methodology. His supposed Kantianism is not some constructivist form of perspectivism, because the external world functions within cognition as a regulating instance. Rather, one could say his view is a monism of multiplicity, in which the multiplicity of subjective Umwelten remains related to the unity of the surrounding, refers to the Planmäßigkeit of the world, and thus is of metaphysical origin.

This constellation gives rise to a number of issues that affect all of his terms for surroundings, though in different ways. What gives a surrounding, or an Umwelt, its place? What lies outside a surrounding—which is itself the outside to an Umwelt? Is there one encompassing surrounding that encircles all surroundings, transforming them into something surrounded? Is there one single surrounding in which all Umwelten have a place? Or are surroundings also centered around a subject? If a surrounding is itself surrounded by something, is it, in this relation, no longer a surrounding but something surrounded? Are there thus unsurrounded surroundings that cannot become Umwelten? These questions bear upon the core of any thinking about what relations define a surrounding, because they concern the scope of the relations engendered by the act of surrounding/ fact of being surrounded. Is this relationship nested, capable of being multiplied? Or is a surrounding something that gives what is surrounded its place, without itself having a place? If a surrounding cannot be surrounded by other surroundings, how does it relate to its own outside? And if a surrounding is surrounded, what is the interrelation between the surrounding and what surrounds it? These questions revolve around the relation between inside and outside, between center and periphery, and around the conditions of their closedness. They furthermore indicate that the relationality of surrounding(s) not only poses epistemological challenges but is also implicated in cosmological, metaphysical, and ultimately political operations, even where Uexküll does not reflect on the matter himself. His distinction between Umwelt and surrounding concerns precisely these questions, which ultimately remain impossible to answer because they reflect aporias, and it is these questions that prove to be the key to the epistemological core of his Umwelt concept.

3. The Aporia of the Surrounded Surrounding

In epistemologies of surrounding(s), a tension repeatedly emerges that poses a fundamental challenge: the question of what surrounds a surrounding. How far, in other words, does the relationality of being surrounded extend? Can it be included in a given relation of surroundedness, thereby expanding that relationship from within? Or it is a simple schema that cannot be multiplied? This tension can be formulated as the aporia of a surrounded surrounding: if a surrounding—which is always only given as a relation to what is surrounded—is itself surrounded by something, then it is more than a surrounding, even if it continues to operate as such. If, on the other hand, the surrounding can only be unsurrounded, then that relation which makes it a surrounding cannot be applied reflexively to itself.

Put simply, there are two ways of resolving this aporia. On the one hand, it is possible that what lies beyond a surrounding is yet another surrounding, whether conceived as an Umwelt, milieu, or environment; and that what is surrounded can itself be surrounded by something in a new relation that can be reiterated without any limit. In this view, the relation of surrounding/being surrounded can be unfolded and relationally multiplied without there being a fixed standpoint allowing surroundings to be compared with each other. This way of arguing ultimately implies a relationality of surrounding(s) in which that which surrounds and that which is surrounded can repeatedly be redetermined. The other possibility is to assume an absolute limit, a universal outside, that cannot become a surrounding. If there is an external, independent point of observation from which the boundary between the surrounded and the surrounding can be drawn, then this implies an outside that lies beyond the surrounding but does not itself surround the surrounding which is being observed. It would thus be possible to clearly determine the boundary of the surrounding from the objective standpoint of the external observer. Uexküll's distinction between Umwelt and Umgebung, of "around-world" and "surrounding," along with his many attempts to justify access to the superordinate surrounding despite the boundedness of every living entity to its Umwelt, reflect this tension inasmuch as it articulates both possibilities.

It is above all his attempts to ground his scientific method in a way that would prevent it from becoming too subjective, along with his assumption of the Planmäßigkeit of nature, that demonstrate the tension between the spatiality of the surrounding and the subject-centeredness of the Umwelt, and between the absoluteness and the relationality of surroundings to what they surround.[18]

This formulation of these two options already indicates that they have philosophical and political consequences which oscillate between idealism and relativism. The two options are not necessarily mutually exclusive and can also be pursued in contradiction; the logic of the Conservative Revolution, for example, forces them to coexist, while tending to silence their contradiction. The question of what surrounds a surrounding is thus not mere sophistry but concerns the question of the outside and its observability. This question of the outside, in turn, lies at the heart of the history of twentieth-century thinking about surrounding(s).[19]

The relation of a surrounding and what its surrounds implies metaphysical questions, which ancient philosophers attempted to grasp with what was likely the first such concept, that of *periechon*.[20] The preposition *peri* means *around*, *about*, or *with*, while as a participle of *echein*, *echon* stands for *to have* or *to*

18 Planmäßigkeit goes beyond the Kantian principle of purposiveness, which Julian Jochmaring has described as a central element of Uexküll's Umwelt theory. See Julian Jochmaring, "Streuen/Strahlen: Negative Ambientialität bei Merleau-Ponty," in *Medienanthropologische Szenen: Die conditio humana im Zeitalter der Medien*, ed. Lorenz Engell, Katerina Kritlova, and Christiane Voss (Munich: Fink, 2018), 68. Planmäßigkeit includes not only the "fitting in" of a living entity into its Umwelt, but also the "fitting in" of all Umwelten into the whole of nature.

19 See Anselm Franke, "Earthrise und das Verschwinden des Außen," in *The Whole Earth: Kalifornien und das Verschwinden des Außen*, ed. Diedrich Diedrichsen and Anselm Franke (Berlin: Sternberg Press, 2013).

20 For a more detailed discussion of this point, see Sprenger, *Epistemologien des Umgebens*, 31–32.

 hold. Accordingly, the Greeks used *periechon* to name that which envelops, encloses, encompasses, or surrounds. The term represents an attempt to define place as something that is not independent of what it contains, just as what is in a place is not independent of what surrounds it. Aristotle defines *periechon* in terms of the circumscribing boundary, which he in turn understands as a conditioning relation. As a *periechon*, the surrounding defines a place by surrounding it. Consequently, there exists no object that is not surrounded, because everything has its place. In the fourth book of his *Physics*, Aristotle defines place, *topos*, as "the boundary of the containing body at which it is in contact with the contained body."[21] Just as a pitcher surrounds the water it contains, so a *periechon* analogously envelops something without itself being part of this things, while at the same time determining its extent. The container is not conceived as a thing, but as something that surrounds and holds, as something whose extent determines what it contains. The surrounding thus forms the boundary of both that which surrounds and that which is surrounded. The surrounding, like a pitcher, is "neither a part of what is in it nor yet greater than its extension."[22] In the same way that the walls of a pitcher close and enclose the water it holds, a surrounding assigns a place to what it surrounds.

For Aristotle, the *periechon* is neither a thing nor a place. Rather, it is a relationship: that which surrounds something. For Aristotle, a surrounding is singular, even though it may contain many

21 Aristotle, *Physics*, trans. Jonathan Barnes, *The Complete Works of Aristotle*, vol. 1 (Princeton: Princeton University Press, 1991), 57 and 212a. See also Benjamin Morison, *On Location: Aristotle's Concept of Place* (Oxford: Clarendon Press, 2002) and Peter Berz, "Contenant Contenu: Anordnungen des Enthaltens," in *Das Motiv der Kästchenwahl: Container in Psychoanalyse, Kunst, Kultur*, ed. Insa Härtel and Olaf Knellessen (Göttingen: Vandenhoeck & Ruprecht, 2012).

22 Aristotle, "Physics," in *The Complete Works of Aristotle*, trans. Jonathan Barnes, vol. 1 (Princeton: Princeton University Press), 211a32–33. *Periechon* is thus, it should be noted here, not identical with the *in-between*, that is to say, it is not a *medium* in the sense of a mediator or in-between, even if the two concepts are related.

components: a fish is surrounded by water, which also surrounds other fish and rocks. All these surrounding things are part of what gives the fish its place. What belongs to something's surrounding, that is to say, what defines the place of something that is surrounded, depends on the respective circumstances and must always be determined anew. Every earthly surrounding is part of other surroundings, ultimately surrounded only by the impassable sphere of the heavens arching overhead. In this respect, as suggested above, the relation of surrounding/being surrounded can either be tied to a fixed limit or thought of as infinitely nested within itself. But what, then, one might ask, going beyond Aristotle, surrounds the surrounding? Surroundings define a place because a place cannot itself have a place, as Aristotle shows: it is neither the form nor the matter of a thing, because then it would have to be at the place of a thing, and a place cannot itself have a place. A surrounding defines a place without itself being one. Therefore—to borrow from Werner Hamacher's explication of this idea—a surrounding limits a thing without being the limit of the thing.[23] If a surrounding, as *periechon*, has no place of its own, but designates a relation and gives a place, then the question arises of how this relation can be referred to itself.

This question is implicit in all terms for surroundings and has, in the twentieth century, prompted especially intensive discussion. That which locates things via relations—which determines dispositions via that which surrounds them, separates inside from outside, and finally makes it possible to name all of this as a place—has diffused throughout history into a number of various concepts and terms. Taking the systematic place of *periechon*, new terms and concepts have arisen that continue, shift, or overwrite its usage in other ways. These modify, in significantly different ways, the idea that *periechon* attempted to sketch in general form: words like Umwelt, milieu, and environment;

23 See Werner Hamacher, "Amphora (Extracts)," *Assemblage* 20 (April 1993): 40–41.

 ambient and ether, sphere and element; augmented in certain historical contexts by medium, aura, habitat, lifeworld, or climate. Up to the present moment, and even in places one would never suspect it, these terms have proven to be deeply ingrained in fundamental metaphysical assumptions, inasmuch as their specific epistemologies of surrounding(s) entail precisely such questions about the relationship of the external surrounding and what it surrounds; about the boundary of what is surrounded; and finally about what lies beyond or outside the surrounding and in turn surrounds it.

4. Surrounding(s) and Umwelt

Umwelt theory, too, can be understood as an attempt to deal with these issues. It treats all living entities as subjects, and this unique approach means that to this day, and especially today, it remains an important theoretical reference for attempts to oppose anthropomorphic descriptions of nature.[24] Uexküll's epistemologically grounded variant of thinking about surrounding(s) plays out different ways of cognizing an Umwelt, and hence different potential locations of the observer. At various points in Uexküll's work, one finds attempts at providing a solution to the aporia of the surrounded surrounding, and it is these attempts that will be presented and contrasted in what follows. In reading Uexküll, the problem is that he does not always work with precisely defined concepts, or even derivatives of concepts, and that he uses terms in divergent meanings. On closer inspection, his connections to philosophical theories often turn out to be attempts to find meaning for questions stemming from a

24 In contrast to Kant, for Uexküll the subject does not have to be a human being, but can also be an animal. As Pobojewska has shown, this extension is possible because subjectivity in Uexküll is not tied to the faculty of thought but rather to the active reception of stimuli (*Merken*) and the active production of effects (*Wirken*). See Aldona Pobojewska, "Die Subjektlehre Jakob von Uexkülls," *Sudhoffs Archiv* 77, no. 1 (1993): 70.

particular way of viewing the world.[25] When read closely, his texts offer more questions than answers, but they are nevertheless revealing precisely because of these inconsistencies.

In his 1909 book *Umwelt und Innenwelt der Tiere* (Umwelt and the inner world of animals), Uexküll introduces this distinction as two ways of surrounding/being surrounded, the subjective Umwelt and the objective outer world or surrounding. Uexküll explains just what distinguishes the two in different ways in various passages, which are moreover not always consistent. The doubling of the surrounding so crucial from a Kantian perspective into one part that is dependent on the organism and another part that is given independently of the organism raises the question of what or how the surrounding is demarcated. The crux of the argument being pursued here is that the Umwelt, as noted above, is created from components of what Uexküll calls the surrounding (or "Umgebung"), which Canguilhem defines as the "banal geographical environment."[26] That is to say: from the abundance of its stimuli, the living entity takes in only those receptor cues that its sensory organs can grasp, with which it can interact in its effector world, and which are of vital significance. An Umwelt is accordingly not an object resulting from passive adaptation like an evolutionary niche but is instead an object that is actively shaped by the respective organism. The concept of being "fitted

25 Martin Heidegger's judgment of Uexküll is clear in this regard: "It would be foolish if we attempted to impute or ascribe philosophical inadequacy to Uexküll's interpretations, instead of recognizing that the engagement with concrete investigations like this is one of the most fruitful things that philosophy can learn from contemporary biology." See Martin Heidegger, *The Fundamental Concepts of Metaphysics*, trans. William McNeill and Nicholas Walker (Bloomington: Indiana University Press, 1995), 263.

26 Canguilhem, *The Knowledge of Life*, 111: "Von Uexküll chooses the words *Umwelt*, *Umgebung*, and *Welt* and distinguishes between them with great care. *Umwelt* designates the milieu of behavior proper to a certain organism; *Umgebung* is the banal geographical environment; *Welt* is the universe of science." It should be noted that this distinction between *Umwelt* and *Umgebung* is rarely found in other linguistic communities, where words for *environment* and *surrounding* are usually used synonymously.

 in" (*Einpassung*, as opposed to *Anpassung* or "adaptation") that Uexküll introduces in this context encompasses the interrelationship of the surrounding and the surrounded, because both are "fitted into" each other, rather than being adapted to each other.

The Umwelt always and necessarily represents the optimal fit, Uexküll argues with recourse to the concept of the "pessimal world" coined by the Jewish biologist Shimon Fritz Bodenheimer:

> Bodenheimer is entirely right when he speaks of a 'pessimal' world, i.e., one as unfavorable as possible, in which most animals live. But this world is not their environment [Umwelt], only their surrounding. An optimal environment [Umwelt], i.e., one as favorable as possible, and pessimal surrounding will obtain as a general rule. For the point is that the species be preserved, no matter how many individuals perish. If the surrounding of a certain species were not pessimal, it would quickly predominate over all other species thanks to its optimal environment [Umwelt].[27]

For Uexküll, then, it is not possible for a "fitting in" to be better or worse than another, which means that each individual Umwelt is both incomparable and in conformity with a plan, i.e., is characterized by Planmäßigkeit.

In its Umwelt, every living entity is for Uexküll an autonomously acting subject. And the relationship between living entities and their Umwelt is always entirely "fitted in," because they mutually constitute each other, meaning that one cannot speak of beings that are better or worse adapted. No Umwelt is deficient and there is no hierarchy of Umwelten. Being "fitted in" thus means something other than the evolutionary observation that the characteristics of living entities correspond to the characteristics

27 Uexküll, *Foray*, 250. On Bodenheimer, see Marco Mazzeo, "Giorgio Agamben: The Political Meaning of Uexküll's 'Sleeping Tick,'" in *Jakob von Uexküll and Philosophy: Life, Environments, Anthropology*, ed. Francesca Michelini and Kristian Köchy (London: Routledge, 2020).

of their surrounding. Adaptation in the Darwinian sense refers, as Julian Jochmaring has put it, to "a prior separation of a living entity and its surrounding that must be overcome through a reactive adaptation made by the living entity."[28] Being "fitted in" for Uexküll, by contrast, consists in the fact that every living entity is "fitted into" its effector world in such a way that the building plan or "Bauplan" of its body and its receptor organs are organized according to natural laws and all Umwelten are harmoniously intermeshed without disturbing one another. All significant Umwelten thus coexist on equal terms, as Uexküll suggests with a theatrical metaphor: "Umwelt theory regards the animal subject as the center of a special world stage."[29] The numerous musical metaphors Uexküll cites also depict this relationship in a similar sense, as a fugue or as a contrapuntal coordination of living entities and Umwelt.[30] This being "fitted in" thus conforms to Planmäßigkeit, necessarily resulting in an optimal relationship in which each living entity has its place with its own Umwelt, and are accordingly "fitted into" each other. Even if this Planmäßigkeit is not reducible to the vitalism of a life force, it guarantees, qua its realization in the building plan, an arrangement of nature in accordance with Planmäßigkeit. Umwelt theory is ultimately concerned with how this Planmäßigkeit is realized in nature.

For Uexküll, the Umwelt of an animal is thus not limited by external surrounding factors such as food cycles or metabolic processes but by its relationship to its receptor world and effector world.[31] Being "fitted in" is thus a relation of the subject

28 Julian Jochmaring, "Im gläsernen Gehäuse: Zur Medialität der Umwelt bei Uexküll und Merleau-Ponty," in *Gehäuse: Mediale Einkapselungen*, ed. Christina Bartz et al. (Munich: Fink, 2017), 261.

29 Jakob von Uexküll and E. G. Sarris, "Das Duftfeld des Hundes," *Zeitschrift für Hundeforschung* 1, 3/4 (1931): 55.

30 See Veit Erlmann, "Klang, Raum und Umwelt: Jakob von Uexkülls Musiktheorie des Lebens," *Zeitschrift für Semiotik* 34, no. 1/2 (2012): 145–58.

31 See Jakob von Uexküll, "Darwin und die englische Moral," *Deutsche Rundschau*, no. 173 (1917): 215–42.

to the world, whereas adaptation is a relation between species and surrounding factors. For Uexküll, being "fitted in" is constitutive of Umwelt, whereas adaptation is a mechanistic effect. Inasmuch as it is "fitted in," every living entity perceives and interacts with its individual Umwelt through the species-specific stimuli of receptor cues; Uexküll writes that "the receptor world and effector world together form the Umwelt."[32] In this regard, Uexküll's concept of Umwelt is more centered around living entities than milieu or environment. At the center of the interrelationship with an Umwelt, one finds, as a cognizing subject, qualified living entities who each have access to an individual Umwelt.

5. From One Umwelt to Another

It is telling that Uexküll's model becomes vague where it concerns exchanges with other living entities, especially with those of one's own species—in other words, exactly where Darwin's concept of competition begins. Other living entities can appear in the animal's Umwelt only as part of the subjective Umwelt. The closedness and isolation of Umwelten from each other leads Uexküll to justify the exchanges, communication, and cooperation between living entities with the elaborate theoretical framework of the functional cycle (fig. 1). Uexküll uses this concept to model the relationship of a subject to an object, without, however, allowing the subject to encounter another subject as subject. In this respect, intersubjectivity constitutes a challenge to Umwelt theory or even, as Florian Höfer writes, a problem for Uexküll that he then ignores.[33] Not only is the inner world of

32 Jakob von Uexküll, "Wie sehen wir die Natur und wie sieht die Natur sich selber?," *Die Naturwissenschaften* 10 (1922): 266.

33 While arguing in a similar vein that Uexküll disregards the phenomenon of communication, Höfer nonetheless remains mostly on a descriptive level in his goal of articulating a theory of communication. See Florian Höfer, "Die Notwendigkeit der Kommunikation: Die Missachtung eines Phänomens bei Jakob von Uexküll" (dissertation, University of Bonn, 2007); see also

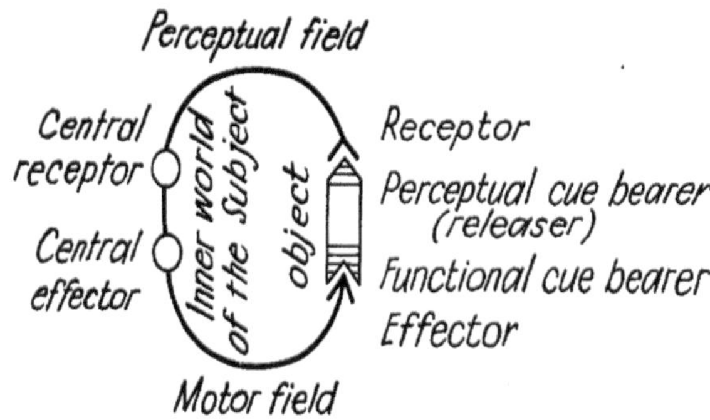

Figure 1: Uexküll's depiction of a functional cycle (*Funktionskreis*) in Uexküll, *Foray*, 49.

other living entities inaccessible; interaction is moreover only possible via the detour of what Uexküll calls the "Merkwelt" and "Wirkwelt," the receptor world and effector world. The objects of the external world, as well as the actions of other living entities, trigger species-specific stimuli in any living entity that appear in its internal world as receptor cues. For Uexküll, interaction with other living entities is therefore always an interaction with signs in one's own Umwelt. All organisms of a species accordingly have an Umwelt that is formally similar but individually specific, determined by their building plan. And it is by means of what Uexküll calls functional cycles that organisms are connected not only to their Umwelt, via their receptor world and effector world, but also to each other when individuals of different species interact. In this case, living entities become part of the Umwelten of other living entities in the form of receptor cues. For Uexküll, the interaction of the functional cycles in turn obeys a Planmäßigkeit in which each individual component is related to the whole. "The entire universe, which consists entirely of Umwelten, is held

Cornelius Borck, "Hans Blumenberg: The Transformation of Uexküll's Bioepistemology into Phenomenology," in Michelini and Köchy, *Jakob von Uexküll and Philosophy.*

 together by functional cycles and joined together, according to an all-encompassing plan, to form a unity we call nature."[34]

Three consequences arise from this observation, which will be unpacked below. *First,* the smallest unit of this biology is the individual in its own Umwelt, but not the species or even the community. The dyad of the surrounded and the surrounding appears in Uexküll as a singularity: every living entity has only one Umwelt. The collective, cooperative, or competitive fabrication of multiple surroundings—and with it, the plethora of ecological questions—plays only a marginal role, insofar as other beings become manifest as receptor cues or effector cues, and as the receptor and effector cues of members of the same species are similar.

Second, it follows that the exchange of signs between living entities is not the rule determining life in Umwelt theory, but the unlikely exception. The exchange of matter or energy is for Uexküll not a subject of biology, but at most of physiology, which he nevertheless does not believe can contribute to the epistemology of Umwelt theory.[35] Umwelt theory is consequently

34 Uexküll, *Theoretische Biologie*, 324. As Georges Canguilhem presents it, the physician Kurt Goldstein turned Uexküll's own ideas against him by arguing that an organism takes in from its Umwelt not only that which corresponds to its receptor world, but also potentially negative stimuli. For Canguilhem, Goldstein sees the Umwelt not as a closed bubble but as shaped by the activities and developments of the organism: this is what supposedly allows Goldstein to explain the development of pathologies and diseases. See Georges Canguilhem, "Das Lebendige und sein Milieu," 260. On the functional cycle, see also Thomas Potthast, "Lebensführung (in) der Dialektik von Innenwelt und Umwelt: Jakob von Uexküll, seine philosophische Rezeption und die Transformation des Begriffs 'Funktionskreis' in der Ökologie," in *Das Leben führen? Das Konzept Lebensführung zwischen Technikphilosophie und Lebensphilosophie*, ed. Nicole Karafyllis (Berlin: Edition Sigma, 2014).

35 See Jakob von Uexküll, "Die Rolle des Subjekts in der Biologie," *Die Naturwissenschaften* 19, May (1931). According to Juan M. Heredia, a division of tasks between physiology and biology was specified by Uexküll in his first book *Leitfaden für das Studium der experimentellen Biologie der Wassertiere* (*Guide to the study of the experimental biology of aquatic animals*): the former was

not compatible with the early systems theory of Ludwig von Bertalanffy, which focused on circulation processes and control cycles, or with the ecology of the second half of the twentieth century, which is largely shaped by the concept of the ecosystem and draws its most important ideas from population biology and limnology. The quantifiable flows of energy and matter used to investigate an ecosystem thus stand in contrast to Uexküll's Umwelt theory, which focuses on the quality of a living entity's relationship to its Umwelt and its purely subjective constitution. Despite its undeniable influences on anthropology, behavioral theory, philosophy, and literature, Uexküll's Umwelt theory remains in this regard an idiosyncratic approach, whereas ecosystem ecology is broadening into a wide-ranging field of research.[36]

Third, and finally, the problem of the observer's point of view becomes particularly vexing in this context: even to the scientific observer, other living entities appear only as part of his Umwelt. To explore the Umwelt of another living entity, the observer must find a way to make inferences from his Umwelt through the surrounding that he shares with the animal. Hence living entities can be meaningfully studied only in their processual interaction with the Umwelt of the researcher, while foreign Umwelten remain categorically inaccessible.

concerned with the energetic and material household of living entities and was accordingly mechanistic in character, while the latter was to investigate its organic unity with a view to the whole. See Juan M. Heredia, "Jakob von Uexküll, an Intellectual History," in Michelini and Köchy, *Jakob von Uexküll and Philosophy.*

36 Dieter Mersch's premise that Uexküll's approach, which does not see itself as ecological, has influenced ecosystem theory can no longer be accepted. See Dieter Mersch, "Ökologie und Ökologisierung," *Internationales Jahrbuch für Medienphilosophie* 4, no 1 (2018): 190. Within ecology, Uexküll's approach, which ceased to be based on experiments by the 1920s at the latest, has been largely ignored for some time now, finding influence mainly in philosophical anthropology, biosemiotics, and cultural studies.

Accordingly, Uexküll is not concerned with objectively determining the factors of a surrounding that determine a living entity, but with describing the relationship of being "fitted in" that dynamically binds all living entities or species to their Umwelten. The approach of his early research—especially in the areas of neuropsychology and anatomical marine biology, the latter focus inspired by the innovative practices of the new marine biology that achieved such great importance in the late nineteenth century—was to study living organisms as much as possible in their natural surroundings, but also in artificial surroundings such as aquariums as well, when necessary.[37] By modifying these surroundings, as Uexküll explained beginning in the 1920s, it is possible to isolate individual stimuli and draw conclusions about the receptor world and/or effector world of organisms without having to make psychological speculations about an animal's inner world, i.e., without having to put oneself in its Umwelt. The fact that such speculations about the external world and about the self-contained inner worlds of other living entities nevertheless pervade Uexküll's writings and form the basis of his scientific methodology shows that Uexküll cannot consistently maintain this isolation of Umwelten.[38] He does not dare to take the step toward a radical perspectivism in which there is no outside world. He answers the question of what surrounds the Umwelt with a surrounding that cannot be transcended; a surrounding that is the same for all living entities, but inaccessible.

With the period's increasing focus on behavioral experiments, Uexküll was faced with the challenge of experimentally

37 On Uexküll's early research, see Kristian Köchy, "Uexküll's Legacy: Biological Reception and Biophilosophical Impact," in Michelini and Köchy, *Jakob von Uexküll and Philosophy*, 52–70.

38 Similar questions also arise, as Julia Gruevska has shown with direct reference to Uexküll, for the biologist Frederik Buytendijk. See Julia Gruevska, "'Mit und in seiner Umwelt geboren': Frederik Buytendijks experimentelle Konzeptualisierung einer Tier-Umwelt-Einheit," *NTM Zeitschrift für Geschichte der Wissenschaften, Technik und Medizin* 27, no. 3 (2019): 343–75.

determining what belongs to a living entity's Umwelt and what does not.[39] An object that is significant for the organism evokes a reaction, that is to say, it is perceived and thus becomes part of the Umwelt because it bears specific receptor cues that are important for the organism's life and to which its receptor organs are oriented. Uexküll attempts to explore these processes—experimentally, on the one hand, through anatomical and neurological research on the sensory organs of sea urchins, cats, and dragonflies; and philosophically, which ultimately means ideologically, on the other. As Uexküll first explains in his 1909 book *Umwelt und Innenwelt der Tiere,* the organism reacts via a response in the form of an action with a particular effect, depending on the possibilities of action that result, in its Umwelt, from the building plan of its physical abilities.[40] Objects that have no receptor cues of importance for the organism—meaning that as receptor cue carriers, they do not speak to the organism's receptor organs—are not perceived and do not belong to the organism's Umwelt; but they do belong to its surrounding. They cannot, however, be reacted to. Hence, depending on the building plan of each living entity, its Umwelt ends where a given object no longer plays a role for it. But what is the place of objects that are not given as part of an Umwelt, but are given as part of a surrounding? Are there objects that do not act as receptor cue carriers for any living entity? Under what conditions can such objects be recognized? Uexküll largely ignores these questions, but they nevertheless make themselves felt again and again in his writings. They are important for the epistemology of surrounding(s) that comes with Umwelt theory, because they coalesce in the question of what is outside the surrounding.

39 See, for example, Stefan Rieger, *Schall und Rauch: Eine Mediengeschichte der Kurve* (Frankfurt am Main: Suhrkamp, 2009) as well as the contributions in Hans-Jörg Rheinberger and Michael Hagner (eds.), *Die Experimentalisierung des Lebens: Experimentalsysteme in den biologischen Wissenschaften 1850/1950* (Berlin: Akademie, 1993).

40 See Jakob von Uexküll, *Umwelt und Innenwelt der Tiere*, ed. Florian Mildenberger and Bernd Herrmann (Berlin: Springer, [1909] 2014).

6. The Science of Umwelt

A biological science of Umwelten necessarily examines its objects from the outside, as a surrounding, via the detour of receptor cues and effector cues. If Uexküll's biology of Umwelten is to claim validity, the observer's methods must be aimed toward identifying the crucial components of the Umwelt of the living entity in question, even though, as Uexküll repeatedly emphasizes in reference to a classic epistemological argument, it will never be possible to capture an animal's Umwelt in the same way that the animal experiences it.

> No attempt to discover the reality behind the world of appearance, i.e. by neglecting the subject, has ever come to anything, because the subject plays the decisive role in constructing the world of appearance, and on the far side of that world there is no world at all.[41]

The Umwelt of a living entity can never be experienced from its point of view, Uexküll argues, because the inner world of other species is categorically inaccessible: "*All reality is subjective appearance*."[42] At best, Uexküll offers a tentative, literary, or artistic approach, as seen with the drawings of his Hamburg collaborator Georg Kriszat in Uexküll's most popular book, *Foray into the World of Animals and Humans* (fig. 2). They attempt to show how animal Umwelten could appear to humans, operating with a visual logic of estrangement. They demonstrate, in other words, Uexküll's procedure of "reduction to the same point of view":[43] the researcher should observe objects from the perspective

41 Uexküll, *Theoretical Biology*, xv.

42 Ibid., italics in the original. Uexküll uses the term "receptor" (*Rezeptor*) instead of "sensory organ" (*Sinnesorgan*) to avoid the appearance of describing inaccessible sensations, drawing attention instead to external stimuli. See Uexküll, "Biologie in der Mausefalle," 215.

43 H. Lassen, "Der Umgebungsbegriff als Planbegriff: Ein Beitrag zu den erkenntnistheoretischen Grundfragen der Umweltlehre," *Sudhoffs Archiv* 27, no. 6 (1935): 482.

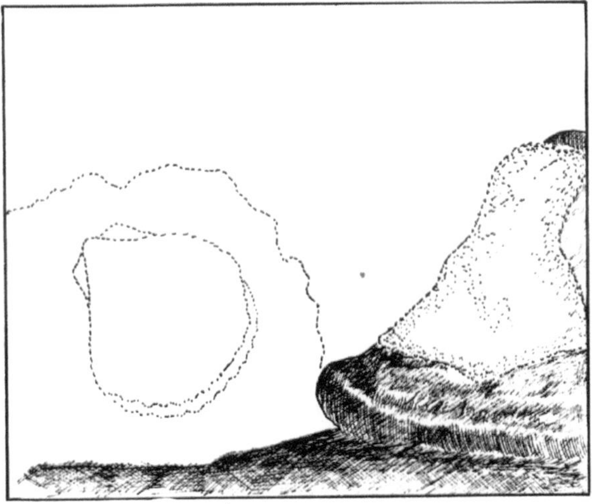

Figure 2: Surroundings (top) and Umwelt (bottom) of the scallop (Uexküll, *Foray*, 2010, 81).

of the other living entity, thereby making it possible to identify receptor cues and effector cues despite the noninterchangeability of viewpoints. Uexküll argues, namely, that with every movement the subject not only changes its place, but also reshapes its Umwelt. It is precisely this assignment of objects to Umwelten that the illustrations are intended to demonstrate.

Uexküll's detailed depictions of animal Umwelten, however, do not limit themselves to simply describing the observer's perspective; instead, they go further in claiming to be scientific assertions with objective validity. Despite the ostensible impossibility of accessing other subjectivities, Uexküll references a world beyond mere appearances, one in which objects belonging to different Umwelten can coincide. When he uses photographs or drawings in *Foray* to illustrate how a human and how a fly perceive a village street, he is explicitly considering the fly's Umwelt through that of the human being. But the fact that he can describe the fly's Umwelt in both the illustrations and the text implies access to a world that is outside of the human Umwelt. If the accessibility of the Umwelten of other beings were radically sealed off, then such representations would be nothing more than speculation, because they would cross an inviolable boundary.[44] But for Uexküll, they demonstrate the essence of his theory and thus have the same functional value as scientific instruments. Even if the inner world of a living entity remains inaccessible, the biologist may succeed in identifying the receptor cues and effector cues of an Umwelt—something Uexküll undertook at the turn of the century primarily in experimental studies, which he then later abandoned in favor of theoretical work. Such an approach requires the assumption of an external world and

44 See Thomas Nagel's classic essay "What Is It Like to Be a Bat?," *The Philosophical Review* 83, no. 4 (1974): 435–50. From a constructivist point of view, Uexküll does not go far enough, because in all his attempts to overcome an inviolable boundary and gain access to an alien sensibility, his descriptions of animal Umwelten still adhere to the vocabulary, available articulations, and media of biology.

access to a surrounding in which objects belonging to different Umwelten can be identified. This procedure may be consistent from a Kantian point of view, inasmuch as the assumption of a common external world is necessary. But the question arises as to what this means for the epistemology of surrounding(s) that underlies Umwelt theory.

This tension is already inherent in the 1909 essay "Die Umwelt," in which Uexküll first explains this concept. Uexküll begins by writing: "All plants and animals, as one can see at any time, are everywhere surrounded by the same objects as we are."[45] He subsequently clarifies that

> though the world surrounding us constitutes only an individual case, it must by no means be regarded as normative. Admittedly, we as humans are forced to start from our human Umwelt if we want to gain an understanding of the Umwelt of animals, because an absolute world, one that would exist for itself without relating at all to any sensory organ, is inconceivable for us; its objects would possess no qualities at all.[46]

Except, one might add here, the quality of surrounding the relevant plants and animals. If an object can be found in different Umwelten, there must be an observer who can detect this correspondence. Since we have access to the world only through our sensory organs, and these "possess the form that is specific to them," we can only assume subjective Umwelten.[47] One can thus interpret Uexküll as follows: the objective external world, in which living entities are "surrounded by the same objects as we are," exists independently of any observation, and within

45 Jakob von Uexküll, "Die Umwelt," *Neue Rundschau* 21, no. 2 (1910): 639.

46 Ibid.

47 Ibid.

his theory, it has the function of ensuring that Umwelten can be compared.[48]

Elsewhere, in the 1934 version of *Foray*, the surrounding in which an animal moves and in which it can be explored is "nothing else but our own, human environment [Umwelt]. The first task of research on such environments [Umwelten] consists in seeking out the animal's receptor cues and, with them, to construct the animal's environment [Umwelt]."[49] These ideas—articulated here as a kind of incipient program for a future biology (in which Uexküll participates at this point only via theoretical works)—are not elaborated elsewhere by Uexküll in any greater detail. He does criticize the "the belief in the existence of one and only one world, in which all living entities are encased."[50] But he does so, contra Kant, by referring to the relativity of space and time, which was being discussed at this time with reference to Einstein's theory of relativity. There is no absolute time and space valid for all living entities, Uexküll writes in a letter to Adolf von Harnack:

> Einstein has, however, now destroyed this unified space of representation by taking away its center. A space cannot exist without a center, and if you give it multiple centers, then you split it into multiple spaces. That is to say, we thus return to subjective spaces.[51]

In this sense, Umwelt theory augments relativity with the centering of a subject in its Umwelt. But this argument does not question the assumption that it is possible to observe the objects in animal Umwelten, from the outside and objectively, even when the relevant animals inhabit other spaces and times.

48 Ibid.

49 Uexküll, *Foray*, 53, translation modified.

50 Ibid., translation modified.

51 Letter to Adolf von Harnack, September 10, 1928, quoted in Jutta Schmidt, "Jakob von Uexküll und Houston Stewart Chamberlain: Ein Briefwechsel in Auszügen," *Medizinhistorisches Journal* 10, no. 2 (1975): 122.

7. The Observer of the Outside

Ecology, like physics, is one of a number of prominent sciences in the first half of the twentieth century in which the figure of the observer is first introduced and then passes through several stages: from an external observer equipped with an objective, analyzing gaze to an involved participant whose observation changes what is observed. Although Uexküll does not understand his theory as ecology, it is nevertheless part of this shift and vacillates between these two conceptions of the observer. As a self-declared, though ultimately quite idiosyncratic Kantian, as was shown above, Uexküll examines the building plan of living entities as an a priori condition for their Umwelt. The question thus arises of how an observer can know anything about the Umwelt, and especially describe the Umwelt, of other living entities?

In this context, passages in which Uexküll describes the methodology of his approach gain a particular importance, because it is here that he responds to the impossibility of direct access to other Umwelten. He opposes both psychologizing attempts to see an animal's Umwelt through its own eyes (even though he makes just such attempts in his *Foray*) and anthropomorphic analogies to animal Umwelten. Terms like "Merkmal" and "Wirkmal," meaning "receptor cue" and "effector cue," are attempts to avoid this psychologization, which is also why they were taken up by semiotics during the last third of the twentieth century.[52] Uexküll's epistemologically grounded methodology thus directly leads to the crux of the epistemology of surrounding(s) that shapes Umwelt theory. In the retrospection of his 1936 autobiography *Niegeschaute Welten* (Never-seen worlds), written at a time when he had long since withdrawn from the day-to-day business of the experimental scientist, Uexküll quite clearly describes his procedure as the subjective

52 See, for instance the special issue of the journal *Semiotica* (134/2001) devoted to Uexküll.

appropriation of the observer's inescapable standpoint: "Umwelt theory is a kind of externally displaced psychology [Seelenkunde] carried out from the observer's point of view."[53]

Contrary to this 1936 statement, Uexküll's 1909 introduction to his *Umwelt und Innenwelt der Tiere* presents a key assertion that still postulates an observer of the animal's Umwelt who can recognize the surrounding that exists outside of it as such: "Of course, it is not difficult to observe any animal in its surrounding. But this by no means solves the challenge. The experimenter must seek to determine what parts of the surrounding affect the animal and in what form this occurs."[54] This assertion has three major implications in terms of what has been argued so far:

First, Uexküll introduces an experimental observer who is capable of observing the surrounding beyond his individual Umwelt without interacting with it and thereby making it into his own Umwelt. Uexküll's methods enable this 1909 observer to step out of his own Umwelt and thus objectively observe how an animal is "fitted into" its surrounding and what is or is not part of the animal's Umwelt.

Second, this introduction of the observer allows Uexküll to provide guidance for the tasks of the biologist. Uexküll's observer has access to precisely the objective gaze that supposedly makes science possible. It is only this objectivity that allows him to rise above the multiplicity of Umwelten and methodically examine the Umwelten of animals from the elevated standpoint of science. Uexküll is accordingly able to write elsewhere: "The life of an animal remains unknown to us until we have walked our way around all of its functional cycles, because is it only then that the animal stands before us in the midst of its Umwelt as a meaningful whole."[55] This instruction to walk around an animal's

53 Jakob von Uexküll, *Niegeschaute Welten*: *Die Umwelten meiner Freunde; Ein Erinnerungsbuch* (Berlin: Fischer, 1936), 25.

54 Uexküll, *Umwelt und Innenwelt der Tiere*, 23.

55 Uexküll, "Biologie in der Mausefalle," 218.

functional cycles presupposes that these can be observed from the outside without the observer becoming part of them. In cases where the diversity and nesting of Umwelten threaten to make comparison and experimentation impossible, this external viewpoint also secures the place of scientific knowledge. If there were only a multiplicity of Umwelten and no access to their surrounding, it would hardly be possible to scientifically examine living entities in their Umwelt or identify their receptor cues and effector cues in the way that Uexküll envisions as a method and an ideal. That is to say: perspectivism's boundary represents, for Uexküll, the beginning of objective science.

Before turning to the *third* implication, it is instructive to look at Uexküll's experimental practices, to the extent they can be reconstructed from his writings.[56]

8. The Umwelt as Laboratory

As Christina Wessely has shown, Uexküll carried out extensive and circumstantial experimental research at the turn of the century, which has tended to be obscured and rendered invisible by the exceptionally clear narratives of the books he wrote for a wider public. In his most prolific period as an experimenter and anatomist during the first two decades of the twentieth century, he followed the aquarists' practice of designing milieus that made it possible for marine organisms to survive in an artificial setting on land. This required, Wessely writes, that "milieus [Umgebungen] . . . be studied very carefully in order for conclusions to be drawn after the systematic modification of individual elements."[57] Wessely argues that the artificial milieu of

56 On Uexküll's experimental practice, see also Astrid Schwarz, "Baron Jakob von Uexküll: Das Experiment als Ordnungsprinzip in der Biologie," in *Das bunte Gewand der Theorie: Vierzehn Begegnungen mit philosophierenden Forschern*, ed. Astrid Schwarz and Alfred Nordmann (Freiburg: Alber, 2009).

57 Christina Wessely, "Watery Milieus: Marine Biology, Aquariums, and the Limits of Ecological Knowledge circa 1900," trans. Nathan Stobagh, *Grey Room* 75 (Spring 2019): 141. The published English translation of Wessely's

the aquarium is thus closely related to the emergence of ecology: Aquariums not only provided observable settings in which living entities could live or die, they also made it possible to control these creatures through their dependence on their surrounding. The figure of the observer is also particularly salient in this research: he stands on the other side of the glass pane, observing the interaction of a surrounding and a living entity from the outside, but he can also intervene and modify the situation, changing the surrounding to suit his interests in order to identify receptor cues and effector cues. What distinguishes the knowledge of a surrounding constituted by an aquarium is that what is surrounded can only be investigated by means of what surrounds it, and vice versa, which makes it necessary to comprehend their mutually entangled relations of regulation and reciprocity. It is in this sense that Uexküll's research can be understood as ecological, even if he would never have called it this himself.

At various stages of his career, in laboratories in Heidelberg, Naples, and Hamburg, Uexküll transferred living entities into a reduced surrounding in this way in order to relate the individual to isolated objects of its receptor world. As Uexküll demonstrates in many of his examples, scientific procedure consists for him in dissecting and isolating. Corresponding to the modern understanding of science, synthesis as the analysis of an animal's building plan and of its organization is only the next step. Uexküll does not believe that an animal's building plan can be grasped by dissecting and isolating individual elements. But he does see these steps as necessary for reaching a position from where it is possible at all to translate an Umwelt into scientific knowledge. What this method is after, however, is not only the composition

article uses "milieu" for the "Umgebungen" of the original German version. For the passage in German, see "Wässrige Milieus: Ökologische Perspektiven in Meeresbiologie und Aquarienkunde um 1900," *Berichte zur Wissenschaftsgeschichte* 36, no. 2 (2013): 141. On this point, see also Mareike Vennen, *Das Aquarium: Praktiken, Techniken und Medien der Wissensproduktion* (Göttingen: Wallstein, 2018).

of each animal's respective Umwelt, but the Planmäßigkeit of nature:

> The task of biology, in addition to the study of individual functions, is therefore also to become familiar with the plan according to which the individual functions of the parts come together to form the total function of the whole. This is called the study of the functional plan or building plan of organisms.[58]

For Uexküll, as Gregor Schmieg has pointed out, the building plan is both a "physiological structural principle of the individual organism" and a "space of action for the concrete manifestation of the organism" in the "order of living nature."[59] Uexküll's methodology attempts to take both of these aspects into account.

The artificial surrounding of the laboratory does make it possible for Uexküll to investigate a living entity in its surrounding, rather than detached from it. But Uexküll's scientific methodology is to dissect the characteristics of the living entity and then to examine their interrelationship with the preselected conditions of this tightly controlled laboratory surrounding via the "workaround of exploring the marks carrying significance for the animal [its 'Bedeutungsträger']."[60] Uexküll's experiments are thus less concerned with the holistic view he foregrounds in his texts than with rationalistic isolation and dissection by means of anatomical studies of sensory and locomotor organs. Furthermore, as Katja

58 Jakob von Uexküll, "Die neuen Fragen in der experimentellen Biologie," *Rivista di Scienza* 4 (1908): 80.

59 Gregor Schmieg, "Die Systematik der Umwelt: Leben, Reiz und Reaktion bei Uexküll und Plessner," in *Das Leben im Menschen oder der Mensch im Leben? Deutsch-französische Genealogien zwischen Anthropologie und Anti-Humanismus*, ed. Thomas Ebke and Caterina Zanfi (Potsdam: Universitätsverlag Potsdam, 2017), 360.

60 Jakob von Uexküll, "Die Bedeutung der Umweltforschung für die Erkenntnis des Lebens," *Zeitschrift für die gesamte Naturwissenschaft* 1 (1935/36): 272.

 Kynast and Inga Pollmann have shown,[61] Uexküll employed the methods of chronophotography (as early as 1900) and cinematography (beginning somewhat later) in order to explore an animal's Umwelt by manipulating its time axis independently of human perception.[62] Uexküll used these different methods to gradually identify the receptor cues and effector cues comprising the Umwelt he was studying. In the case of the tick, arguably Uexküll's most influential example from his *Foray*, three receptor cues and effector cues suffice to characterize its Umwelt: heat, butyric acid, and the mechanical stimulus of the host animal's skin surface. These three elements, Uexküll argues, are enough to extrapolate the Umwelt of the tick. However, studying an Umwelt not only entails identifying receptor cues and effector cues. Insofar as this biology is concerned with the study of Planmäßigkeit, it presupposes the existence, in the Umwelten it investigates, of precisely what it aims to study:

> All that we can ascertain is an incredibly rich fabric of overlapping and interfitted subjective Umwelten. This fabric of Umwelten is governed by a Planmäßigkeit that is beyond all doubt, which we encounter at every turn once we have learned to pay attention to biological relationships.[63]

9. The Guide Dog

Returning to the quote from Uexküll cited above, its *third* and final implication is the existence of a surrounding that encompasses all Umwelten. It may be that there is a multitude of

61 Katja Kynast has argued that the contouring of Uexküll's subject is closely linked to cinematographic metaphors. See Katja Kynast, "Kinematografie als Medium der Umweltforschung Jakob von Uexkülls," *Kunsttexte.de* 4 (2010): 1-12. On Uexküll's use of media metaphors, see Julian Jochmaring, "Im gläsernen Gehäuse."

62 Inga Pollmann, "Invisible Worlds, Visible: Uexküll's Umwelt, Film, and Film Theory," *Critical Inquiry* 39, no. 3 (2013): 798.

63 Uexküll, "Die Bedeutung der Umweltforschung für die Erkenntnis des Lebens," 269.

equally legitimate Umwelten inhabited by different living entities, but Uexküll's statement also posits an objective surrounding that encompasses all of them, to which the scientist alone has access via his research. The scientist is able to recognize objects that are present in different Umwelten as receptor cue carriers and then to isolate these objects and dissect them in order to identify the specific receptor cues they carry so as to enable a synthesis. The tension between the spatial surrounding and the subjective Umwelt clearly emerges here: although the qualities of sensation necessarily remain beyond the access of the scientist, an Umwelt appears as a component of a surrounding that is defined by its relation to a particular living entity, from which it is then extracted by the observer according to the living entity's building plan.

> In order to investigate the subject of the animal in that part of the external world to which it alone relates, and which I call its 'Umwelt,' the biologist has at his disposal both the physical factors of the external world and the physiological factors of the animal's body; he must dispense with the psychological factor.[64]

The psychological inaccessibility of alien Umwelten—the impossibility of putting oneself in an animal's place and knowing the world with its sensory organs—does not mean that this Umwelt cannot be studied by other methods. The degree to which Umwelten can be investigated depends on their Planmäßigkeit, that is to say, on the predetermined order that structures them. But this assumption also renders fragile the distinction between Umwelt and surrounding for the scientific observer: on the one hand, it is maintained as an epistemological barrier, and on the other, it is overcome experimentally.

64 Jakob von Uexküll, "Biologische Briefe an eine Dame, Brief 4–12," *Deutsche Rundschau*, no. 179 (1919): 144. "The building plan of every living entity is expressed not only in the structure of its body, but also in the relations of the body to the world around it." See Uexküll, *Umwelt und Innenwelt der Tiere*, 4.

All this becomes particularly clear in Uexküll's work on guide dogs from the 1930s.[65] Uexküll's premise here is that a guide dog must not only move through its innate Umwelt—it must also avoid those obstacles that could be dangerous to the blind person but which are not part of the canine Umwelt that is its own. Even before Uexküll began researching guide dogs, dogs in general had caught his interest because their territory-marking behavior is accessible to humans and thus offers insight into their receptor world. In his 1931 essay *Das Duftfeld des Hundes* (The olfactory field of dogs), coauthored with Emmanuel G. Sarris, Uexküll explains how the "relationship of the dog to the cornerstone" on a map of the Hamburg Zoological Garden can be used to reconstruct the Umwelt of four dogs that Uexküll was able examine by analyzing the frequency with which they urinated at specific locations in relation to the presence of other dogs.[66] In the experiment, Uexküll used wooden blocks functioning as moving receptor signs (*Merkzeichen*) for the dog. The aim of this empirical study, he writes, is to clarify "the subjective toning ('Ich-Tönung') of the dog's worlds" that they used to declare everything in their territory as belonging to them.[67]

The practical dimension within such applications of Umwelt theory becomes clear when Uexküll presents the training of guide dogs as a philosophical problem in which the deep abyss between Umwelten must be overcome: as part of its training, a guide dog must add to its own Umwelten a number of receptor cues that are significant for the blind person and then coordinate them with its own effector world. The texts that Uexküll publishes in this context deal with the necessary practical crossings

65 Since Katja Kynast has examined this research in detail, I am focusing here on just one aspect. See Katja Kynast, "Personalerweiterung: Gefüge von Menschen, Phantomen und Hunden in der Blindenführhundausbildung nach Jakob von Uexküll und Emanuel Sarris," in *Animal Encounters: Kontakt, Interaktion und Relationalität*, ed. Alexandra Böhm and Jessica Ullrich (Berlin: Metzler, 2019), 323–42.

66 Uexküll and Sarris, "Das Duftfeld des Hundes," 53.

67 Ibid., 68.

between Umwelten that occur not through a merging of subjectivities, but through detailed instructions for controlling effector cues and receptor cues. Not only must the dog be trained to behave in a certain way, but its Umwelt must be imprinted with receptor signs that are not part of the original canine Umwelt. The dog must then carry these conditions into the Umwelt of the blind person.

> In the dog world there are only dog things, in the dragonfly world there are only dragonfly things, and in the human world there are only human things. And even more radically: Mr. Schulz will only come into contact with Schulz things, and not with Meyer things; conversely, Meyer will never come into contact with Schulz things. Each person must build his world around himself with the help of the lens provided by his senses.[68]

As Uexküll describes it, obstacles are imprinted upon the guide dog during training that are not part of the dog's Umwelt, and that can be seen only by the trainer and not by the blind person. Uexküll calls for trainers to incorporate into their training the overlap of the dog's Umwelt with that of the blind person, in order to teach the dog to be independent in its modified Umwelt.[69] Uexküll gives practical instructions for achieving this goal by suggesting a special training wagon in the size of a human being that is to be pulled by the dog.[70] This would allow the dog's receptor world to be extended to that of human beings—or as Stefan Rieger writes, for "human things to become dog things"[71]—through the direct effect of collisions on the movements of the

68 Jakob von Uexküll, "Zum Verständnis der Umweltlehre," *Deutsche Rundschau* 256, no. 7 (1938): 64.

69 See Uexküll and Sarris, "Das Duftfeld des Hundes."

70 See Jakob von Uexküll and Emmanuel G. Sarris, "Dressur und Erziehung der Führhunde für Blinde," *Der Kriegsblinde* 16, no. 6 (1932): 93–94.

71 See also Stefan Rieger, "Bipersonalität: Menschenversuche an den Rändern des Sozialen," in *Kulturgeschichte des Menschenversuchs im 20. Jahrhundert*, ed. Birgit Griesecke et al. (Frankfurt am Main: Suhrkamp, 2009), 196.

 dog. These considerations make clear that the determination envisioned by Uexküll presupposes precisely the overlapping of both worlds that it means to uncover, and thus that both can be observed as a surrounding, that is to say, from the perspective of a higher point of view.

10. The Metaphysics of Planmäßigkeit

For Uexküll's observer, the Umwelt in this sense is surrounded by a surrounding that is itself not surrounded, but is rather the site for external observation. If a surrounding were surrounded, it would be an Umwelt that would not allow the observation of other Umwelten because it would necessarily be perspectival. Uexküll's assumption of an unsurrounded surrounding is precisely what makes it so important for him to establish the observability of Umwelten from the standpoint of the surrounding, and this enables him to account for the difference between the subjectively produced Umwelt and a spatial surrounding that is independent of the subject. But with this distinction, he then also generates the problem of having to clarify how a subject can grasp this surrounding.

In the passages quoted above, Uexküll thus postulates a surrounding of all Umwelten, an idea he had denied in *Theoretical Biology*, from which the Umwelten of animals are accessible to the scientific observer via the study of effector cues and receptor cues. This assumption of a surrounding of all Umwelten has a unifying function within his theory because it captures the diversity of Umwelten without postulating that their subjective quality is accessible. Even if this barrier remains, the surrounding—precisely in the sense of the ancient *periechon*—ensures that all Umwelten have their place, even when they themselves do not indicate spatial relations. Their diversity, as can be seen from Uexküll's *Foray*, is organized by a unity that provides a meaningful framework to the Umwelten, which exist independently of their surrounding:

> The role Nature plays as an object in the various environments [Umwelten] of natural scientists is highly contradictory. If one wanted to sum up its objective characteristics, only chaos would result. And yet, all these different environments [Umwelten] are fostered and borne along by the One that is inaccessible to all environments [Umwelten] forever. Forever unknowable behind all of the worlds it produces, the subject—Nature—conceals itself.[72]

Uexküll's science is ultimately concerned with knowing this nature that is conceived as a subject. Uexküll describes it as the order behind all phenomena and thus as the principle that gives all Umwelten their place. It is unknowable and therefore not an object but a subject. Knowledge of nature is possible because the building plan of the animals he means to investigate follows a Planmäßigkeit that makes nature itself accessible to knowledge: "The central subject is replaced by a plan that connects and governs all subjects."[73] The building plan of all living entities is a "purposive connection" of the relations between living entities and Umwelten, which gives each part its place in the whole.[74] Every living entity is "fitted into" its world from the very start. Evolution is unnecessary. Uexküll's assumption of Planmäßigkeit is also a criticism of Darwinism, because it sees an Umwelt and a living entity as necessarily being "fitted into" each other, which means that they do not need to adapt. An observer can accordingly marvel at the

> seamless harmony between the organization of bodies and the Umwelt. Nothing is left to chance—everything fits together. The Umwelt's sun is matched to the measure of the eye, and the living entity's eye is matched to the measure of its world's sun. . . . A supraspatial and supratemporal

72 Uexküll, *Foray*, 135.

73 Uexküll, "Wie sehen wir die Natur und wie sieht die Natur sich selber?," 316.

74 Uexküll, "Die Umwelt," 640.

> power carries, moves, and forms everything—namely, Planmäßigkeit.[75]

Since, in this monadological order, all subjects have their place and are "fitted in," Uexküll concludes that the multiplicity of building plans merges into the whole and thereby constitutes the subjectivity of nature itself. Uexküll alludes at this point, as previously demonstrated, to the harmony of nature postulated by Goethe, in which the nature of the eye corresponds to that of the sun precisely to enable it to see this source of light. The building plan, in this sense, "is an incomplete unity until the objects of the Umwelt are included in its consideration."[76] But this requires an observer to recognize the objects of the external world and to select, on the basis of experimental research, those that belong to the Umwelt of the animal: "This rest of the world forms our Umwelt."[77] For Uexküll, biology is first and foremost the science of the building plans of living entities and thus of their Planmäßigkeit.

The knowing, cognizing subject who would make its surrounding into an Umwelt is replaced by the subject of nature, evincing a Planmäßigkeit and unity that are the reasons why a multiplicity of Umwelten are related to a single surrounding. For Uexküll, the surrounding does not need a surrounding precisely because it is part of nature, which surrounds it. With this sublation of multiplicity into a singular nature encompassing all Umwelten, Uexküll thus allows multiplicity to merge into unity, taking the differences between inaccessible Umwelten and replacing them with nature as a subject. The Planmäßigkeit of nature, in which everything has its place, thereby makes it possible to move beyond the closedness of an Umwelt: "Only the knowledge that everything in Nature is created according to its meaning and that all environments [Umwelten] are composed into the world-score opens

75 Uexküll, "Biologische Briefe an eine Dame, Brief 4–12," 148.
76 Uexküll, "Die Umwelt," 641.
77 Ibid.

up a path leading out of the confines of one's own environment [Umwelt]."[78] Uexküll's Umwelt theory is unthinkable without this metaphysics of Planmäßigkeit.

In *Foray*'s discussion of Planmäßigkeit, there is a telling misspelling, unintended by Uexküll, that has crept into the text: In the original edition published by Julius Springer in 1934, the text speaks of the "subject Nature" as being "unerkennbar"—"unknowable" or "unrecognizable"; but in the later edition prepared for Rowohlt's Deutsche Enzyklopädie of 1956, with an introduction by Adolf Portmann, this reads with an added letter v as "unverkennbar"—i.e., "unmistakable."[79] The fact that Uexküll's sentence makes sense in both variants points to the concept of *Anschaulichkeit*, as the quality of being seeable, perceivable, or clearly intuitable, that was outlined in the previous chapter: the point of this concept for Uexküll is to render self-evident what is invisible. It also shows just how close these two assumptions are. The fact that the "subject Nature" is *unerkennbar*, unknowable or unrecognizable, is itself *erkennbar unverkennbar*, recognizably unmistakable. The building plan's orderly structure, one in which everything is "fitted into" everything else, testifies to the unquestionable harmony of nature—a harmony that remains inaccessible from the point of view of Umwelten, even though everything

78 Uexküll, *Foray*, 250. Benjamin Bühler has pointed out the rhetorical strategy by which Uexküll succeeds in generating "the phantasm of an organismic wholeness whose hypostasis opened the way to Umwelt theory." Benjamin Bühler, "Das Tier und die Experimentalisierung des Verhaltens: Zur Rhetorik der Umwelt-Lehre Jakob von Uexkülls," in *Wissen: Erzählen: Narrative der Humanwissenschaften*, ed. Arne Höcker, Jeannie Moser, and Philippe Weber (Bielefeld: Transcript, 2006), 49.

79 See Jakob von Uexküll and Georg Kriszat, *Streifzüge durch die Umwelten von Tieren und Menschen: Ein Bilderbuch unsichtbarer Welten* (Reinbek: Rowohlt, 1956), 101. Both the 1957 and 2010 English translations adhere to the earlier word "unerkennbar": Jakob von Uexküll, "A Stroll Through the Worlds of Animals and Men: A Picture Book of Invisible Worlds," in *Instinctive Behavior: The Development of a Modern Concept*, ed. Claire Schiller (New York: International Universities Press, 1957), 80: "eternally beyond the reach of knowledge"; and Uexküll, *Foray*, 135: "Forever unknowable."

 is part of its orderliness. In this sense, Umwelt theory is holistic: the whole gives the parts their place in the overall organization. As individual parts, they are isolated and without any effect. Only as part of the whole do they gain their meaning, in being attached to a fixed place. This structural conservatism, which draws equally from Uexküll's anti-Darwinism and from his political stance, is also rooted in Umwelt theory.

The Planmäßigkeit of nature as a subject that is *un/v/erkennbar* gives Umwelt theory a place within a harmonious philosophy of nature that strives toward universal unity: "Planmäßigkeit is the world-defining power that creates subjects."[80] As shown in the previous chapter, this position of the observer who is involved in what he observes, in the sense worked out in German-language biology by Goethe and Haeckel, implies the possibility of a universal connectedness. This includes not only all components of nature but also the unity of the observer with what he observes. In contrast, Uexküll's assumption of a subject-independent, unsurrounded surrounding suggests that this surrounding exists as a condition of all Umwelten, one that is subjective to itself but objective for others.

The supposedly subjective quality of the Umwelt according to Uexküll, in which every living entity, including the biologist, produces its own Umwelt, is thus counteracted by Uexküll's observer from 1909 who stands outside the Umwelt, as well as by the equally *unerkennbar* and *unverkennbar*, unknowable and unmistakable, assumption of a Planmäßigkeit of nature. Although Uexküll introduces a subjective observer at various points, it does not impinge upon the difference between Umwelt and surrounding. In the following quotation from *Foray* (reflecting Uexküll's 1934 thinking), this issue also emerges quite clearly: "There are thus purely subjective realities in environments [Umwelten]. But the objective realities of the surrounding [Umgebung] never appear as such in the environments

80 Uexküll, "Biologische Briefe an eine Dame, Brief 4–12," 281.

[Umwelten]."[81] Accordingly, there are objective realities even if they do not appear in the subjective Umwelten. The observer has access to these objective realities insofar as he operates outside of an Umwelt. In this passage, composed a quarter of a century after *Umwelt und Innenwelt der Tiere*, the surrounding in which a scientist observes the Umwelt of an animal reappears as the scientist's own Umwelt and hence as the possibility of accessing the surrounding. This closes the circle in which the subjectivity of the observer who makes the surroundings into an Umwelt in turn enables the exploration of other Umwelten. Yet the question still remains of how scientific knowledge could be possible. It is true that Uexküll's examples demonstrate in extenso the ways in which Umwelt remains, for him, a world a subject cannot transcend—the Umwelt of the tick remains inaccessible to human beings. And one can cite a number of passages from his work arguing for the multiplicity of Umwelten. The objective observability of the surrounding in Uexküll's books nonetheless remains a central pillar for the methodological foundation of his Umwelt theory. Uexküll does not need, for this theory, to assume an objective external world; in fact, he denies such a thing. But he does need to provide his theory with a methodical foundation and to structure it around the metaphysics of Planmäßigkeit. For him, the assumption of an external world is necessary for establishing the validity of scientific observation, one aimed at acquiring knowledge of the Planmäßigkeit of nature while also preventing this knowledge from being lost to an infinite perspectivism in which there is no fixed point of view. This kind of epistemological relativism makes sense for Uexküll only if its relativity is contained through its subordination to Planmäßigkeit.

Planmäßigkeit implies the assumption that each living entity has its place within the nesting of Umwelten. In this framework, changes—if even possible—can only happen in minute incremental steps, and they represent a danger to the stability of

81 Uexküll, *Foray*, 125, translation modified.

 the structure. Evolutionary adaptation, the variability of species, the historicity of positions, and social change are unthinkable in such a model. This is also reflected in Uexküll's attempt to extend his theories into politics with his book *Staatsbiologie*—which did so abstractly in the 1920 edition, but then concretely by praising Nazism in the 1933 edition. Here, the isolation of Umwelten from one another becomes the ordering principle underlying a state model based on Uexküll's theory, a principle that also underlies his pathologization of democratic culture. Uexküll's state organism draws its strength from the fact that everyone does just what they are meant to do; that they fulfill their function and do not leave their innate place. This is why Uexküll can easily transform this theory into a doctrine of the total state. Only when everyone performs their function can this state develop its full potential. In this model of order, as Leander Scholz has shown, the Planmäßigkeit of nature guarantees the stability of the state.[82] There is only one predetermined order, which remains stable as long as no individual deviates from their role. The "world-defining power" of Planmäßigkeit,[83] which in this epistemology of surrounding(s) gives everything surrounded its place and relates every part to the whole, is thus inseparable from Uexküll's extension of biology to politics. This is also the foundation for his attempts to ingratiate himself with Nazism.

11. The Unity of the Umwelt

The reception of Uexküll's writings has often ignored the metaphysics of Planmäßigkeit and the aporia of (the) surrounding(s), especially in recent attempts to open up Umwelt theory for emancipatory theorizing. In the process, these interpretations of Uexküll have at times lost sight of Umwelt theory's problematic aspects, which in turn has led them to ignore or

82 See Leander Scholz, "Karl August Möbius und die Politik der Lebensgemeinschaft," *Zeitschrift für Medien- und Kulturforschung* 7, no. 2 (2016): 206–20.

83 Uexküll, "Biologische Briefe an eine Dame, Brief 4–12," 281.

downplay Uexküll's political stance. However, his holism and his commitment to Nazism cannot be separated from each other, neither biographically nor theoretically.

Uexküll's recurring assertion of a multiplication of Umwelten in an "inscrutable abundance of overlapping and contradictory worlds"[84] is currently being claimed as a politically viable foundation for a range of theories that include a relational epistemology, a philosophy of multiplicity, a "pluralistic ontology,"[85] a "milieu of pure relationality and perspectivism,"[86] and an account of "multispecies relationships."[87] His rejection of a human-

84 Uexküll, *Theoretische Biologie*, 221.

85 Thorsten Rüting, "Ohne biologische Körper kein intelligentes Modell der Welt: Wissenschaftshistorische Betrachtungen zur Rezeption Jakob von Uexkülls und zur Kritik an der Entwicklung Künstlicher Intelligenz (KI)," in *Modelle*, ed. Ulrich Dirks and Eberhard Knobloch (Frankfurt am Main: Peter Lang, 2008), 265.

86 Leonie A. de Vries, "Political Life beyond the Biopolitical?" *Theoria* 60, no. 134 (2013): 61.

87 Sara A. Schroer, "Jakob von Uexküll: The Concept of Umwelt and its Potentials for an Anthropology Beyond the Human," *Ethnos* 6, no. 3 (2019): 2. Also see, for example, Tom Greaves, "A Silent Dance: Eco-Political Compositions after Uexküll's Environmental Biology," in *An [Un]Likely Alliance: Thinking Environment[s] with Deleuze|Guattari*, ed. Bernd Herzogenrath (Newcastle upon Tyne: Cambridge Scholars Publishing, 2008), 98–115. The multiplicity of Umwelten is taken as a starting point, for instance, in the following texts: Ian G. R. Shaw, John P. Jones, and Melinda K. Butterworth, "The Mosquito's Environment, or One Monster's Standpoint Ontology," *Geoforum* 48 (2013): 260–7; Stephen Loo and Undine Sellbach, "A Picture Book of Invisible Worlds: Semblances of Insects and Humans in Jakob von Uexküll's Laboratory," *Angelaki* 18, no. 1 (2013): 45–64; Thom van Dooren, *Flight Ways: Life and Loss at the Edge of Extinction* (New York: Princeton University Press, 2016), 67. Referring to the chapter "Magical Environments" ("Die magischen Umwelten") from *Foray*, Graham Harman has suggested that all attempts by a subject to reach beyond the limits of its Umwelt should be called magic. With this term, Harman argues, Uexküll means a "non-perceptual access to the world." See Graham Harman, "Magic Uexküll," in *Living Earth: Field Notes from the Dark Ecology Project 2014–2016*, ed. Mirna Belina (Amsterdam: Sonic Acts Press, 2016), 128. Why Harman ignores the notion of Planmäßigkeit, which Uexküll uses to explain behaviors that cannot be accounted for by the interplay of receptor cues and effector cues, remains unclear. Uexküll writes: "Now, in concluding, we have come upon the magical phenomenon of the

 centered perspective makes him an icon for a nondualistic world-view in which human and animal life forms stand side by side as equals.[88] Uexküll's work on the functional cycles of sea urchins, snails, and dogs, which takes these creatures seriously in their complexity, has unquestionably inspired these perspectives. And his "radical dehumanization of nature" has conversely served as a guide for abolishing the difference between humans and nonhumans.[89] As Geoffrey Winthrop-Young has shown, the plausibility of Uexküll's theory for posthumanism and for animal studies rests on its rejection of an elevated position for humans, a positioning that would be the very definition of humanism.[90] Winthrop-Young writes: "Animals are promoted by virtue of their human-like ability to construct their environment; humans are demoted by virtue of our animal-like inability to transcend our environment."[91] And in his book *The Open*, Giorgio Agamben, whose reading of Uexküll clearly does not extend beyond *Foray*, takes the aforementioned sentence in which Uexküll equates the animal's surrounding with the scientist's Umwelt as evidence of the fact that "in reality, the *Umgebung* is our own *Umwelt*, to which Uexküll does not attribute any particular privilege and which, as such, can also vary according to the point of view from which we

inborn path, which mocks any and all objectivity and yet intervenes in the environment [Umwelt] according to a plan [i.e. according to Planmäßigkeit]" (Uexküll, *Foray*, 125). Harman draws an analogy between Uexküll and object-oriented ontology, which pursues access to the external world through aesthetic and magical channels in a manner similar to Uexküll.

88 See, for example, Matthew Chrulew, "Reconstructing the Worlds of Wildlife: Uexküll, Hediger, and Beyond, *Biosemiotics* 13, no. 1 (2020): 137–49. The fact that this antianthropocentrism always remains committed to Uexküll's Kantianism has been pointed out by Julian Jochmaring; see Jochmaring, "Im gläsernen Gehäuse.'"

89 Giorgio Agamben, *The Open: Man and Animal* (Stanford: Suhrkamp, 2003), 45.

90 For an analysis of this kind of interpretation of Uexküll, see Jussi Parikka, *Insect Media: An Archaeology of Animals and Technology* (Minneapolis: University of Minnesota Press, 2010), 66; Buchanan, *Onto-Ethologies*; and Schroer, "Jakob von Uexküll."

91 Geoffrey Winthrop-Young, "Afterword," 222.

observe it."[92] Or take Bruno Latour, who states that there is no Umwelt encompassing all Umwelten:

> Being alive means not only adapting to but also modifying one's surroundings, or, to use Julius Von Uexküll's [sic] famous expression, there exists no general Umwelt (a term to which we will have to return) that could encompass the Umwelt of each organism.[93]

With both Agamben and Latour, a closer look at the sources reveals that these interpretations are insupportable. Though Uexküll does not in fact prioritize the human Umwelt in his *Foray*, even here the human observer has access, via the detour of the scientific method, to a surrounding that is the basis for a multiplicity of Umwelten. But what is more important in these two prominent examples is that Uexküll is used as a placeholder for a perspective that is actually at odds with the planned unity of all Umwelten—and also at odds with the resulting political consequences. With both of these texts, it becomes impossible to see the problematic aspects of Umwelt theory: indeed, Agamben declares Uexküll's political entanglements to be trivial.

In all of the commentaries cited so far, Uexküll's name is used to affirm a multiplicity and relativity of all Umwelten. But upon closer examination, this is only one side of the coin. Even where Uexküll emphasizes multiplicity, his solution to the aporia of (the) surroundings(s) is unity, not multiplicity. The "multispecies relationships" being described today with recourse to Uexküll are something entirely different from the ethnonational order determined by Planmäßigkeit as outlined in Uexküll's worldview.[94] It is possible to derive from Uexküll's works an infinite perspectivism leading to a multiplicity of worlds. This nevertheless

92 Agamben, *The Open*, 40–41.

93 Bruno Latour, "Gifford Lectures: Facing Gaia—Six Lectures on the Political Theology of Nature," last accessed November 24, 2013, http://www.bruno-latour.fr/sites/default/files/downloads/GIFFORD-ASSEMBLED.pdf, 67.

94 Schroer, "Jakob von Uexküll," 2.

 remains entirely outside the ambit of his thought, inasmuch as Planmäßigkeit reintegrates all diversity back into unity. The interplay of the relation between the surrounded and the surrounding in the "inscrutable abundance of overlapping and contradictory worlds" remains, for him, the central object of research.[95] But this is only possible from the elevated perspective of a biologist whose position as an observer is removed from any feedback loop with the observation. This is what allows the multiplicity and unity of Umwelten to coexist in contradiction.

Uexküll's theory is thus not compatible with constructivist theories—or if it is, then only to a very limited extent, because he does posit the existence of a single, all-encompassing and unifying surrounding, quite to the contrary of what Agamben or Latour suggest. He invokes an absolute limit secured by the objective gaze of the scientist and a Planmäßigkeit of nature in which the cognizing, the knowing of Umwelten follows a given template. As a consequence, both a relationality and mixing of Umwelten are incompatible with Uexküll's structural conservatism, even though he himself emphasizes the diversity of Umwelten. Yet different Umwelten are precisely *not* of equal importance, because there is no subject freed from accepting, and thus imposing, the absolute priority of its own Umwelt.

By combining the diversity of Umwelten with the structural conservatism of Umwelt theory, Uexküll is thus able to take a position in favor of diversity with a gesture that appears magnanimous, while at the same time excluding all Umwelten that for him have no place in the state organism. This is also what allows Uexküll to stand by his Jewish friends and pay the highest respect to the achievements of Judaism, while at the same time cultivating an antisemitism of placelessness. For Uexküll, then, the plurality of Umwelten always has this flip side: while everyone has their own Umwelt, not everyone has the right to live this Umwelt at the place where they currently are—especially not in

95 Uexküll, *Theoretische Biologie*, 221.

Germany. Uexküll can affirm the diversity of Umwelten while also denying that they are in the right place—with clear consequences that emerge beginning in 1933, the year of Hitler's takeover.

The aporia of (the) surrounding(s) is entangled with structural conservatism—and for this reason, no reading of Uexküll should separate his theoretical work from his commitment to Nazism, or rather what he hoped that Nazism would accomplish. Beyond any political concerns, however, it is also important to maintain the aporia of (the) surrounding(s) as an aporia, and to neither smooth it out nor prioritize one side over the other. This is the only way to make clear the fault lines within his Umwelt theory. If one decides for the pure multiplicity of Umwelten, for their relativity and inaccessibility, one loses sight of the metaphysics of the building plan, the holism of Planmäßigkeit, and thus the deeply conservative assumption of a planned harmony of nature resistant to any change—not only of living entities, but also of culture and society. The deconstruction of the metaphysical assumptions underlying Umwelt theory that has been proposed here, by contrast, clarifies the theory's architecture and uncovers its foundations. And today, it is precisely these foundations that are being used once again as the building plan, the blueprint or guide, for a right-wing worldview.

[5]

Conclusion: Politics and the Future of Umwelt Theory

Gottfried Schnödl and Florian Sprenger

As the three chapters of this book have shown, Uexküll's Umwelt theory cannot be separated from the problematic premises of its underlying holistic metaphysics any more than it can be extricated from the historical constellations in which it arose and into which it flowed in 1933, the year of Hitler's takeover. Its structural conservatism and identitarian logic are not historical aberrations that can simply be ignored; they are instead embedded in its very foundations.

What many readings of Uexküll today see as an emancipatory decentering of the anthropos, a relativization of all places, and an unhierarchical arrangement of autonomous individuals, also proves to be a rejection of any change (whether evolutionary, social, or historical) and thus to be highly compatible with right-wing positions—both old and new. In Uexküll's framework, it is precisely because every Umwelt is self-sufficient and autonomous on a microlevel that it can be subsumed into an already given order on a macrolevel as a completely dependent part of it. This allowed his theory to become a theory of the organic "total state," a concept that underpinned Uexküll's 1934 participation in

Nazism's attempts to define a legal philosophy of its own. This is also why Uexküll's opposition to democracy and his antisemitism cannot be detached from his Umwelt theory and should instead be critically investigated in their twofold trajectory, with a tolerant gesture toward Umwelt pluralism on the one hand and a rhetoric of placelessness and parasitism on the other.

From this, it follows that Uexküll's work is not riven by a fissure and that the attempted separation of a progressive side from a problematic side is in itself problematic. The two sides do not diverge from one another—and so they should not be separated in order for one side to be further developed on its own. Despite all its internal contradictions, Uexküll's work contains—as this book has shown—an essentially closed doctrine in which the "biology of the state" and its attendant political implications are the complement of his "forays" and his openness to a multiplicity of worlds. If one side is split away and carried forward, the other side does not simply wither from neglect but is implicitly carried along as well. The progressive side and the conservative-to-fascist side are not mutually exclusive: on the contrary, Uexküll is a good example of how they can be combined in an at least somewhat logically consistent manner. There are both explicit and implicit connections between Umwelt theory and New Right, ethnonationalist, and racist identitarian ecologies, a fact that justifies the former's current topicality.

This close relationship is the spur that motivated our investigation, a call to keep looking back at the history of ecology with a fresh perspective. We have consequently focused on the how Umwelt self-sufficiency and autonomy are entangled with Umwelt multiplicity while also looking at how geographic rootedness and placelessness relate to the overarching Planmäßigkeit of a nature understood in subjective terms. What the analysis shows is that Uexküll's biocentrism involves not only a decentralized expansion of a solipsism that exists according to Planmäßigkeit, but also an anthropocentric narrowing or privation of the same. The geographic rootedness of this solipsistic subject and the placelessness of the "other" are both effects of the structural conservatism that permeates Umwelt theory and that makes it highly compatible with the ideology of "blood and soil."

However, the evidence of Uexküll's involvement in Nazism should not lead one to abandon his work (and its reception) as an object of study. Instead, taking a fresh look at Uexküll's work can prove to be highly worthwhile (and virtually indispensable for politically understanding right-wing usage of his ideas) while also reminding us how ecology and its attendant fields have always represented arenas of political action—and continue to do so. Investigators guided by this understanding are faced with the task not only of describing the past anew, but also of reconstructing the lines of connection that extend into the present day. Holistic thinking is not necessarily fascist, but it can well be used in a fascist way and grows better in this type of political environment than anywhere else. In order to take a position regarding recent instrumentalizations of ecological thought, it is important to acknowledge that ecology is not inherently left-wing in itself. This is the only way that tomorrow's scholars of ecology can arm themselves against the ghosts of their own history.

Despite these complications, it is certainly possible to be inspired by Uexküll's detailed comparisons of different Umwelten while still rejecting his political stance. However, the more affirmative readings of Uexküll, even ones that stick to the unproblematic aspects of his theory while pushing aside the politically problematic ones, do little in terms of tackling the political challenge that his Umwelt theory represents. In order to address this, future investigations of ecological thought by scholars in cultural studies and the history of knowledge should take seriously the past and present entanglements of holism and right-wing ideology while also advancing this as a topic of discussion. This entanglement is not a situation from which Umwelt theory needs to be rescued, but something that should be critically investigated. Instead of being set aside, it should be read once again with fresh eyes, differently than before.

Jakob Johann von Uexküll: Biographical Overview

1864	Born on an estate in Keblas (today Estonia)
1884	Study of zoology at the University of Dorpat
1888	Moves to Heidelberg, studies physiology
1899–1900	Study visit to Dar es Salaam (East Africa)
1903	Marriage to Gudrun von Schwerin
1905	*Leitfaden in das Studium der experimentellen Biologie der Wassertiere* (*Guide to the study of the experimental biology of aquatic animals*)
1907	Awarded an honorary doctorate by the Heidelberg Medical Faculty
1909	*Umwelt und Innenwelt der Tiere* (*Umwelt and the inner world of animals*)
1917	Loss of all property in Estonia following the expropriation of aristocratic estates
1918	Becomes a German citizen
1919	*Biologische Briefe an eine Dame* (*Biological letters to a lady*)
1920	*Theoretische Biologie* (published in English in 1926 as *Theoretical Biology*) and *Staatsbiologie: Anatomie – Physiologie – Pathologie des Staates* (*State biology: anatomy, physiology, and pathology of the state*)
1924	Research assistant at the Medical Faculty of the University of Hamburg

1925–1940	Director of the Institut für Umweltforschung (Institute for Umwelt Research), University of Hamburg
1928	*Natur und Leben* (*Nature and life*)
1932	Member of the German Academy of Sciences Leopoldina
1933	Signing of the *Bekenntnisses der deutschen Professoren zu Adolf Hitler*, (published in English as the *Vow of Allegiance of the Professors of the German Universities and High-Schools [sic., Institutions of Higher Education] to Adolf Hitler and the National Socialistic State*). 2nd edition of *Staatsbiologie* (*State biology*).
1934	Honorary doctorate from the Faculty of Philosophy at Kiel University
May 3, 1934	Opening of the Committee for Legal Philosophy within the Academy for German Law in Weimar
May 26, 1934	Second meeting of the Committee for Legal Philosophy, Berlin
1936	*Niegeschaute Welten - Die Umwelten meiner Freunde* (*Worlds never seen: the Umwelten of my friends*), honorary doctorate in scientific natural history from the University of Utrecht
1940	*Bedeutungslehre* (*Theory of meaning*), retirement, move to Capri (Italy)
1944	Death on Capri

Bibliography

Adorno, Theodor W. "Spengler nach dem Untergang." *Der Monat* 20 (1950): 115–28.

Agamben, Giorgio. *The Open: Man and Animal*. Stanford, CA: Stanford University Press, 2004.

Allen, Garland E. "Mechanism, Vitalism and Organicism in Late Nineteenth and Twentieth-Century Biology: The Importance of Historical Context." *Studies in History and Philosophy of Science Part C: Studies in History and Philosophy of Biological and Biomedical Sciences* 36, no. 2 (2005): 261–83.

Alverdes, Friedrich. "Organizismus und Holismus." *Der Biologe* 5, no. 4 (1936): 121–28.

Amidon, Kevin S. "Adolf Meyer-Abich, Holism, and the Negotiation of Theoretical Biology." *Biological Theory* 3, no. 4 (2008): 357–70.

Amrine, Frederick. "The Music of the Organism: Uexküll, Merleau-Ponty, Zuckerkandl, and Deleuze as Goethean Ecologists in Search of a New Paradigm." *Goethe Yearbook* 22 (2015): 45–72.

Anderson, Dennis L. *The Academy for German Law: 1933–1944*. New York: Taylor & Francis, 1987.

Anonym. "Niederschrift für die Sitzung vom 3.5.1934." In *Akademie für Deutsches Recht, 1933–1945. Protokolle der Ausschüsse: Weitere Nachträge (1934–1939)*. Vol. XXIII, edited by Werner Schubert, 45-6. Berlin: De Gruyter, 2019.

———. "Thüringische Staatszeitung vom 4.5.1934." In *Akademie für Deutsches Recht, 1933-1945. Protokolle der Ausschüsse: Weitere Nachträge (1934–1939)*. Vol. XXIII, edited by Werner Schubert, 53-6. Berlin: De Gruyter, 2019.

Aristotle. *Physics*. Translated by Jonathan Barnes. *The Complete Works of Aristotle*. Vol. 1. Princeton: Princeton University Press, 1991.

Ash, Mitchell G. *Gestalt Psychology in German culture, 1890–1967: Holism and the Quest for Objectivity*. Cambridge: Cambridge University Press, 2007.

Bassin, Mark. "Blood or Soil? The Völkisch Movement, the Nazis, and the Legacy of Geopolitik." In *How Green were the Nazis? Nature, Environment, and Nation in the Third Reich*, edited by Franz-Josef Brüggemeier, Mark Cioc, and Thomas Zeller, 204–42. Athens: Ohio University Press, 2005.

Bauch, Jost, "Gibt es eine konservative Ökologie?" *Herbert-Gruhl-Gesellschaft*. Last accessed October 10, 2020. http://herbert-gruhl.de/gibt-es-eine-konservative-oekologie/.

Bäumer, Änne. *NS-Biologie*. Stuttgart: S. Hirzel, 1990.

Beever, Jonathan and Morten Tønnessen. "'Darwin und die englische Moral': The Moral Consequences of Uexküll's Umwelt Theory." *Biosemiotics* 6, no. 3 (2013): 437–47.

Behrens, Kilian, Vera Henßler, Ulli Jentsch, Jessica Kieck, Frank Metzger, Eike Sanders, and Patrick Schwarz, "Ökologie von rechts – Teil 1." *Antifaschistisches Pressearchiv und Bildungszentrum*. Last accessed 8, 2020. https://www.apabiz.de/2019/oekologie-von-rechts-teil-1/.

Bein, Alexander. "'Der jüdische Parasit': Bemerkungen zur Semantik der Judenfrage." *Vierteljahreshefte zur Zeitgeschichte* 13, no. 2 (1965): 121–49.

Beleites, Michael. *Umweltresonanz: Grandzüge einer organismischen Biologie*. Treuenbriezen: Telesma, 2014.

Beleites, Michael. "Wir haben gelernt: Sachsen 2030 – Ein Zukunftsmanifest." *Tumult* Frühjahr (2014): 90–2.

———. "Vorwort." In Sebastian Hennig. *PEGIDA. Spaziergänge über den Horizont*. Neustadt: Arnshaugk Verlag, 2015: 11–22.

———. "Die menschengemachte Überhitzung: Zur Entropie der Industriegesellschaft." *Die Kehre*, no. 1 (2020): 7–13.

Bennett, Jane. *Vibrant Matter: A Political Ecology of Things*. Durham, NC: Duke University Press, 2010.

Benoist, Alain de. *Mein Leben: Wege eines Denkens*. Berlin: JF Edition, 2014.

———. *View from the Right. Volume 1: Heritage and Ideas*. London: Arkos, 2017.

———. *View from the Right. Volume 2: Systems and Debates*. London: Arkos, 2018.

Bensch, Margit. "Blut und Boden: Welche Natur bestimmt den Rassismus." In *Landschaftsentwicklung und Umweltforschung*, edited by Stefan Körner et al., 37–51. Berlin: Schriftenreihe im Fachbereich Umwelt und Gesellschaft, TU Berlin, 1999.

———. *Rassismus als kulturelle Entwicklungstheorie: Formen biologischen Denkens im Sozialdarwinismus*. Dissertation, TU Berlin, 2009.

Berz, Peter. "Contenant Contenu: Anordnungen des Enthaltens." In *Das Motiv der Kästchenwahl: Container in Psychoanalyse, Kunst, Kultur*, edited by Insa Härtel and Olaf Knellessen, 133–54. Göttingen: Vandenhoeck & Ruprecht, 2012.

Bhatt Chetan. "White Extinction: Metaphysical Elements of Contemporary Western Fascism." *Theory, Culture & Society* 38, no. 1 (2021): 27–52.

Biehl, Janet, and Peter Staudenmaier. *Ecofascism Revisited: Lessons from the German Experience*. Porsgrunn: New Compass Press, [1995] 2011.

Bierl, Peter. *Grüne Braune: Umwelt-, Tier- und Heimatschutz von Rechts*. Münster: Unrast, 2010.

Block, Katharina. *Von der Umwelt zur Welt: Der Weltbegriff in der Umweltsoziologie*. Bielefeld: Transcript, 2015.

Blumenberg, Hans. *Quellen*. Edited by Ulrich von Bülow and Dorit Krusche. Marbach am Neckar: Deutsche Schillergesellschaft, 2009.

Bogner, Thomas. "Zur Bedeutung von Ernst Rudorff für den Diskurs über Eigenart im Naturschutzdiskurs." In *Projektionsfläche Natur: Zum Zusammenhang von Naturbildern und gesellschaftlichen Verhältnissen*, edited by Ludwig Fischer, 105–34. Hamburg: Hamburg University Press, 2004.

Böhnigk, Volker. "Die nationalsozialistische Kulturphilosophie Erich Rothackers." In *Philosophie im Nationalsozialismus*, edited by Hans J. Sandkühler, 191–218. Hamburg: Meiner, 2009.

Bölsche, Wilhelm. *Stirb und Werde! Naturwissenschaftliche and kulturelle Plaudereien*. Jena: Diederichs, 1913.

———. *Die naturwissenschaftlichen Grandlagen der Poesie: Prolegomena einer realistischen Ästhetik*. Leipzig: Carl Reissner, 1887.

Borck, Cornelius. "Hans Blumenberg: The Transformation of Uexküll's Bioepistemology into Phenomenology." In *Jakob von Uexküll and Philosophy: Life,*

Environments, Anthropology, edited by Kristian Köchy and Francesca Michelini, 188–204. London: Routledge, 2020.

Borrmann, Norbert. "Ökologie ist rechts." *Sezession*, no. 56 (2013): 4–7.

Boterman, Frits. *Oswald Spengler und sein "Untergang des Abendlandes."* Cologne: S.H.-Verlag, 2000.

Bowler, Peter. *The Eclipse of Darwinism. Anti-Darwinian Evolution Theories in the Decades around 1900*. Baltimore, MD: John Hopkins University Press, 1983.

———. *The Non-Darwinian Revolution. Reinterpreting a Historical Myth*. Baltimore, MD: John Hopkins University Press, 1988.

Bramwell, Anna. *Blood and Soil: Richard Walther Darré and Hitler's Green Party*. Abbotsbrook: Kensal Press, 1985.

Brauckmann, Sabine. "From the Haptic-Optic Space to our Environment: Jakob von Uexküll and Richard Woltereck." *Semiotica* 134, no. 1/4 (2001): 293–309.

Breidbach, Olaf. "Blumenbachs Vorfeld und Umfeld – Wolff und Goethe und auch etwas Hegel." In *Wissenschaft und Natur: Studien zur Aktualität der Philosophiegeschichte. Festschrift für Wolfgang Neuser zum 60. Geburtstag*, edited by Klaus Wiegerling and Wolfgang Lenski, 149–71. Nordhausen: Bautz, 2011.

Brentari, Carlo. "Konrad Lorenz's Epistemological Criticism towards Jakob von Uexküll." *Sign Systems Studies* 37, no. 3/4 (2009): 662–37.

———. *Jakob von Uexküll: The Discovery of the Umwelt Between Biosemiotics and Theoretical Biology*. Berlin: Springer, 2015.

Breuer, Stefan. *Anatomie der konservativen Revolution*. Darmstadt: Wissenschaftliche Buchgesellschaft Darmstadt, 1995.

Brock, Friedrich. "Jakob Johann von Uexküll zum 70. Geburtstag." *Sudhoffs Archiv* 27 (1934): 193–203.

Brüggemeier, Franz-Josef, Mark Cioc, and Thomas Zeller, eds. *How Green were the Nazis? Nature, Environment, and Nation in the Third Reich*. Athens: Ohio University Press, 2005.

Buchanan, Brett. *Onto-Ethologies: The Animal Environments of Uexküll, Heidegger, Merleau-Ponty, and Deleuze*. New York: University of New York Press, 2008.

Bühler, Benjamin. "Das Tier und die Experimentalisierung des Verhaltens: Zur Rhetorik der Umwelt-Lehre Jakob von Uexkülls." In *Wissen. Erzählen: Narrative der Humanwissenschaften*, edited by Arne Höcker, Jeannie Moser, and Philippe Weber, 41–52. Bielefeld: Transcript, 2006.

———. Ökologische *Gouvernementalität: Zur Geschichte einer Regierungsform*. Bielefeld: Transcript, 2018.

Canguilhem, Georges. "Das Lebendige und sein Milieu." In *Die Erkenntnis des Lebens*, edited by Georges Canguilhem, 242–79. Berlin: August, 2009.

———. "The Living and its Milieu." In *Knowledge of Life*, Georges Canguilhem, 98–120. New York: Fordham University Press.

Cassin, Barbara, ed. *Dictionary of Untranslatables*. Translated by Steven Randall et al. Princeton: Princeton University Press, 2014.

Chamberlain, Houston Stewart. *Natur und Leben*. Edited by Jakob von Uexküll. Munich: Bruckmann, 1928.

Cheung, Tobias. "Cobweb Stories: Jakob von Uexküll and the Stone of Werder." *Place and Location. Studies in Environmental Aestethics and Semiotics* V (2006): 231–53.

Chrulew, Matthew. "Reconstructing the Worlds of Wildlife: Uexküll, Hediger, and Beyond." *Biosemiotics* 13, no. 1 (2020): 137–49.

Dahn, Ryan. "Big Science, Nazified? Pascual Jordan, Adolf Meyer-Abich, and the Abortive Scientific Journal Physis." *Isis* 109, no. 4 (2018): 68–90.

Darwin, Charles. *The Origin of Species by Means of Natural Selection, or the Preservation of Favoured Races in the Struggle for Life*. 6th ed. London: John Murray, 1876; Cambridge: Cambridge University Press, 2009.

Deichmann, Ute. *Biologists under Hitler.* Cambridge, MA: Harvard University Press, 1996.

Deleuze, Gilles, and Félix Guattari. *Tausend Plateaus: Kapitalismus und Schizophrenie*. Berlin: Merve, 1992.

Dieke, Thom. "Der Ökologische Komplex: Möglichkeiten für die deutsche Rechte." Last accessed October 10, 2020. https://gegenstrom.org/der-oekologische-komplex-moeglichkeiten-fuer-die-deutsche-rechte/.

Di Paolo, Ezequiel A. "A Future for Jakob von Uexküll." In *Jakob von Uexküll and Philosophy: Life, Environments, Anthropology, edited by* Kristian Köchy and Francesca Michelini, 252–56. London: Routledge, 2020.

Dohrn, Alfred. "Vorwort des Herausgebers." In *Fauna und Flora des Golfes von Neapel 1, Ctenophorae*. Edited by Alfred Dohrn. Leipzig: W. Engelmann, 1880.

———. "Publications of the Zoological Station at Naples." *Nature* 48 (1883).

Driesch, Hans. "Kant und das Ganze." *Kant-Studien* 29 (1924): 365–76.

Engelhardt, Wolf von. "Der Versuch als Vermittler zwischen Objekt und Subjekt. Goethes Aufsatz im Licht von Kants Vernunftkritik." *Athenäum. Jahrbuch für Romantik* 10 (2000): 9–28.

Emge, Carl A. "Erinnerungen eines Rechtsphilosophen an die Umwege, die sich schließlich doch als Zugänge nach Berlin erwiesen, an die dortige rechtsphilosophische Situation und Ausblicke auf Utopia." In *Studium Berolinense: Aufsätze und Beiträge zu Problemen der Wissenschaft und zur Geschichte der Friedrich-Wilhelms-Universität zu Berlin*, edited by Georg Kotowski, Eduard Neumann, and Hans Leussink, 108–37. Berlin: De Gruyter, 1960.

———. "Ansprache von Prof. Dr. C.A. Emge, Weimar." In *Akademie für Deutsches Recht, 1933–1945. Protokolle der Ausschüsse: Weitere Nachträge (1934–1939).* Vol. XXIII, edited by Werner Schubert, 52–3. Berlin: De Gruyter, 2019.

———. "Ideen über die Aufgaben der wissenschaftlichen Rechtsphilosophie." In *Akademie für Deutsches Recht, 1933–1945. Protokolle der Ausschüsse: Weitere Nachträge (1934–1939).* Vol. XXIII, edited by Werner Schubert, 73–9. Berlin: De Gruyter, 2019.

Erlmann, Veit. "Klang, Raum und Umwelt: Jakob von Uexkülls Musiktheorie des Lebens." *Zeitschrift für Semiotik* 34, no. 1/2 (2012): 158–45.

Espahangizi, Kijan M. *Wissenschaft im Glas: Eine historische Ökologie moderner Laborforschung*. Dissertation, ETH Zurich, 2010.

Esposito, Maurizio. "Kantian Ticks, Uexküllian Melodies, and the Transformation of Transcendental Philosophy." In *Jakob von Uexküll and Philosophy: Life,*

Environments, Anthropology, edited by Kristian Köchy and Francesca Michelini, 36–51. London: Routledge, 2020.

Esposito, Roberto. *Bíos: Biopolitics and Philosophy*. Minneapolis: University of Minnesota Press, 2008.

Fábregas-Tejeda, Alejandro, Abigail Nieves Delgado, and Jan Baedke. "Reconstructing 'Umkonstruktion': Hans Böker's Organism-Centered Approach to Evolution." *Classics in Biological Theory* 16 (2021): 63–75.

Farías, Victor. *Heidegger and Nazism*. Philadelphia: Temple University Press, 1990.

Feuerbach, Ludwig. *Anthropologischer Materialismus: Ausgewählte Schriften I*. Edited by and with an introduction from Alfred Schmidt. Frankfurt am Main: Ullstein, 1985.

Feuerhahn, Wolf. "Du milieu à l'Umwelt: Enjeux d'un changement terminologique." *Revue philosophique de la France et de l'étranger* 134, no. 4 (2009): 419–38.

———. "A Specter Is Haunting Germany – the French Specter of Milieu: On the Nomadicity and Nationality of Cultural Vocabularies." *Contributions to the History of Concepts* 9, no. 2 (2014): 33–50.

Foucault, Michel. *The Order of Things*. London: Routledge Classics, 2002.

Frank, Hans. "Ansprache von Hans Frank." In *Akademie für Deutsches Recht, 1933–1945. Protokolle der Ausschüsse: Weitere Nachträge (1934–1939)*. Vol. XXIII, edited by Werner Schubert, 46–8. Berlin: De Gruyter, 2019.

Franke, Anselm. "Earthrise und das Verschwinden des Außen." In *The Whole Earth: Kalifornien und das Verschwinden des Außen*, edited by Diedrich Diedrichsen and Anselm Franke, 12–20. Berlin: Sternberg Press, 2013.

Friederichs, Karl. "Vom Wesen der Ökologie." *Sudhoffs Archiv* 27 (1934): 285–77.

———. Ökologie als Wissenschaft von der Natur oder biologische Raumforschung. Leipzig: Barth, 1937.

———. "Über den Begriff der ‚Umwelt' in der Biologie." *Acta Biotheoretica* 7 (1943): 147–62.

Fultot, Martin, and Michael T. Turvey. "von Uexküll's Theory of Meaning and Gibson's Organism–Environment Reciprocity." *Ecological Psychology* 31, no. 4 (2019): 289–315.

Gebhard, Walter. *Der Zusammenhang der Dinge: Weltgleichnis und Naturverklärung im Totalitätsbewußtsein des 19. Jahrhanderts*. Tübingen: Max Niemeyer, 1984.

Geden, Oliver. *Rechte* Ökologie*: Umweltschutz zwischen Emanzipation und Faschismus*. Berlin: Elefanten, 1999.

Geulen, Eva. "Urpflanze (und Goethes *Hefte zur Morphologie*)." In *Urworte: Zur Geschichte und Funktion erstbegründender Begriffe*, edited by Michael Ott and Tobias Döring, 155–71. Munich: Fink, 2012.

———. *Aus dem Leben der Form: Goethes Morphologie und die Nager*. Berlin: August, 2016.

Goebbels, Joseph. *Tagebücher: Teil 1. Aufzeichnungen 1923–1941, Band 2/I Dezember 1929–Mai 1931*. Edited by Elke Fröhlich. Munich: Saur, 2008.

Goethe, Johann Wolfgang von. "Reine Begriffe." *Goethes Schriften zur Naturwissenschaft, Leopoldina-Ausgabe*, LA I 3, 290–91. Weimar: Böhlau, 1951.

———. "Bildungstrieb." *Hefte zur Morphologie*. Vol. 1 (1817–1822), 399–568. In *Johann Wolfgang Goethe. Sämtliche Werke*. Vol. 24. Frankfurt am Main: Deutscher Klassiker-Verlag, 1987.

———. *Scientific Studies*. Edited and translated by. Douglas Miller. New York: Suhrkamp, 1988.

———. "Significant Help Given by an Ingenious Turn of Phrase." In *Scientific Studies*, edited and translated by Douglas Miller, 39–41. New York: Suhrkamp, 1988.

Greaves, Tom. "A Silent Dance: Eco-Political Compositions after Uexküll's Umwelt Biology." In *An [Un]Likely Alliance: Thinking Environment[s] with Deleuze|Guattari*, edited by Bernd Herzogenrath, 98–115. Newcastle upon Tyne: Cambridge Scholars Publishing, 2008.

Groß, Felix. "Einleitung." In *Bausteine zu einer biologischen Weltanschauung*, edited by Jakob von Uexküll. 9–13. Munich: Bruckmann, 1913.

Gruevska, Julia. ",mit und in seiner Umwelt geboren': Frederik Buytendijks experimentelle Konzeptualisierung einer Tier-Umwelt-Einheit." *NTM Zeitschrift für Geschichte der Wissenschaften, Technik und Medizin* 27, no. 3 (2019).

Günzel, Stephan. "Philosophie des Führens: Carl August Emge in Jena und Weimar." In *Angst vor der Moderne: Philosophische Antworten auf Krisenerfahrungen: Der Mikrokosmos Jena 1900–1940*, edited by Klaus-Michael Kodalle, 157–82. Würzburg: Königshausen & Neumann, 2000.

Guidetti, Luca. "The Space of the Living Beings. Umwelt and Space in Jakob von Uexküll." In *The Changing Faces of Space*, edited by Maria Teresa Cantena and Felice Masi, 3–18. Cham: Springer, 2017.

Haas, Maximilian. *Tiere auf der Bühne: Eine ästhetische Ökologie der Performanz*. Berlin: Kadmos, 2018.

Haeckel, Ernst. *Die Radiolarien (Rhizopoda radiaria): Eine Monographie mit einem Atlas von fünf und dreissig Kupfertafeln*. 2 vols. Berlin: Georg Reimer, 1862.

———. *Gott-Natur (Theophysis): Studien über monistische Religion*. Leipzig: Alfred Kröner, 1914.

———. *Die Lebenswunder*. Stuttgart: Kröner, 1905.

Hamacher, Werner. "Amphora (Extracts)." *Assemblage* 20, April (1993): 40–1.

———. "Arbeiten. Durcharbeiten." In *Archäologie der Arbeit*, edited by Dirk Baecker, 155–200. Berlin: Kadmos, 2002.

Haraway, Donna J. *Crystals, Fabrics, and Fields: Metaphors of Organicism in Twentieth-Century Developmental Biology*. New Haven, CT: Yale University Press, 1976.

Harman, Graham. "Magic Uexküll." In *Living Earth: Field Notes from the Dark Ecology Project 2014–2016*, edited by Mirna Belina, 115–30. Amsterdam: Sonic Acts Press, 2016.

Harrington, Anne. *Reenchanted Science: Holism in German Culture from Wilhelm II to Hitler*. Princeton: Princeton University Press, 1999.

Harwood, Jonathan. "Weimar Culture and Biological Theory: A Study of Richard Woltereck (1877–1944)." *History of Science* 34, no. 3 (1996): 347–77.

Heidegger, Martin. *The Fundamental Concepts of Metaphysics*. Translated by William McNeill and Nicholas Walker. Bloomington: Indiana University Press, 1995.

———. Ontology—*The Hermeneutics of Facticity.* Translated by John van Buren. Bloomington: Indiana University Press, 1999.

———. *Ponderings VII–XI: Black Notebooks 1938–1939*. Translated by Richard Rojcewicz. Bloomington: Indiana University Press, 2014.

Hein, Hilde. "The Endurance of the Mechanism-Vitalism Controversy." *Journal of the History of Biology* 5, no. 1 (1972): 159–88.

Heinrich, Gudrun, Klaus D. Kaiser, and Norbert Wiersbinski, eds. *Naturschutz und Rechtsradikalismus: Gegenwärtige Entwicklungen, Probleme, Abgrenzungen und Steuerungsmöglichkeiten*. Bonn: Bandesamt für Naturschutz, 2015.

Helbach, Charlotte. *Die Umweltlehre Jakob von Uexkülls: Ein Beispiel für die Genese von Theorien in der Biologie des 20. Jahrhanderts*. Dissertation, RWTH Aachen, 1999.

Herder, Johann G. *Ideen zur Philosophie der Geschichte der Menschheit: Dritter Teil.* Riga: Johann Friedrich Hartknoch, 1787.

Heredia, Juan M. "Jakob von Uexküll, an Intellectual History." In *Jakob von Uexküll and Philosophy: Life, Environments, Anthropology, edited* by Kristian Köchy and Francesca Michelini, 17–35. London: Routledge, 2020.

Herrmann, Bernd. "...mein Acker ist die Zeit." Aufsätze zur Umweltgeschichte. Göttingen: Universitätsverlag Göttingen, 2011.

Hitler, Adolf. *Mein Kampf*. Translated by Ralph Manheim. Boston: Houghton Mifflin, 1943.

Höfer, Florian. *Die Notwendigkeit der Kommunikation: Die Missachtung eines Phänomens bei Jakob von Uexküll*. Dissertation, Rheinische Friedrich-Wilhelms-Universität Bonn, 2007.

Horkheimer, Max. "Materialismus und Metaphysik." *Zeitschrift für Sozialforschung* II/1 (1933): 1–33.

Hornacek, Milan. *Politik der Sprache in der ‚konservativen Revolution'*. Dresden: Thelem, 2015.

Inda, Jonathan. "Foreign Bodies: Migrants, Parasites, and the Pathological Nation." *Discourse* 22, no. 3 (2000): 46–62.

Ingensiep, Hans Werner. "Metamorphosen der Metamorphosenlehre – Zur Goethe-Rezeption in der Biologie von der Romantik bis in die Gegenwart." In *Goethe and die Verzeitlichung der Natur*, edited by Peter Matussek, 259–75. Munich: C.H. Beck, 1988.

Institut für Staatspolitik. *Die Grünen: Die zersetzende Kraft der Emanzipation.* Steigra: Verein für Staatspolitik, 2013.

Jahn, Thomas, and Peter Wehling, eds. *Ökologie von rechts: Nationalismus und Umweltschutz bei der neuen Rechten und den ‚Republikanern'*. Frankfurt am Main, New York: Campus Verlag, 1991.

———. "‚Wir sind die nationalen Umweltschützer...': Konturen einer Ökologie von rechts in der Bandesrepublik Deutschland." *Soziale Welt* 42, no. 4 (1991): 473–88.

Jax, Kurt. "Holocoen and Ecosystem: On the Origin and Historical Consequences of Two Concepts." *Journal of the History of Biology* 31, no. 1 (1998): 113–42.

———. "‚Organismic' Positions in Early German-Speaking Ecology and Its (Almost) Forgotten Dissidents." *History and Philosophy of the Life Sciences* 42, no. 4 (2020): 44.

Jochmaring, Julian. "Im gläsernen Gehäuse: Zur Medialität der Umwelt bei Uexküll und Merleau-Ponty." In *Gehäuse: Mediale Einkapselungen*, edited by Christina Bartz et al., 253–70. Munich: Fink, 2017.

———. "Streuen/Strahlen: Negative Ambientialität bei Merleau-Ponty." In *Medienanthropologische Szenen: Die conditio humana im Zeitalter der Medien*, edited by Lorenz Engell, Katerina Kritlova, and Christiane Voss, 57–75. Munich: Fink, 2018.

Johe, Werner. *Die gleichgeschaltete Justiz: Organisation des Rechtswesens and Politisierung der Rechtsprechung 1933–1945, dargestellt am Beispiel des Oberlandesgerichtsbezirks Hamburg*. Hamburg: Christians, 1983.

Johnson, Steven. *Emergence. The Connected Lives of Ants, Brains, Cities, and Software*. New York: Scribner, 2001.

Jünger, Ernst. "Revolution und Idee." *Völkischer Beobachter* 23 (24.9.1923).

———. "Der Pazifismus." *Die Standarte (Sonderbeilage des Stahlhelm)* (15.11.1925).

———. "Der Neue Typ des Deutschen Menschen" *Stahlhelm-Jahrbuch* (1926).

———. *The Worker: Dominion and Form*. Edited by Laurence P. Hemming. Translated by Bogdan Costea and Laurence P. Hemming. Evanston, IL: Northwestern University Press, 2017.

Kant, Immanuel. "On a Recently Prominent Tone of Superiority in Philosophy." In *Theoretical Philosophy after 1781*, edited by Henry Allison and Peter Heath, translated by Gary Hatfield et al., 425–46. Cambridge: Cambridge University Press, 2002.

———. *The Educational Theory of Immanuel Kant*. Translated and edited by Edward Franklin Buchner. Philadelphia: J. B. Lippincott, 1904.

Kellerer, Sidonie and François Rastier. "Den Völkermördern entgegen gearbeitet." *FORVM*. Last accessed August 15, 2020. http://forvm.contextxxi.org/den-volkermordern-entgegen.html.

Keulartz, Jozef. *Struggle for Nature: A Critique of Radical Ecology*. London: Routledge, 1998.

Kittsteiner, Heinz Dieter. "Die Heroische Moderne" [Manuskript], *Nachlass*, Sig. 10.

Kjellén, Rudolf. *Grundriss zu einem System der Politik*. Leipzig: S. Hirzel, 1920.

Klages, Ludwig. *Der Geist als Widersacher der Seele*. Leipzig: Barth, 1929.

Kleeberg, Bernhard. "Evolutionäre Ästhetik" In *Text und Wissen: Technologische und Anthropologische Aspekte*, edited by Stefan Rieger and Renate Lachmann, 153–79. Tübingen: G. Narr, 2003.

———. *Theophysis. Ernst Haeckels Philosophie des Naturganzen*. Cologne: Böhlau, 2005.

Kockerbeck, Christian. *Die Schönheit des Lebendigen: Ästhetische Naturwahrnehmung im 19. Jahrhundert*. Vienna: Böhlau, 1997.

Köchy, Kristian. "Helmuth Plessners Biophilosophie als Erweiterung des Uexküll-Programms." In *Zwischen den Kulturen: Plessners "Stufen des Organischen" im zeithistorischen Kontext*, edited by Kristian Köchy and Francesca Michelini, 25–64. Freiburg: Verlag Karl Alber, 2016.

Köchy, Kristian. "Uexküll's Legacy: Biological Reception and Biophilosophical Impact." In *Jakob von Uexküll and Philosophy: Life, Environments, Anthropology,* edited by Kristian Köchy and Francesca Michelini, 52–70. London: Routledge, 2020.

Koktanek, Anton. *Oswald Spengler in seiner Zeit*. Munich: Beck, 1968.

Kross, Matthias. "Engineering Phenomena: Wittgenstein and Goethe on Scientific Method." In *Goethe and Wittgenstein: Seeing the World's Unity in its Variety*, edited by Fritz Breithaupt, Richard Raatzsch, and Bettina Kremberg, 27–46. Frankfurt am Main: Peter Lang, 2003.

Krüger, Hans Peter. "Closed environment and open world: On the significance of Uexküll's biology for Helmuth Plessners natural philosophy." In *Jakob von Uexküll and Philosophy: Life, Environments, Anthropology*, edited by Kristian Köchy and Francesca Michelini, 89–105. London: Routledge, 2020.

Kubitschek, Götz, "Entortung und Masse sind per se destruktiv, nivellierend, unorganisch, unökologisch. Interview mit Götz Kubitschek." *Die Kehre*, no. 4 (2020): 30–5.

Kudszus, Winfried. "Linguistic-Literary Reflections on the Science of Light: Sensory Emergence in Goethe's *Theory of Colours* and Jakob von Uexkülls Metaphoricity of Semiotic *Scaffolding*." In *Studies about Languages* 26 (2015): 83–109.

Kull, Kalevi. "Jakob von Uexküll: An introduction." *Semiotica* 134, no. 1/4 (2001): 1–59.

Kynast, Katja. "Kinematografie als Medium der Umweltforschung Jakob von Uexkülls." *Kunsttexte.de* 4 (2010).

———. "Personalerweiterung: Gefüge von Menschen, Phantomen und Hunden in der Blindenführhandausbildung nach Jakob von Uexküll und Emanuel Sarris." In *Animal Encounters: Kontakt, Interaktion und Relationalität*, edited by Alexandra Böhm and Jessica Ullrich, 323–42. Berlin: J.B. Metzler, 2019.

Lassen, Harald. "Der Umgebungsbegriff als Planbegriff: Ein Beitrag zu den erkenntnistheoretischen Grandfragen der Umweltlehre." *Sudhoffs Archiv* 27, no. 6 (1935): 480–93.

———. "Leibniz'sche Gedanken in der Uexküll'schen Umweltlehre." *Acta biotheoretica* A5 (1939–1941): 41–50.

Latour, Bruno. "Gifford Lectures: Facing Gaia – Six lectures on the Political Theology of Nature." Last accessed November 24, 2013. http://www.bruno-latour.fr/sites/default/files/downloads/GIFFORD-ASSEMBLED.pdf.

Lehmann, Ernst. "Rezension." *Der Biologe* 3 (1934): 25.

———. "Rezension J. von Uexküll, Staatsbiologie." *Der Biologe* 3, no. 1 (1934): 25.

Lilienfeld, Paul von. *Gedanken über die Sozialwissenschaft der Zukunft. Erster Theil: Die menschliche Gesellschaft als realer Organismus*. Mitau: E. Behre, 1873.

Liggieri, Kevin. *‚Anthropotechnik': Zur Geschichte eines umstrittenen Begriffs*. Constance: Konstanz University Press, 2020.

Loo, Stephen and Andine Sellbach. "A Picture Book of Invisible Worlds: Semblances of insects and humans in Jakob von Uexküll's laboratory." *Angelaki* 18, no. 1 (2013): 45–64.

Luhmann, Niklas. *Introduction to Systems Theory*. Translated Peter Gilgen. Cambridge: Polity Press, 2013.

Malm, Andreas. *Fossil Capital The Rise of Steam-Power and the Roots of Global Warming: The Rise of Steam-power and the Roots of Global Warming*. London: Verso, 2015.

Mann, Gunter, Dieter Mollenhauer et. al., eds. *In der Mitte zwischen Natur und Subjekt. Johann Wolfgang von Goethes Versuch, die Metamorphose der Pflanze zu erklären. 1790–1990*. Frankfurt am Main: Waldemar Kramer, 1990.

Mann, Thomas. *Essays II, 1914–1926*. Vol. 1. Frankfurt am Main: S. Fischer, 2002.

Maturana, Humberto and Francisco Varela. *Der Baum der Erkenntnis: Die biologischen Wurzeln des menschlichen Erkennens*. Bern: Scherz, 1987.

Mazzeo, Marco. "Giorgio Agamben: The Political Meaning of Uexküll's ‚Sleeping Tick'." In *Jakob von Uexküll and Philosophy: Life, Environments, Anthropology*, edited by Kristian Köchy and Francesca Michelini, 205–20. London: Routledge, 2020.

Merleau-Ponty, Maurice. *Nature: Course Notes from the Collège de France*. Edited by Dominique Séglard. Translated by Robert Vallier. Evanston, IL: Northwestern University Press, 2003.

Mersch, Dieter. "Ökologie und Ökologisierung." *Internationales Jahrbuch für Medienphilosophie* 4, no. 1 (2018): 187–220.

Meyer-Abich, Adolf. "Hauptgedanken des Holismus." *Acta Biotheoretica* 5, no. 2 (1940): 85–116.

———. *Biologie der Goethezeit*. Stuttgart: Hippokrates, 1949.

Meyer-Abich, Klaus Michael. *Wege zum Frieden mit der Natur: Praktische Naturphilosophie für die Umweltpolitik*. Munich: Carl Hanser, 1984.

Michelini, Francesca. "Introduction: A Foray into Uexküll's Heritage." In *Jakob von Uexküll and Philosophy: Life, Environments, Anthropology, edited* by Kristian Köchy and Francesca Michelini, 1–14. London: Routledge, 2020.

Michelini, Francesca, and Kristian Köchy, eds. *Jakob von Uexküll and Philosophy: Life, Environments, Anthropology*. London: Routledge, 2020.

Mildenberger, Florian. "Überlegungen zu Jakob von Uexküll (1864–1944): Vorläufiger Forschungsbericht." *Österreichische Zeitschrift für Geschichtswissenschaften* 13, no. 3 (2002): 145–49.

———. "Race and Breathing Therapy: The Career of Lothar Gottlieb Tirala (1886–1974)." *Sign Systems Studies* 32, no. 1–2 (2004): 253–75.

———. *Umwelt als Vision: Leben und Werk Jakob von Uexkülls (1864–1944)*. Wiesbaden: Steiner, 2007.

Mildenberger, Florian and Bernd Herrmann. "Nachwort." In *Umwelt und Innenwelt der Tiere*, edited by Florian Mildenberger and Bernd Herrmann, 261–330. Berlin: Springer, 1909/2014.

Mohler, Armin. *Die konservative Revolution in Deutschland 1918–1932: Ein Handbuch*. Darmstadt: Wissenschaftliche Buchgesellschaft, 1989.

Mohr, Volker. "Ökologie im Spiegel der Ortlosigkeit." *Die Kehre*, no. 4 (2020): 6–13

Moore, Jason W. *Capitalism in the Web of Life: Ecology and the Accumulation of Capital*. London: Verso, 2015.

Morison, Benjamin. *On Location: Aristotle's Concept of Place*. Oxford: Clarendon Press, 2002.

Müller-Funk, Wolfgang: *Die Rückkehr der Bilder: Beiträge zu einer ‚romantischen Ökologie'*. Vienna: Böhlau, 1988.

Musolff, Andreas. *Metaphor, Nation and the Holocaust: The Concept of the Body Politic*. London: Routledge, 2010.

Nagel, Thomas. "What Is It Like to Be a Bat?" *The Philosophical Review* 83, no. 4 (1974): 435–50.

Nassirin, Kaveh. "Martin Heidegger und die ‚Rechtsphilosophie' der NS-Zeit." *FORVM*. Aufgerufen August 15., 2020. http://forvm.contextxxi.org/martin-heidegger-und-die.html.

———. "Den Völkermördern entgegengearbeitet?" *Frankfurter Allgemeine Zeitung*, July 11, 2018.

Neuffer, Moritz, and Morton Paul. "‚Rechte Hefte': Rightwing Magazines in Germany after 1945." *Eurozine*, Oktober 12, 2020. https://www.eurozine.com/rechte-hefte-rightwing-magazines-germany-1945/.

oekom e.V., ed. *Ökologie von rechts: Braune Umweltschützer auf Stimmenfang*. Munich: Oekom Verlag, 2012.

Parikka, Jussi. *Insect Media: An Archaeology of Animals and Technology*. Minneapolis: University of Minnesota Press, 2010.

Penzlin, Heinz. "Jakob von Uexküll legte die Grundlagen zu seiner Umweltlehre" *Biologie in unserer Zeit* 39, no. 5 (2009): 349–52.

Phillips, D. C. "Organicism in the Late Nineteenth and Early Twentieth Centuries." *Journal of the History of Ideas* 31, no. 3 (1970): 413–32.

Pichinot, Hans-Rainer. *Die Akademie für deutsches Recht: Aufbau und Entwicklung einer öffentlich-rechtlichen Körperschaft des Dritten Reichs*. Dissertation, University Kiel, 1981.

Plessner, Helmut. *The Levels of Organic Life and the Human: Introduction to Philosophical Anthropology*. Translated by Millay Hyatt. New York: Fordham University Press, 2019.

Pobojewska, Aldona. "Die Subjektlehre Jakob von Uexkülls." *Sudhoffs Archiv* 77, no. 1 (1993): 54–71.

Pollmann, Inga. "Invisible Worlds, Visible: Uexküll's Umwelt, Film, and Film Theory." *Critical Inquiry* 39, no. 3 (2013): 777–816.

Portmann, Adolf. "Vorwort: Ein Wegbereiter der neuen Biologie." In Jakob von Uexküll and Georg Kriszat, *Streifzüge durch die Umwelten von Tieren und Menschen. Ein Bilderbuch unsichtbarer Welten. Bedeutungslehre*, edited by Adolf Portmann, 7–17. Hamburg: Rowohlt, 1956.

Potthast, Thomas. "Wissenschaftliche Ökologie und Naturschutz: Szenen einer Annäherung." In *Naturschutz und Nationalsozialismus*, edited by Joachim Radkau and Frank Uekötter, 225–56. Frankfurt am Main: Campus, 2003.

———. "Lebensführung (in) der Dialektik von Innenwelt und Umwelt: Jakob von Uexküll, seine philosophische Rezeption und die Transformation des Begriffs ‚Funktionskreis' in der Ökologie." In *Das Leben führen? Das Konzept Lebensführung zwischen Technikphilosophie und Lebensphilosophie*, edited by Nicole Karafyllis, 197–218. Berlin: Edition Sigma, 2014.

Radkau, Joachim, and Frank Uekötter, eds. *Naturschutz und Nationalsozialismus*. Frankfurt: Campus, 2003.

Rastier, François. "Heidegger, théoricien et acteur de l'extermination des juifs?" *The Conversation*, August 15, 2020. https://theconversation.com/heidegger-theoricien-et-acteur-de-lextermination-des-juifs-86334.

Reinert, Sophus. "Darwin and the Body Politic: A Note on Schäffle, Veblen and the Shift of Biological Metaphor in Economics." In *Albert Schäffle (1821–1903): The Legacy of an Anderestimated Economist*, edited by Jürgen Backhaus, 129–52. Frankfurt am Main: Haag and Herchen, 2010.

Rheinberger, Hans-Jörg, and Michael Hagner, eds. *Die Experimentalisierung des Lebens: Experimentalsysteme in den biologischen Wissenschaften 1850/1950*. Berlin: Akademie, 1993.

Rheinberger, Hans-Jörg, "Entwicklung als "Prozess ohne Subjekt." In *Rekurrenzen: Texte zu Althusser*, edited by Hans-Jörg Rheinberger, 97–112. Berlin: Suhrkamp, 2014.

Richards, Robert. *The Tragic Sense of Life: Ernst Haeckel and the Struggle over Evolutionary Thought*. Chicago: University of Chicago Press, 2008.

Rieger, Stefan. "Bipersonalität: Menschenversuche an den Rändern des Sozialen." In *Kulturgeschichte des Menschenversuchs im 20. Jahrhandert*, edited by Birgit Griesecke et al., 181–98. Frankfurt am Main: Suhrkamp, 2009.

———. *Schall und Rauch: Eine Mediengeschichte der Kurve*. Frankfurt am Main: Suhrkamp, 2009.

Ritterbush, Philip C. *The Art of Organic Forms*. Washington, DC: Random House, 1968.

Rogalla von Bieberstein, Johannes. *‚Jüdischer Bolschewismus' – Mythos und Realität*. 4. Edition Schnellroda: Edition Antaios, 2004.

Rohan, Karl Anton Prinz. *Umbruch der Zeit 1923–1930*. Berlin: Stilke, 1930.

Rosenberg, Alfred. *Letzte Aufzeichnungen: Ideale und Idole der nationalsozialistischen Revolution*. Göttingen: Plesse, 1955.

Rothacker, Erich. *Geschichtsphilosophie*. Munich: Oldenbourg, 1934.

Ruddick, Susan M. "Rethinking the Subject, Reimagining Worlds." *Dialogues in Human Geography* 7, no. 2 (2017): 119–39.

Rüting, Thorsten. "Ohne biologische Körper kein intelligentes Modell der Welt: Wissenschaftshistorische Betrachtungen zur Rezeption Jakob von Uexkülls und zur Kritik an der Entwicklung Künstlicher Intelligenz (KI)." In *Modelle*, edited by Ulrich Dirks and Eberhard Knobloch, 259–76. Frankfurt am Main, New York: Peter Lang, 2008.

Sagan, Dorion. "Introduction: Umwelt after Uexküll." In Jakob von Uexküll, *A Foray into the Worlds of Animals and Humans: With a Theory of Meaning*, translated by Joseph D. O'Neill, 1–34. Minneapolis: University of Minnesota Press, 2010.

Sandmann, Jürgen. "Ernst Haeckels Entwicklungslehre als Teil seiner biologistischen Weltanschauung." In *Die Evolution von Rezeptionstheorien im 19. Jahrhandert*, edited by Eve-Marie Engels, 326–46. Frankfurt am Main: Suhrkamp, 1995.

Sarasin, Philipp. *Darwin und Foucault. Genealogie und Geschichte im Zeitalter der Biologie*. Frankfurt am Main: Suhrkamp, 2009.

Sax, Boris and Peter H. Klopfer. "Jakob von Uexküll and the Anticipation of Sociobiology." *Semiotica* 134, no. 1/4 (2001): 767–78.

Schäfer, Martin Jörg. *Die Gewalt der Muße: Wechselverhältnisse von Arbeit, Nichtarbeit, Ästhetik*. Zurich: Diaphanes, 2013.

Scheerer, E. "Organische Weltanschauung und Ganzheitspsychologie." In *Psychologie im Nationalsozialismus*, edited by C. F. Graumann, 15–54. Berlin: Springer, 1985.

Schick, Jonas. "Die Kehre." Aufgerufen Oktober 10, 2020. https://die-kehre.de/2020/04/28/die-kehre/.

———. "Editorial." *Die Kehre*, no. 4 (2020): 1.

Schmidt, Jutta. "Jakob von Uexküll und Houston Stewart Chamberlain: Ein Briefwechsel in Auszügen." *Medizinhistorisches Journal* 10, no. 2 (1975): 121–29.

Schmieg, Gregor. "Die Systematik der Umwelt: Leben, Reiz und Reaktion bei Uexküll und Plessner." In *Das Leben im Menschen oder der Mensch im Leben? Deutsch-französische Genealogien zwischen Anthropologie und Anti-Humanismus*, edited by Thomas Ebke and Caterina Zanfi, 355–68. Potsdam: Universitätsverlag Potsdam, 2017.

Schmitt, Carl. *Der Begriff des Politischen*. Berlin: Duncker & Humblot, [1932] 2009.

———. *The Concept of the Political*. Chicago: Chicago University Press, 2009.

———. "Die Staatsphilosophie der Gegenrevolution." In *Archiv für Rechts- und Wirtschaftsphilosophie* 16 (1922): 121–31.

———. *Land and Sea*. Translated by and with a foreword from Simona Draghici. Washington, DC: Plutarch Press, 1997.

Schneider, Manfred. "Der Jude als Gast." In *Gastlichkeit: Erkundungen einer Schwellensituation*, edited by Peter Friedrich and Rolf Parr, 49–69. Heidelberg: Synchron, 2009.

Scholz, Leander. "Karl August Möbius und die Politik der Lebensgemeinschaft." *Zeitschrift für Medien- und Kulturforschung* 7, no. 2 (2016): 206–20.

———. *Die Menge der Menschen: Eine Figur der politischen Ökologie*. Berlin: Kadmos, 2019.

Schroer, Sara A. "Jakob von Uexküll: The Concept of Umwelt and its Potentials for an Anthropology Beyond the Human." *Ethnos* 6, no. 3 (2019): 1–21.

Schubert, Werner, ed. *Akademie für Deutsches Recht, 1933–1945. Protokolle der Ausschüsse: Weitere Nachträge (1934–1939)* XXIII. Berlin: De Gruyter, 2019.

———. "Einleitung." In *Akademie für Deutsches Recht, 1933–1945. Protokolle der Ausschüsse: Weitere Nachträge (1934–1939)*. Vol. XXIII, edited by Werner Schubert, 9–44. Berlin: De Gruyter, 2019.

Schwarz, Astrid. "Baron Jakob von Uexküll: Das Experiment als Ordnungsprinzip in der Biologie." In *Das bunte Gewand der Theorie: Vierzehn Begegnungen mit philosophierenden Forschern*, edited by Astrid Schwarz and Alfred Nordmann, 207–34. Freiburg: Alber, 2009.

Sieferle, Rolf Dieter. *Die konservative Revolution: Fünf biographische Skizzen*. Frankfurt am Main: Fischer, 1995.

Shaw, Ian G.R., John P. Jones, and Melinda K. Butterworth. "The Mosquito's Umwelt, or One Monster's Standpoint Ontology." *Geoforum* 48 (2013): 260–67.

Serres, Michel. *The Parasite.* Minneapolis: University of Minnesota Press, 1982.

Sontheimer, Kurt. "Antidemokratisches Denken in der Weimarer Republik." In *Vierteljahreshefte für Zeitgeschichte* 5, no. 1 (1957): 42–62.

———. *Antidemokratisches Denken in der Weimarer Republik: Die politischen Ideen des deutschen Nationalismus zwischen 1918 und 1933*. Munich: Nymphenburger Verlagshandlung, 1962.

Spann, Othmar. *Der wahre Staat – Vorlesungen über Abbruch und Neubau des Staates.* Leipzig: Quelle und Meyer, 1921.

Spengler, Oswald. *Der metaphysische Grandgedanke der Heraklitischen Philosophie*, Inaugural-Dissertation zur Erlangung der Doctorwürde. Halle a.d. Saale: Hofdruckerei v. C.A. Kaemmerer, 1904.

———. *Preußentum und Sozialismus*. Munich: Beck, 1919.

———. *Der Untergang des Abendlandes: Umrisse einer Morphologie der Weltgeschichte.* Mit einem Nachwort von Detlef Felken. Munich: dtv, 2006.

———. *Man and Technics: A Contribution to a Philosophy of Life*. Translated by Charles Francis Atkinson. London: George Allen & Unwin, 1932.

———. *The Decline of the West, vol. 1: Form and Actuality.* Translated by Charles Francis Atkinson. New York: Alfred A. Knopf, 1926.

———. *The Hour of Decision, Part One: Germany and World-Historical Evolution.* Translated by Charles Francis Atkinson. London: George Allen & Unwin, 1934.

Spitzer, Leo. "Milieu and Ambiance." *Essays in historical Semantics*, 179–316. New York: Vanni, 1948.

Sprenger, Florian. "Zwischen Umwelt und milieu: Zur Begriffsgeschichte von environment in der Evolutionstheorie." *Forum interdisziplinäre Begriffsgeschichte* 3, no. 2 (2014). http://www.zfl-berlin.org/tl_files/zfl/downloads/publikationen/forum_begriffsgeschichte/ZfL_FIB_3_2014_2_Sprenger.pdf.

———. *Epistemologien des Umgebens: Zur Geschichte, Ökologie und Biopolitik künstlicher Environments*. Bielefeld: Transcript, 2019.

———. "Neben-, Mit-, In- und Durcheinander: Zur Wissensgeschichte der Symbiose." *Zeitschrift für theoretische Soziologie* 9, no. 2 (2020): 274–91.

———. "Zirkulationen des Kreises: Von der Regulation zur Adaption." *Zeitschrift für Medienwissenschaft* 23 (2020): 41–54.

———. "Zur rechten Ökologie-Zeitschrift 'Die Kehre'." *Pop-Zeitschrift*, August 5, 2020. https://pop-zeitschrift.de/2020/08/03/zur-rechten-oekologie-zeitschrift-die-kehreautorvon-florian-sprenger-autordatum3-8-2020-datum/.

Stein, Philip. "Ökomanifest von rechts." *Sezession*, Oktober 10, 2020. https://sezession.de/46543/oekomanifest-von-rechts.

———. "Das organische Welt und die ökologische Revolution." Last accessed October 10, 2020. https://www.youtube.com/watch?v=-bUTKgmV9x8.

Steinbömer, Gustav. "Betrachtungen über den Konservatismus." *Deutsches Volkstum* 14 (1932): 25–30.

Steinmayr, Markus. "Fridays for Yesterday: Ein Kommentar zur politischen Ökologie." *Merkur* 74, no. 855 (2020): 20–30.

Stella, Marco, and Karel Kleisner. "Uexküllian Umwelt as Science and as Ideology: The Light and the Dark Side of a Concept." *Theory in Biosciences* 129, no. 1 (2010): 39–51.

Stullich, Heiko. "Parasiten, eine Begriffsgeschichte." *Forum interdisziplinäre Begriffsgeschichte* 2, no. 1 (2013): 21–9.

Szilasi, Wilhelm. *Wissenschaft als Philosophie*. Zurich: Europa-Verlag, 1945.

Thienemann, August. *Leben und Umwelt*. Leipzig: Barth, 1941.

Tilitzki, Christian. "Der Rechtsphilosoph Carl August Emge: Vom Schüler Hermann Cohens zum Stellvertreter Hans Franks." *Archiv für Rechts- und Sozialphilosophie* 89, no. 4 (2003): 459–96.

Toepfer, Georg, ed. *Historisches Wörterbuch der Biologie*. Stuttgart: Metzler, 2011.

———. "Parasitismus." In *Historisches Wörterbuch der Biologie*. Vol. 3, edited by Georg Toepfer, 1–11. Stuttgart: Metzler, 2011.

———. "Umwelt." In *Historisches Wörterbuch der Biologie*. Vol. 3, edited by Georg Toepfer, 566–607. Stuttgart: Metzler, 2011.

Tønnessen, Morten. "Umwelt Transitions: Uexküll and Environmental Change." *Biosemiotics* 2, (2009): 47–64.

Trepl, Ludwig, and Annette Voigt. "Von einer Kulturaufgabe zur angewandten Ökologie: Welche Verwissenschaftlichung hat der Naturschutz nötig?" *Jahrbuch des Vereins zum Schutz der Bergwelt* 73 (2008): 165–81.

Uexküll, Jakob von. "Psychologie und Biologie in ihrer Stellung zur Tierseele." *Ergebnisse der Physiologie, II. Abteilung: Biophysik und Psychophysik* 1 (1902): 212–33.

———. *Leitfaden in das Studium der experimentellen Biologie der Wassertiere*. Wiesbaden: Bergmann, 1905.

———. "Die Umrisse einer kommenden Weltanschauung." *Neue Rundschau* 18, no. 1 (1907): 641–61.

———. "Die neuen Fragen in der experimentellen Biologie." *Rivista di Scienza* 4, no. 2 (1908): 72–84.

———. *Umwelt und Innenwelt der Tiere*. Berlin: Springer, 1909.

———. "Die Umwelt." *Neue Rundschau* 21, no. 2 (1910): 638–49.

———. "Die Merkwelten der Tiere." *Deutsche Revue* 37, no. 9 (1912): 349–54.

———. *Bausteine zu einer biologischen Weltanschauung*. Munich: Bruckmann, 1913.

———. "Volk und Staat." *Neue Rundschau* 26, no. 1 (1915): 52–66.

———. "Darwin und die englische Moral." *Deutsche Rundschau*, no. 173 (1917): 215–42.

———. "Biologie und Wahlrecht." *Deutsche Rundschau* 174, no. 1 (1918): 183–203.

———. "Biologische Briefe an eine Dame, Brief 4–12." *Deutsche Rundschau*, no. 179 (1919): 132–48, 276–92, 451–68.

———. *Biologische Briefe an eine Dame*. Berlin: Paetel, 1920.

———. *Staatsbiologie: Anatomie – Physiologie – Pathologie des Staates*. 1st ed. Paetel: Berlin, 1920.

———. *Theoretische Biologie*. Berlin: Paetel, 1920.

———. *Theoretical Biology*, New York: Harcourt, Brace & Co., 1926.

———. "Leben und Tod." *Deutsche Rundschau*, no. 190 (1922): 173–83.

———. "Mensch und Gott." *Deutsche Rundschau*, no. 190 (1922): 85–7.

———. "Trebitsch und Blüher über die Judenfrage." *Deutsche Rundschau*, no. 193 (1922): 95–7.

———. "Wie sehen wir die Natur und wie sieht die Natur sich selber?" *Die Naturwissenschaften* 10 (1922): 265–71, 296–301, 316–22.

———. "Die Stellung des Naturforschers zu Goethes Gott-Natur." *Die Tat. Monatsschrift für die Zukunft deutscher Kultur* 15/2 (1923): 492–506.

———. "Die Aristokratie in Wissenschaft und Politik." *Das Gewissen*, 5. März 1923: 1.

———. "Weltanschauung und Gewissen." *Deutsche Rundschau*, no. 197 (1923): 253–66.

———. "Die Biologie des Staates." *Nationale Erziehung* 6, no. 7/8 (1925): 177–81.

———. *Theoretischen Biologie*. 2nd ed. Berlin: Springer, 1928.

———. "Die Rolle des Subjekts in der Biologie." *Die Naturwissenschaften* 19, Mai (1931): 385–91.

———. "Das Duftfeld des Hundes." In *Bericht über den XII. Kongreß der Deutschen Gesellschaft für Psychologie in Hamburg vom 12.–16. April 1931*, edited by Gustav Kafka, 431–4. Jena: Gustav Fischer, 1932.

———. *Staatsbiologie: Anatomie – Physiologie – Pathologie des Staates*. 2nd ed. Hamburg: Hanseatische Verlagsanstalt, 1933.

———. "Biologie oder Physiologie." (1933). In *Kompositionslehre der Natur: Biologie als undogmatische Naturwissenschaft. Ausgewählte Schriften*, edited by Thure von Uexküll, 122–29. Frankfurt am Main: Propyläen, 1980.

———. "Die Universitäten als Sinnesorgane des Staates." *Ärzteblatt für Sachsen, Provinz Sachsen, Anhalt und Thüringen* 13, no. 1 (1934): 145–46.

———. "Die Bedeutung der Umweltforschung für die Erkenntnis des Lebens." *Zeitschrift für die gesamte Naturwissenschaft* 1 (1935/36): 257–72.

———. *Niegeschaute Welten: Die Umwelten meiner Freunde. Ein Erinnerungsbuch*. Berlin: Fischer, 1936.

———. "Biologie in der Mausefalle." *Zeitschrift für die gesamte Naturwissenschaft* 2 (1936/37): 213–22.

———. "Antwort von Prof. Dr. Jakob von Uexküll vom 9.5.1934." In *Akademie für Deutsches Recht, 1933–1945. Protokolle der Ausschüsse: Weitere Nachträge (1934–1939)*. Vol. XXIII, edited by Werner Schubert, 615. Berlin: De Gruyter, 2019.

———. *Staatsbiologie: Anatomie – Physiologie – Pathologie des Staates*. 2nd ed. Hamburg: Hanseatische Verlagsanstalt, 1933.

———. "Zum Verständnis der Umweltlehre." *Deutsche Rundschau* 256, no. 7 (1938): 64–6.

———. *Bedeutungslehre*. Leipzig: Barth, 1940.

———. "A Stroll Through the Worlds of Animals and Men: A Picture Book of Invisible Worlds." In *Instinctive Behaviour: The Development of a Modern Concept*, edited by Claire Schiller, 5–80. New York: International Universities Press, 1957.

———. "Vorschläge zu einer subjektbezogenen Nomenklatur in der Biologie." In *Kompositionslehre der Natur: Biologie als undogmatische Naturwissenschaft. Ausgewählte Schriften*, edited by Thure von Uexküll, 129–42. Frankfurt am Main: Propyläen, 1980.

———. *Kompositionslehre der Natur. Biologie als undogmatische Naturwissenschaft. Ausgewählte Schriften*. Edited by Thure von Uexküll. Frankfurt am Main: Propyläen, 1980.

———. *A Foray into the Worlds of Animals and Humans: With a Theory of Meaning*. Minneapolis: University of Minnesota Press, 2010.

Uexküll, Gudrun von. *Jakob von Uexküll, seine Welt und seine Umwelt*. Hamburg: Wegner, 1964.

Uexküll, Jakob von and E. G. Sarris. "Das Duftfeld des Hundes." *Zeitschrift für Hundeforschung* 1, no. 3/4 (1931): 55–68.

Uexküll, Jakob von and Emmanuel G. Sarris. "Dressur und Erziehung der Führhunde für Blinde." *Der Kriegsblinde* 16, no. 6 (1932): 93–4.

Uexküll, Jakob von and Georg Kriszat. *Streifzüge durch die Umwelten von Tieren und Menschen*. Berlin: Springer, 1934.

———. *Streifzüge durch die Umwelten von Tieren und Menschen: Ein Bilderbuch unsichtbarer Welten*. Reinbek: Rowohlt, 1956.

———. *A Foray into the Worlds of Animals and Humans, with A Theory of Meaning*. Edited by Geoffrey Winthrop-Young. Translated by Joseph D. O'Neil. Minneapolis: University of Minnesota Press, 2010.

Vagt, Christina. "‚Umzu Wohnen': Umwelt und Maschine bei Heidegger und Uexküll." In *Ambiente: Das Leben und seine Räume*, edited by Thomas Brandstetter and Karin Harrasser, 91–108. Vienna: Turia + Kant, 2010.

van Dooren, Thom. *Flight Ways: Life and Loss at the Edge of Extinction*. New York: Columbia University Press, 2016.

Vennen, Mareike. *Das Aquarium: Praktiken, Techniken und Medien der Wissensproduktion*. Göttingen: Wallstein, 2018.

Vinx, Lars, ed. and trans. *The Guardian of the Constitution: Hans Kelsen and Carl Schmitt on the Limits of Constitutional Law*. Cambridge: Cambridge University Press, 2015.

Vogt, Carl. *Ocean und Mittelmeer. Reisebriefe*. 2 vols. Frankfurt am Main: J. Rütten, 1848.

Vries, Leonie A. de. "Political Life beyond the Biopolitical?" *Theoria* 60, no. 134 (2013): 50–68.

Wagner, Jannis. "Spengler in der heroischen Moderne: Zu Heinz Dieter Kittsteiners Spengler-Rezeption." In *Spenglers Nachleben: Studien zu einer verdeckten Wirkungsgeschichte*, edited by Christian Voller, Gottfried Schnödl, and Jannis Wagner, 245–64. Springe: zu Klampen, 2018.

Weber, Andreas. *Die Natur als Bedeutung*. Würzburg: Königshausen & Neumann, 2003.

Weber, Hermann. "Der Umweltbegriff der Biologie und seine Anwendung." *Der Biologe* 8, 7/8 (1939): 245–61.

———. "Organismus und Umwelt." *Der Biologe*, no. 11 (1942): 57–68.

Weingart, Peter, Jürgen Kroll, and Kurt Bayertz. *Rasse, Blut und Gene: Geschichte der Eugenik und Rassenhygiene in Deutschland*. Frankfurt am Main: Suhrkamp, 1992.

Weiss, Helene. "Aristotle's Theology and Uexküll's Theory of Living Nature." In *The Classical Quarterly* 42, no. 1/2 (1948): 44–58.

Wessely, Christina. "Wässrige Milieus: Ökologische Perspektiven in Meeresbiologie und Aquarienkande um 1900." *Berichte zur Wissenschaftsgeschichte* 36, no. 2 (2013): 128–47.

Wessely, Christina. "Watery Milieus: Marine Biology, Aquariums, and the Limits of Ecological Knowledge circa 1900." *Grey Room* 75, no. 6 (2019): 36–59.

Wildenauer, Miriam. "Grandlegendes über den Ausschuss für Rechtsphilosophie der Akademie für Deutsches Recht." Last accessed August 15, 2020. https://entnazifiziert.com/.

Winthrop-Young, Geoffrey. "Afterword: Bubbles and Webs: A Backdoor Stroll through the Readings of Uexküll." In *A Foray into the Worlds of Animals and Humans: With a Theory of Meaning*, edited by Geoffrey Winthrop-Young. 209–43. Minneapolis: University of Minnesota Press, 2010.

Woltereck, Richard. *Grandzüge einer allgemeinen Biologie: Die Organismen als Gefüge/Getriebe, als Normen und als erlebende Subjekte*. Stuttgart: Enke, 1932.

Wuketits, Franz M. *Außenseiter in der Wissenschaft: Pioniere – Wegweiser – Reformer.* Berlin: Springer, 2015.

www.ingramcontent.com/pod-product-compliance
Ingram Content Group UK Ltd.
Pitfield, Milton Keynes, MK11 3LW, UK
UKHW041951190726
13854UKWH00005B/1907

9 783957 962010